New Versions of Victims

New Versions of Victims

Feminists Struggle with the Concept

EDITED BY

Sharon Lamb

New York University Press

NEW YORK AND LONDON

NEW YORK UNIVERSITY PRESS
New York and London

Copyright © 1999 by New York University
All rights reserved

Library of Congress Cataloging-in-Publication Data
New versions of victims : feminists struggle with the concept /
edited by Sharon Lamb.
p. cm.
Includes bibliographical references and index.
ISBN 0–8147–5152–0 (cloth : alk. paper)
ISBN 0–8147–5153–9 (pbk. : alk. paper)
1. Women—Crimes against. 2. Victims—Psychology.
3. Women—Psychology. 4. Feminist theory. I. Lamb, Sharon.
HV6250.4.W65N45   1999
362.88′082—dc21   99-17521
CIP

New York University Press books are printed on acid-free paper,
and their binding materials are chosen for strength and durability.

Manufactured in the United States of America

10 9 8 7 6 5 4 3 2 1

Contents

Acknowledgments

The contributors would like to thank several people for reading over various chapters and giving comments: Johanna Brennan; Peggy Brick; Richard De Grandpre; Norah Feeny; Lisa Handler; Rachel Hare-Mustin; Mark Jackson; Susan Kuntz; Monica Kellow; Paul Orgel; Geri Phillips; Esther Rothblum; the University of Auckland Psychology Discourse Research Unit; Christina Walulik; and one another, for helpful discussions and reading of the chapters.

As editor of the volume, I also extend warm thanks to Jennifer Hammer, associate editor at New York University Press, for her smart and generous editing and her support, availability, and flexibility.

Contributors

Chris Atmore has worked for the New Zealand government as a child abuse researcher and educator and has also been involved in various forms of feminist activism, especially against sexual violence. At present she teaches feminist theory and cultural and media studies in Australia, in the Department of Anthropology and Sociology at Monash University. Her great preference is for interdisciplinary scholarship and engagement, although she often finds herself exchanging ideas with feminist psychologists in particular. Her articles have been published in an eclectic range of journals and books, including *Feminist Review, Feminism and Psychology, Child Abuse Review, Journal of Homosexuality*, and *Media Information Australia*. She is currently working on an analysis of cultural representations of child sexual abuse and rape at the end of the millennium, including their relationship to the politics of contemporary feminist theory.

Nicola Gavey is a lecturer in the Psychology Department at the University of Auckland in New Zealand. She is the author of numerous articles on such topics as the recovered memory debate and heterosexual coercion, including "In the Name of Science: Commentary on 'On the recovered memory debate'" in *Health Care Analysis*, 1997 and "Women, sexual freedom, and the 'coital imperative,'" with Allanah Ryan, in DuPlessis, R. & Alice, L. (eds.), *Feminist Thought in Aotearoa/New Zealand* (Oxford: Oxford University Press, forthcoming).

Janice Haaken is professor of psychology at Portland State University, Oregon; a clinical psychologist in private practice; and an activist in the fields of reproductive rights and family violence. She has published widely on gender and psychopathology, psychoanalysis and feminism, and the psychology of social movements. Haaken is author of *Pillar of Salt: Gender, Memory and the Perils of Looking Back* (New Brunswick, N.J.: Rutgers University Press, 1998).

Sharon Lamb is associate professor of psychology at St. Michael's College in Colchester, Vermont. She is the author of *The Trouble with Blame: Victims, Perpetrators, and Responsibility* (Cambridge, Mass.: Harvard University Press, 1996). She has worked as a therapist for children and adults who have been victimized and has served as an expert witness in cases of sexual abuse and custody. She is currently working on a qualitative study of women's memories for the "hidden" games they played as girls—the sexual, aggressive, and transgressive activities of girlhood.

Jeanne Marecek is professor of psychology and head of women's studies at Swarthmore College, Swarthmore, Pennsylvania. She is the coauthor (with Rachel Hare-Mustin) of *Making a Difference: Psychology and the Construction of Gender* (New Haven, Conn.: Yale University Press, 1990). She works on theory and metatheory in psychology, especially the intersections of feminist theory, postmodern thought, and discursive psychology. Trained as a clinical psychologist, she is collaborating with Diane Kravetz on the study of feminist-identified therapists, on which her chapter in this book is based. She also works in Sri Lanka, where her interests focus on narrative accounts of suicide and interpersonal and communal violence.

Lynn M. Phillips has been involved in advocacy and research on issues pertaining to girls and women for the past fifteen years. She is the author of *Flirting with Danger: Young Women's Reflections on Sexuality and Domination* (forthcoming, New York University Press). Her recent publications include *The Girls Report: What We Know and Need to Know about Growing Up Female*, commissioned by the National Council for Research on Women, and Planned Parenthood's *Unequal Partners: Exploring Power and Consent in Adult-Teen Relationships*. A social and developmental psychologist, she studies sexuality, victimization, and social injustice. She teaches psychology and gender studies at Eugene Lang College of the New School for Social Research in New York City.

Claire Renzetti is professor and chair of sociology at St. Joseph's University in Philadelphia. She is editor of the international, interdisciplinary journal *Violence Against Women*; coeditor of the Violence against Women Book Series (Sage); and editor of the Gender, Crime and Law Book Series (Northeastern University Press). She has written or edited ten books and is the author of numerous book chapters and journal articles. She also chairs the board of directors of the National Clearinghouse for the Defense of Battered Women. Her current research focuses on women's use of violence in intimate relationships and on violence against women living in public housing projects.

Carol Rambo Ronai is assistant professor of sociology at the University of Memphis in Memphis, Tennessee. She has written in the *Journal of Contemporary Ethnography* about using a "layered account" to examine and understand child sexual abuse. She is currently in the process of conducting life-history interviews with adult female and male subjects who have experienced childhood sexual abuse. Her primary interests focus on the intersection of identity, discourse, narrative practices, and interpretive theory.

Introduction

Sharon Lamb

The media won't like this book. It's too reasonable. And too educated. We make no exaggerated claims about victimization—for example, that it is *impossible* for someone to repress abuse and remember it later, or that date rape is *an invention* of whining college students, or even that we're a nation of *complainers* and "everyone wants to be a victim." We make no exaggerated claims about rape, date rape, and sexual abuse victims; we don't say, for example, that all women who've experienced these events are "survivors" or tragically wounded for life. To be honest, we're choosing not to practice today's "look-at-me" feminism, in which young feminists do tricks on the media's jungle gym, showing their panties to compete for (often male) attention by coming up with outrageous antiwomen and antifeminist claims.

But although we don't support this aspect of look-at-me feminism, we join these women in saying that we don't like what has become of feminism's interest in victims. We are unhappy with what some therapists, victim advocates, TV talk-show hosts, and others have done with the movement to portray victimization as a women's issue and to bring activist efforts to bear on the problem. No, the media won't like this book. And neither will those people who believe they are advocating women's right to sexual freedom when they make accusations about the nonexistence of abuse and the harm it causes. They won't like this book because it knocks down their straw women—whom they call "victim-feminists," whom they claim are out there teaching women to be victims. We are not victim-feminists.

But those who have been dubbed "victim-feminists" and some therapists who treat victims may not like this book either. The most extreme among them will be challenged to re-examine their deeply held beliefs about the harm of victimization and required to look at harm they may have caused in their exaggerations and their ways of labeling and treating women who have been abused. When the topic of *victimization* divides women so, who will be served by a book that plants itself squarely in the middle of the debate? Perhaps those thinkers, students, and therapists who fall through the cracks. We suspect there are a great many of them: those who surreptitiously said of Katie Roiphe or Camille Paglia, possibly in a tone of self-disgust, "Well, she has a small point there, maybe. . . . "; perhaps also, those victims who have resisted seeing themselves as part of a "survivors'" movement but who also deny that they are "in denial" with regard to their abuse. Those who have questioned the usefulness of current therapeutic practices may like this book. And those who worry that the activism has gone out of feminism, we hope will be prompted to return to activist and educational efforts. Those who have complained about the narrowness of the version of "victim" that is popular today may find confirmation through the authors in this book. And finally, those readers who both love and fear language, who see in it the power to transform as well as to maintain the status quo, to punish and reward, to include and to exclude, will find sisterhood with these authors.

Our Frame of Reference

The contributors (myself among them) believe that abuse and victimization of women exist and take place too frequently; but we also worry about what happens (and has happened) after the recognition of the abuse. Cultural forces have shaped the meaning of this abuse, and we can no longer simply state the basic point, that abuse is bad and harmful to women.

In this book, we take what has been referred to in academia as a "constructionist," and sometimes a "poststructuralist," view. We also take an interdisciplinary perspective, and this requires us to define and examine terminology that comes out of this approach. One of the criticisms of women's studies programs and feminism today is that they speak an exclusionary language that can be unfathomable, not only to regular folk but even to academics in other disciplines. This is the language of postmodernism, and more often than not it is from works such as those of French philosopher Michel Foucault and culture theorist Judith Butler.

The incomprehensibility of academic or postmodern language is one more valid criticism of feminist studies made by backlash critics (although it is more often than not the humanities, rather than feminist studies per se, that supports this language). It is, however, a problem we wish to escape in writing this book. The book aims to show that, when done carefully, it is possible to think and express "deep thoughts" in simple language that women in all disciplines can understand. We want nonacademic feminists to think about what we write, and we want to bring graduate students into this work without requiring them to take an additional course in postmodern theory.

Thus, when I claim that most of the contributors to this book write from a postmodern or constructionist perspective, I want to spell out exactly what I mean. Basically, the contributors question the meaning of abusive events to the ones who have been victimized and to the culture at large. This doesn't mean we analyze who is lying or what is real; rather, we explore what the language of abuse and victimization and the practices associated with the recognition and treatment of abuse mean at this time in our culture. We see a victim as someone not only made a victim by her victimization but also made a "victim" by our culture's understanding of what that word means, of social practices (such as therapy or heterosexual sex or raising children), and of gender relations. A constructionist analysis also sees categories and labels such as "victim" as shifting, changing frequently. We can never pinpoint the precise definition, and the label will mean different things in different contexts, depending on who is using the label and to what end. I hope this explains the title *New Versions of Victims*; we see all understandings of "victim" as "versions" that have different meanings and different ideals for the future. They are alternative ways of seeing the label. In any case, the term *victim* is a product of social relations, culture, and language.

The difficulty in talking about the creation of categories such as "victim," "rape," and "abuse" is that to victim advocates it sounds as if we are denying the existence of these experiences, implying that they are "mere" creations. Unfortunately, backlash critics may see in our analysis support for their views: for example, when we speak of "rape" as a creation, they may assume we mean it actually does *not* exist, that rape victims are lying. This is exactly the kind of simplistic thinking we aim to get away from.

We begin to do this by asserting that categories such as "victim" and "rape" are "constructed," which by no means is the same as "made up." The terms *rape, victim*, and *abuse* are like any other cultural constructs, such as gender, race, emotion. Depending on the culture, historical period, and social context, they can mean various things. There is always *some* basis for the category in what is observed—raw data, if you will. But we must also always be aware that even what we observe is seen through cultural and historical lenses. We can never study "raw" data, because it is always articulated, under certain circumstances, at particular times.

Moreover, the construction of categories such as "rape," "date rape," and "sexual abuse" is thoroughly mixed up with notions of power. This is to say that the analyses we do here examine the relationship between what is given the status of truth and the process of getting access to, as well as exercising, power (Bernauer 1988). Different groups (therapists, backlash critics, the False Memory Syndrome Foundation, victim advocates, law and order) compete to define the victim, to teach us ways to think about and understand victimization. (Postmodern writers would put it this way: victimization is a highly contested space.) The naming and defining of terms is indeed a power struggle.

The power to label or call someone a "victim" or to label or call some act a "rape" is never unitary. A unitary explanation of dominance would be: "Men, because of their power, have minimized and denied that rape exists." It is unitary because it describes one source of power that, in addition to being unitary, is unidirectional: men exercise power over women. This kind of one-sided explanation has led backlash critics to see victim advocates as "man haters."

But the act of labeling and the exercise of power to label or to call a deed a deed, come not only from "the patriarchy" or from men. They are embedded in social relationships and also internalized in women, including those who are victimized. This means that victims are imprisoned in cultural constructions of their victimization imposed from within as well as from without.

Our Writing

The reader will probably notice that in addition to trying to make the language more accessible, to explain our thoughts in the simplest terms we can, the contributors sometimes include our own experiences. This is purposeful and means several things.

There is a long-standing tradition in feminist writing that values experience. This valuing of experience reflects several feminist claims. First, the idea that women, as an oppressed group, have been silenced is deeply connected with the idea of "coming to voice" and making the personal political. Second, feminists have challenged male authority as the final arbiter of history, psychology, and other disciplines; sharing women's particular experiences is thus a way of bringing about a fuller range of accounts of reality. Third, the methodology of science, which claims to be objective and analytical, itself has been criticized as an enterprise in which variables are taken out of natural context and studied under artificial, laboratory conditions to produce a sterile form of knowledge. Feminists claim that qualitative methods—interviewing, listening, making the subject the arbiter of her own truth—are a means of giving voice to oppressed women.

Although the contributors to this book don't always overwhelmingly support these claims, we show an allegiance to this kind of thinking by including our personal experiences in our writing. The absence of the author-as-a-person from theory building has been a problem. The "objective," more "distant" style of writing has been criticized not only for its lack of warmth but also for the pretense that it is *the* truth. By including our own experiences, we recognize that in writing, one exercises power and subverts that power at the same time by making oneself more "readable" for the audience.

We also write about our own experiences when possible because it is important to avoid setting "them" against "us," that is, women who experience abuse against those who comment on it. We argue against those who claim that "objectivity" is lost if experience is included. Furthermore, if we set ourselves up as "experts," we reproduce the power dynamic we critique in the medical field, the media, and the field of psychology: we become the experts who tell women how to view their victimization. We aim for more humility and prefer to expose and criticize cultural constructions, rather than teach or educate victims about themselves.

We also share some personal history in the hopes of sisterhood, an idea that has lost support in recent years. If sisterhood is to be powerful, we must fight against hierarchical distinctions and look for commonalities in our differences. Some of the writing deals directly with the fact that feminists differ greatly from one another in experience and philosophy, just as victims differ greatly from one another in the degree of abuse that they have experienced and how they make sense of this abuse. Yet such differences do not preclude solidarity around issues of abuse.

Ultimately, we share personal experiences because we do not want to be hypocritical. Therapists have argued that people should disclose, that victims need not be ashamed of their abuse, and that disclosure is healing. But how many authors, therapists, and doctors actually reveal their own abuse? By not revealing it, they preserve abuse as a special category to write about and obfuscate the notion that abuse is simply a part of most individual women's history (see chapter 5, note 1) and women's collective history. As such, we can name it "those things most women have to endure" rather than "horrible abusive experiences that have silenced women for centuries." Our solidarity need not come from seeing ourselves as tortured captives but may derive from having to endure, in varying degrees, the verbal, physical, and sexual humiliation and assaults that have become too commonplace in so gender divided a culture as our own. Certainly, men perpetrate verbal, physical, and sexual humiliation on one another as well as on women. But this book is primarily about female victims and sees such abuse from a straightforward feminist perspective, as hostility toward women.

Our Chapters

The chapters in this book focus on specific areas of abuse, such as sexual abuse, domestic violence, acquaintance rape, and rape. They also focus on broader issues, such as teen-adult relationships, victims and agency, the media and the victim, therapists, and backlash critics.

Janice Haaken's chapter begins the book, with an analysis of *The Courage to Heal* and other "heretical texts" in the incest recovery movement. *The Courage to Heal*, written as a guide for survivors of sexual abuse, has been central in the "memory wars" (the debate about whether or not a sexually abused child can repress or forget her abuse and later recollect such experiences). Rather than taking sides in this debate, Haaken examines its dynamics from a cultural perspective.

Working from a feminist perspective, Haaken acknowledges the larger meaning of recognizing repressed memory: that it symbolizes the suppression of women's history of oppression and abuse. But Haaken is interested in the process of remembering as a socially constructed, not an empirical, event, and she explores the narrative structuring of memory as a transformative process. She writes that one need not minimize the anguish of recalling sexual abuse to recognize how such recollections may serve multiple functions for and arouse myriad responses in tellers and listeners alike. This is Haaken's focus—a search not for the factual truth but for the truth that lies in the structure of narrative and in the multiplicity of meanings such a narrative evokes.

Haaken sees the stories of survivorship in *The Courage to Heal* as standing for a larger set of female grievances. Its authors' emphasis on literal truth has cost them an opportunity to speak more broadly about the range of personal violations that girls endure through development, the "quieter assaults of everyday life." While Haaken sees "progressive insights" in *The Courage to Heal*, she scrutinizes its blind spots: the disavowal of fantasy elements of memory, the infantilizing of female sexuality, and the denial of erotic arousal and voyeurism in the readers and therapists in the field of sexual victimization. She ends her chapter with a nuanced look at storytelling, as culturally prescribed narrative and also as a foundation for solidarity.

Claire Renzetti grapples with a topic that has been confusing for feminists: women's use of violence in intimate relationships. Backlash authors might be quick to say that women's violence in relationships is proof that women are truly equals with men and that feminists have been exaggerating the extent and damage of domestic abuse. But Renzetti argues, "Not so fast!" Her analysis explains the various ways in which we need to examine the statistics of women's use of violence and warns feminists not to shy away from such an examination.

Women's violence calls into question the version of the victim as powerless. Some earlier writings on the topic underscore the problem of statistical interpretation: often women's violence is in self-defense; husbands and boyfriends initiate the violence more often than women do; and men's violence toward women is more likely to result in great bodily harm than women's violence toward men (Das Dasgupta, forthcoming; Saunders 1989). But Renzetti brings into the discussion other elements that allow us to see that women truly can be agents as well as victims in these scenarios.

Central to Renzetti's chapter are the examples of women's violence from cultures other than the white U.S. "mainstream," as well as examples of the meanings women ascribe to their violence. Using examples of Indian immigrants, Australian Aboriginal women, and lesbians in Euro-American culture, she shows readers how to "read" women's violence in a contextualized and feminist way. Most important, Renzetti argues that it is possible to have a feminist theory of women's violence and to acknowledge that women can be offenders as well as survivors.

Nicola Gavey, in her chapter "I Wasn't Raped, but . . . ," takes on the issues of rape, date rape, and the "unacknowledged" rape victim. In specific, she challenges empirical research on the topic. She also explores whether being the object of violence necessarily makes one a victim of violence and to what extent it is in women's best interest to be called a "victim."

Gavey identifies early feminist strategies to include a wide range of experiences as "rape" and acknowledges the importance of such an overinclusive strategy. Still, she asks, why do victims resist such a label? Are we serving them well when we label their experiences for them? She sees their reluctance to label certain acts "rape" as more than denial or the wish to protect the perpetrator. For better or worse, this reluctance reflects a victim's understanding of what heterosexual sex entails. And feminists' accounts of rape, she argues, don't always take into account women's experiences that are contradictory—"normal" and coercive heterosexual sex.

Finally, Gavey discusses the difficult intricacies of date rape, which show it is not always easy to demarcate rape and sexual coercion from normative heterosexual practice—which privileges men's sexual interests over women's. If we accept this theoretical continuity, we can no longer separate our research on victimization from our research on gender relations.

Lynn M. Phillips's chapter on adult-teen relationships challenges the idea that when older men date teenage girls, the girls are necessarily passive victims. By interviewing a racially diverse group of girls who are currently in adult-teen relationships, as well as adult women reflecting on their teenage years and their involvement then in adult-teen relationships, Phillips juxtaposes two versions of these relationships. While the teens describe themselves as full agents who enjoy social as well as material benefits, the adult women tend to look back on the relationships as harmful and exploitative. In her chapter, Phillips avoids taking sides with either the girls or the women but explores what is missing in each version of what is happening in these relationships. In retrospect, it is clear that the girls are discounting the abusive and domineering treatment of their adult boyfriends, under whose "guidance" they choose to put themselves. But the adult women's narratives also do not tell the whole story. Have they forgotten the sense of choice, power, and esteem they experienced as teenagers dating "older men"? How can feminists, eager to assert women's agency, accept a version of the teenage partner as being so helpless, with so little agency or power to make choices? Yet how can they accept teen girls' versions of events outside a critical analysis of power dynamics? These are the difficult questions with which Phillips grapples in her chapter.

In my chapter, I revisit the label of "victim." I examine the current cultural requirements for being a victim, including the pathology, the diagnoses, and the expectation of long experience of suffering. Being victimized no longer stands for suffering an insult of oppression but is now equivalent to having a chronic mental illness; it is a diagnosis, of sorts. Such a version of victim is both damaging to the victim herself and exclusionary in terms of the other everyday forms of oppression that women and girls endure. More important, it robs victims of agency.

After examining the ways in which victims become "convincing" victims, I turn my attention to the labels "victim" and "survivor," raising questions about their meaning and function for victims and for feminism. Through the analysis of two women's experiences, I explore how the culture's expectations of victims enter into and shape the women's own conceptualizations of their experience. I note that victims are starting to avoid the label "victim" because of these associations. Victims struggle to remain agents of their acts as they describe their victimization in a culture that has grown to call victims "whiners."

In the final section of my chapter, I analyze the paradox of the agentic victim and the metaphor of "voice." My version of victim recognizes agency as well as passivity, strength as well as harm, resistance as well as dissociation. Although the metaphor of "voice" seems particularly applicable to understanding the agency of victims, it can also work against victims and women. I conclude with a discussion of the politics of abuse and a call for repoliticizing abuse-talk so that it speaks to the pervasiveness and "normality" of abuse.

In her chapter, Carol Rambo Ronai explores a form of writing she calls the "layered approach." This is a narrative form designed to be a continuous dialectic of experience, one that emerges from a multiplicity of identities that simultaneously produce and interpret the text. While traditional narratives force a certain authority or particular understanding onto the reader, Ronai's narrative decenters any one authoritative voice. It is a personal narrative, systematic introspection, and theoretical reflection all in one. It integrates and holds together both objective and subjective moments.

The topic of her chapter is her personal experience in relation to being asked to appear on the CBS show *Public Eye* as a daughter of a mentally retarded mother and the author of works pertaining to this experience. Ronai reflects on how the makers of the show seemed to try to make her into a "victim," and only a victim, of this experience. In her "layered" approach, she tries to preserve her multiple identities: as "victim" and benefiter of victimization (past and present), as loving daughter and betrayer of her mother, and as academic theorist and representative of her institution. The personal narrative she produces is one that mimics and plays around with aspects of "date rape" narratives; yet Ronai subverts this story by inserting her own introspective reflections and theoretical understandings of what else is going on.

Jeanne Marecek, like Lynn M. Phillips, works from interviews. She is interested in the stories that some forty feminist therapists tell with regard to their work with victims and perpetrators. What she labels "trauma talk" is the system of terms, metaphors, and modes of representation that enables therapists to construct accounts of their clients' lived experiences.

Marecek, in her analysis, examines both the dominant and subterranean discourses. The dominant discourse in the interviews (ones that are granted some elevated status of truth) enlarges the category of abuse to include even some forms of clinical practice and sees "trauma stories" as the privileged way to narrate women's lives. Marecek notes the irony that even though many respondents repudiated the medical model, trauma talk replicates it in significant ways.

Subterranean, or marginal, discourses (those that appear only fleetingly) appear in the form of speakers' acknowledgment of several aspects of clinical work that they identify as counter to received wisdom. Some, for example, acknowledge the need to work with perpetrators. Some hesitatingly state that sometimes boundaries are important in clinical practice. And some imply that it may be impossible and sometimes unwise to equalize power in the client-therapist relationship.

Marecek ends her chapter with a look at why "trauma talk," among all possible narratives of clients' lives, has such appeal for feminist therapists. She calls for diversity in narratives and skepticism with regard to psychology's claims of access to a single truth.

In her chapter, Chris Atmore specifically addresses some claims by Camille Paglia, Katie Roiphe, Christina Hoff Sommers, and Naomi Wolf, comparing their characterization of feminist analyses of rape as "victim feminism" with what some radical feminists actually argue. While largely rejecting the views of Paglia and the others, Atmore, like the other contributors to this book, suggests that it is unhelpful simply to dismiss the ideas of these women as part of a backlash. We need to take a far more nuanced approach, one that is culturally and historically attuned. Atmore points out how, at the end of the twentieth century and after more than three decades of feminist work against rape, it is not so easy to oppose "them" against "us." She uses the arguments of Paglia and others as a springboard to examine what it is crucial to retain from the theories of such radical feminists as Catharine MacKinnon and what in her theory tends to be ignored, misinterpreted, and misrepresented by the "backlash" writers.

At the same time, Atmore suggests that some elements of radical feminist theory about rape need rethinking. Feminist postmodernism—which has been condemned alongside radical feminism by the backlash critics—can combine with the core of radical feminist analysis to give us the theoretical tools we need to continue the fight against rape in the present, rather different, era. Atmore argues that this potential alliance is just one illustration of the need for feminists to try to avoid being caught in the easy generalizations all too typical of the backlash critics.

Atmore gives a rich rendition of the plurality of feminisms and sexual violences that exists today. She also takes on the mass media as a site in which extreme, inaccurate, and exaggerated opinions are played out because of the need to set up an issue as an either-or debate.

Our Book as a Site of Ambivalence

We contributors are sometimes unsure of what we say, even though we say it with appropriate authorial confidence. What we suspect, however, is that the general public, graduate students, and victims themselves are also uncertain about several things: Which version of victim can we live with today? Which version of victim will be most helpful in addressing gender inequities as well as victims' suffering? Rather than join backlash critics in their media gymnastics, writers, researchers, students, and other women must seek answers to the following questions: How do we acknowledge all kinds of victimizations and continue to see women's agency and strengths? How do we acknowledge some of the backlash critics' claims without losing ground? How do we proceed to a more nuanced approach toward victimization while retaining our feminist politics and our sensitivity to those who have suffered?

Most prevalence studies of harassment, sexual abuse, domestic battering, and rape show that for each category, one-third to one-half of all women report at least one incident. Given that these categories don't necessarily overlap, we can assume that most women have experienced some kind of gender-related abuse.

REFERENCES

Bernauer, J. 1988. Michael Foucault's ecstatic thinking. In J. Bernauer and D. Rasmussen (eds.), *The final Foucault* (pp 45–82). Cambridge, MA: MIT Press.

Das Dasgupta, S. Forthcoming. Violence by women—A critical view. In Shepard, M., and Pence, E. (eds.), *Coordinating community response to domestic violence: Lessons from the Duluth model.* Thousand Oaks, CA: Sage.

Saunders, D. G. 1989. Who hits first and who hurts most? Evidence for greater vicitmization of women in intimate relationships. Paper presented at the Annual Meeting of the American Society of Criminology, Reno, NV.

Chapter One

Heretical Texts

The Courage to Heal and the
Incest Survivor Movement

Janice Haaken

"The world has split open. Women have broken the silence." These were the exhortatory opening words of Ellen Bass before a rapt audience of therapists at a 1993 annual conference for treating sexual abuse survivors. After two days of tedious clinical presentations by several male therapists who have colonized the field of sexual abuse recovery training, Bass spoke from the heart of the survivors' movement and from its soul in feminism.

As the first woman to address the audience in the five-day conference—made up predominantly of female therapists—Bass projected a mixture of feminine softness and commanding authority. She called us to arms, to political activism, in countering the pernicious silencing of survivors spearheaded by the False Memory Syndrome Foundation (FMSF) and its allies. The FMSF had mobilized against what its members claimed was an epidemic of false allegations of sexual abuse, based on therapeutically "implanted" memories. Bass read of threats against her, even letters calling for her death. But she spoke with steady calm, with warm intonations that comforted the audience of worried therapists, shell-shocked by the memory war.

Many FMSF members describe Bass and Davis—the authors of *The Courage to Heal*, the "bible" of the survivors' movement—as promoters of hate (Goldstein and Farmer 1992; Merskey 1995; Pendergrast 1996). For some critics, these women are wolves in sheep's clothing, seducing women away from loving families. Bass mocks this vilification, adding that the fact that she and Davis are lesbians underlies much of the contempt for the book. And in a sense, coming out of the closet about sexual abuse is related to other transgressive acts for women—other strivings for sexual independence from men.

Given the intense loyalties and the deep hostilities aroused by *The Courage to Heal*, it is surprising that there has been so little exegesis of its content. Defenders and critics alike offer general pronouncements concerning the book's persuasive power, while diverging widely in the moral tone of their pronouncements. For both sides in the recovered memory debate, *The Courage to Heal* has acquired the status of a heretical text, particularly in that it embraces and advances the idea that long-forgotten childhood events may be unearthed and later recollected with considerable accuracy (see Loftus and Ketcham 1994).

From a feminist perspective, the idiom of repressed and recovered memory has persuasive appeal because women's experiences, indeed, have been "hidden from history." For all oppressed groups, emancipation involves struggling to achieve a more authentic account of the past, out from under the dominant, repressive accounts of the more powerful. Creating change involves a reworking of the past and the *objectifying* of that which was formerly invisible. Yet objectification may easily slide into reification, as the passion of discovery gives way to protective measures and to defending singular versions of the truth. The very precariousness of oppositional knowledge—ideas, images, desires, and memories contrary to "received wisdom"—may generate anxiety and uncertainty as well as a liberating sense of freedom.

For women, who have been denied authority to define the cultural past, a discourse that emphasizes the ambiguity of remembering may seem threatening, even counter to the assertion of an emergent female voice. Yet memories of distant events are created out of a complex fabric of mental imagery, generated both by external events and by internal elaborations and interpretations of those events. Emotions and ideas weave through the fragments of the past to create color, texture, shadow, and design out of the contours of retained experience. While this model—which emphasizes the *reconstructive* over the *reproductive* aspects of remembering—introduces doubt concerning the stability and certainty of recollections, it also makes central the creative, generative capacities of mind. If the mind is viewed as merely a holding tank for memory, as passive receptacle to the imprints or residue of past encounters, then a basis for conceiving of social change, a grounding for an active subject capable of breaking out of the oppressive cycles of history, is diminished.

In the feminist-informed field of sexual abuse, there has been a tendency to grant an exalted status to subjective, experiential knowledge and to adopt a literalist approach to memory. The truth of the memory is thought to lie in its factual accuracy and in the subjective conviction underlying it. This literalist model of mind implies that unconscious memories are stored in the recesses of the mind, frozen in time, and waiting to be revealed at opportune moments. In the context of psychotherapy or of life events evocative of past trauma, memories flood consciousness in an unbidden manner. This experiential/literalist approach could also be described as a naive realism: essence and appearance are conceived as one and the same. From this perspective, recovered memories are presented as representations of actual events, with little attention to how meanings are altered in the course of telling and retelling. The storyteller moves the listener through the "eyewitness" account of vivid, experientially realized suffering.

One of the limits of this approach is that we are captured—mesmerized, in a sense—by the immediacy of the drama and by the subjective, personal conviction that underlies it. The first-person narrator may be unaware of various influences on the telling and interpreting of the story, bound as she/he is to its particularities and to one's own inevitable ego-involvement in the unfolding narrative. Yet, if the project of feminism involves the "recovery" of critical consciousness, this same project must attend to the various social influences that work their way through the fabric of our memories.

This chapter enters the debate over recovered memories of childhood sexual abuse by deconstructing *The Courage to Heal*—this master narrative of the late 1980s—and by exploring the basis of its populist appeal.[1] Its progressive insights and its blind spots are explored, particularly in explaining the complex, conflictual currents of *female* sexuality. My exposition extends into an analysis of the historical context in which the book achieved tremendous currency and takes up the question of why remembering incest emerged as the "master narrative" of feminism in the late 1980s and early 1990s. I argue that childhood sexual abuse narratives, and specifically incest, acquired a legendary power within feminism as stories moved beyond the concrete suffering and voices of actual incest survivors to encompass a broad range of more ambiguous grievances. In other words, stories of incest took on a potent social symbolic loading as they broke through the barrier of cultural denial and traversed across the cultural landscape.

In introducing terms such as *legendary* and *symbolic*, my intent is not to minimize the suffering of survivors or to downplay the strength of cultural resistance to acknowledging child sexual abuse. Rather, I suggest that the social symbolic power of incest narratives derives from the very historical realities that gave rise to the survivors' movement. At the same time, there is a problematic side to this genre of feminist storytelling, particularly in its neglect of the layered, textured, and imaginative elements of remembering.

In widening the field of interpretive possibilities for understanding women's narratives of abuse, this chapter makes use of a concept that I term *transformative remembering* (see Haaken 1998). This term suggests that a recollected event may serve as a psychological marker from an early to a later form of self-knowledge. Since memory may be true, false, or somewhere in between as a representation corresponding to some referent event, the interest here is in mental activity that is *judged* to be memory, either by the subject or by some observer. Transformative remembering refers to event schemata that have supra-ordinate explanatory power, serving as phenomenological anchors in autobiographical recall. From this perspective, the truth of the memory may lie less in its factual content than in its narrative structure of shifting plots and subplots and of changing subject positions that emerge out of the landscape of memory.

Text and Subtext

In the preface to the second edition of *The Courage to Heal,* Bass and Davis underscore the transformative power of their heretical text. Excoriating the mental health industry, endorsements include survivors' scathing indictments of professionals: "I've been in treatment since I was six. I've been in mental hospitals. I've been given shock treatments. I've been on meds. I've seen counselors up the wazoo, but [your book] is the first real help I've ever received" (p. 13).

Offering testimonials attesting to the book's life-saving powers is not merely an act of self-promotion or grandstanding on the part of its authors. A best-seller for years, *The Courage to Heal* finds a responsive chord in the lives of vast numbers of women. Like so much of the self-help recovery literature that flooded the market in the 1980s, *The Courage to Heal* combines personal accounts, presented in a confessional vernacular, and a step-by-step path to recovery, peppered with commonsense psychology. Much like the booming co-dependence literature of the late 1980s, which similarly addresses the weariness and emotional binds of modern women (see Beattie 1987; Schaef 1986; Haaken 1993), *The Courage to Heal* is an inspirational text. And like the authors of healing manuals dealing with the aftermath of alcoholic, dysfunctional families, Bass and Davis encourage sexual abuse survivors to disengage from excessive preoccupation with the needs of others. For women who continue to bear primary responsibility for the household, often while working long hours in low-status, underpaid jobs, such prescriptive advice feels like welcome medicine. While many self-diagnosed survivors who recover new memories of sexual abuse may not have been literally abused by their fathers, they are likely to find some of the truth of their experiences embedded in the narratives in this lengthy text. This feminist apocrypha inspires, comforts, and anoints believers with heroic powers. And indeed, for women to speak up about their own oppression, to refuse to continue to serve as guardians of fathers' and husbands' secrets, requires courage and solidarity.

Bass and Davis fail to understand, however, that once sexual survivorship moves from the realm of the particular abuses of women to that of legendary truth, it speaks to a much broader set of female grievances. The incest survivor stands for Every Woman's seductions under patriarchy, for the myriad daily violations of her sense of self, and for the estrangement so many women experience from their own bodies. In locating the source of a range of emotional ailments, such as depression and eating disorders, in a forgotten sexual trauma, Bass and Davis grant dramatic force to the discontents of women. "When you were abused, your boundaries, your right to say no, your sense of control in the world, were violated. You were powerless. The abuse humiliated you, gave you the message that you were of little value. Nothing you did could stop it" (p. 39). Bass and Davis's recuperative message is moving to many women because it affirms the depths of female grievances. In an era when child sexual abuse has come to represent the violation of the self at the deepest level, this imagery may be employed to objectify a pervasive sense of anguish under patriarchy.

Take, for example, the belief—widely circulated in the mental health community in the 1980s—that eating disorders are an indicator of repressed memories of sexual abuse. While empirical studies indicate no clear causal connection between a history of child sexual abuse and eating disorders (Steiger and Zanko 1990), the link between them has a certain ring of truth. It is difficult to disentangle empirically single background factors from the web of determinants that contribute to difficulties in adult womanhood (Edwards and Alexander 1992). Phenomenologically, however, sexual abuse assumes priority as a causal factor in female disturbances because it symbolizes dilemmas more common to women: specifically, vulnerability to masculine invasions and subjugation to male assertions of sexual en-

titlement. Unlike the "acting out" disorders common among men, expressed in aggressive or antisocial behavior, women's ailments are more apt
to be carried privately, hidden behind the domesticated behavior cultivated
in female development. If incest is the secret crime, it would seem to explain the sense of private shame that often accompanies the female journey
out of childhood and the extent to which women's maladies, such as eating
disorders, center on the body.

In the third edition of *The Courage to Heal*, Bass and Davis qualify their
earlier, controversial statement that "if you think you were abused, then you
were." In this new edition, the authors reiterate the message while conceding some ground to the opposition, replacing the definitive "you were" with
the qualified "strong likelihood":

> It is rare that someone thinks she was sexually abused and then later discov-
> ers she wasn't. The progression usually goes the other way, from suspicion to
> confirmation. If you genuinely think you were abused and your life shows
> the symptoms, there's a strong likelihood that you were.   (p. 15)

The gripping stories of survivors' journeys into remembering, which include the recent genre of satanic ritual abuse accounts, are granted authority by the authors because they "feel true." Women's own subjective
sense of truth—the emotional conviction attached to a personal discovery—emerges as the final arbiter in the memory war. And for women, who
have lacked authority in adjudicating claims in so many public arenas,
emotional conviction may seem like the only weapon available in fighting
back.

Bass and Davis fail to extend the power of their legendary discovery,
however, into the far reaches of female development. If, as the authors assert, women experience a range of personal violations in the course of development—from sexual harassment to neglect and deprecating treatment—might the identity of child sexual abuse survivor also provide an organizing thematic, a vivid urgency, to the quieter assaults of everyday life?
The very cultural repression of incest and child sexual abuse gives such allegations, once they break through public consciousness, a tremendous
emotional valence and evocative power. More mundane forms of female
suffering do not mobilize the same level of moral outrage or empathic concern in American society as does child sexual abuse. It is not surprising,
then, that child sexual abuse emerges as a "master narrative" within feminism during an era when social supports for women and families are de-
clining. Sexual violations may serve as a conduit for the more mundane

grievances of women, for forms of suffering that fall below the threshold of public concern.

By focusing exclusively on sexual abuse as the source of disturbing sexual imagery for women, Bass and Davis also fail to explore the other side of patriarchal oppression: the repression of female sexuality. Underlying the text is an implicit assumption that unwholesome thoughts are imported into the female psyche entirely through abuse experiences, that nice girls don't have dirty thoughts. Anxieties centering on the body may indeed originate in abusive sexual experiences. But they also may be intertwined with sexual prohibitions that are more difficult to identify or locate in a discrete past encounter.

Transformative Remembering

Many of the stories of sexual survivorship in *The Courage to Heal* may be employed to illustrate the process of transformative remembering. They include a dramatic turning point where a recovered memory of sexual abuse becomes a means of escaping diffuse forms of suffering and the troubling binds of growing up female. The new memory provides a developmental landmark, a movement out of the darkness of feminine madness to the new light generated by the recovered trauma scene. One of the costs of this idea of dramatic transformation, however, is its blinding adherence to a new mythology with its own repressive demands.

The story of Gizelle, included in *The Courage to Heal*, exemplifies the power of this transformative remembering. A forty-year-old woman from an Irish Catholic family, Gizelle remembers, during the course of therapy, a violent rape by her father at the age of three. Prior to the recovery of this memory, she had suffered various psychiatric and physical ailments. Hospitalized for a series of tests, "with needles in my back" and under heavy sedation, Gizelle begins to have flashbacks. In a state of mental crisis, she calls her therapist, who then conducts a five-hour session during which he administers MDMA. (More commonly known as Ecstasy, MDMA is a drug initially designed and prescribed by some sex therapists for enhancement of lovemaking.) Gizelle's therapist uses the drug to "lower the level of fear" in cases such as hers, which indicated "severe repression" (p. 466). Like the devil, the repressed truth is a formidable opponent that the therapist exorcises. Gizelle describes the marathon therapy scene, where she wrestles with the emerging memories:

But, even then, the denial was so strong . . . And then I'd go into hysteria where I couldn't breathe. And then I'd start choking. And then I would be numb and I wouldn't feel anything. We went around like that for three hours. I said to Frank (the therapist), "You know what I'm feeling? I feel like I'm lying."   (p. 467)

Lying is a complicated matter. Truth may be conveyed through a conscious fiction, or a truth may be told with a deceiving intent. Here, we are led to believe that Gizelle feels as though she is lying even as the truth wells up from the bowels of her unconscious. There may be, however, a complex interplay of fact and fiction, truth-telling and deception, embedded in this narrative of memory retrieval. The memory that results from this therapeutic trial by fire may draw some of its dramatic potency from the context of discovery—the context both of the hospitalization that produced the flashbacks and of the marathon therapy session that followed. Gizelle reports that she felt invaded by the medical procedures that she had also experienced frequently in her early years in her bouts with illness. Her father, we learn early on in the narrative, is a surgeon and was involved in her medical care as a child. In a striking parallel, her present therapist administers a drug during an extensive session that was, itself, a highly seductive and invasive situation.

The new memory recovered under these dramatic conditions may have elements of historical truth, but much of its emotional power may be drawn from its immediate context, the influence of which may well have been overdetermined by myriad past associations. Gizelle's more recent hospitalization may have evoked childhood memories of invasive procedures, with her father as the fantasied or real agent of her pain. Young children often experience frightening procedures as sadistic assaults, which may be woven into the fabric of memory as abuse. The memory of the father's rape when Gizelle was three may vivify and, more important, concretize more ambiguous struggles with a father who let his daughter down in countless other unarticulated ways. And the contemporary context of therapeutic probing for a dramatic revelation—and the special treatment of a five-hour session in a drug-induced state—may give incest memories a metaphorical immediacy. Like daddy having his way with his "special girl," many therapists make exceptions to their own rules in meeting the "unique needs" of suspected incest survivors.

These influences may or may not be important to the meaning of this recovered memory. But in presenting the memory as a straightforward account of a recovered memory of sexual abuse, Bass and Davis fail to appreciate the rich, textured nature of memory or the multiple possible meanings and interpretations of representations of the past.

Fundamentalist Feminism

As a didactic text, *The Courage to Heal* actually blunts the critical edge of feminism, even as it advances feminist aims. Its portrayals of therapeutic ventures are mesmerizing and unreflective. The assumption in the story of Gizelle is that the source of truth lies in the depths of the unconscious and that this emerging truth may be trusted more than any rational processes of mind. Through this resurrection of the buried past, remembering takes on the power of a conversion experience. Gizelle describes her own recovered memory in these terms:

> Since it's come out, it's been the difference of night and day, of living in hell and living on the earth. Everything in me has changed—my perception of myself, of others, of the earth, of my power, of my strength, of my abilities, of my sanity—of everything. It's been so fast. I can't believe it. In just three and a half months, there's incredible healing.   (Bass and Davis 1994, p. 471)

The religious subtext of Gizelle's narrative is based on the idea of transfiguration through a ritualized encounter with evil. Like any conversion experience, the creation of a transformative memory grows out of real human suffering and out of efforts to overcome it. Taking the everyday assaults on the human spirit and elevating them to the realm of the diabolical or the divine ennobles the human quest for solace and meaning. In many "born again" stories, the former life of degradation—of a descent into hell— serves as dramatic counterpoint to the conversion experience. The most convincing of evangelists have wrestled with the devil, and this devil is cast as a full rival with God in the spiritual cosmology. In this religious worldview, rebellion and transgressive impulses are central motifs, even though they are experienced as the "work of the devil," requiring the transmutive taming of a supreme power.

For many women, recovered memory narratives offer a powerful mythology because they contain many of the same religious or moralistic elements. Emergent memories are felt to be hot and dangerous and as containing the imprints of past sexual invasions. To some extent, this imagery allows women to recover a sense of goodness and positive capacities, in that it separates the sense of personhood—the "good" aspects of the self—from the residue of past destructive experiences. But this dichotomized imagery marks the boundary between good self and bad memory too definitively, stripping women of psychological complexity, including ambivalence and countervailing desires.

If the concepts of God and Satan are the heirs of the child's ambivalence toward the father, as Freud once asserted, the shift from father worship to demonology in Bass and Davis's feminist mythology operates as a de-idealization of paternal authority. Indeed, Gizelle's journey is from the position of an idealized love for her father (her recovered memory begins with shouts of "I love you, Daddy. I love you, Daddy") to a rupture in this emotional tie, brought about by the new memory. Since raping one's child is the most egregious of parental violations, it permits a definitive, morally sanctioned bridge out of the father's world.

The Courage to Heal is, then, the "bible" of a very fundamentalist feminism, with some of the same costs for believers as those exacted by religious fundamentalism. Both provide an emotionally vivid, dramatic encounter with evil and righteousness that breaks through the deadening effects of everyday life. As cosmologies, both fundamentalisms unify believers around an emotionally gratifying but simplified universe. All of the bad, disturbing aspects of oneself and one's group of believers can be reassuringly placed beyond the gate of the new kingdom, protecting the faithful from both real and imagined threats. *The Courage to Heal* provides women a reassuring message that nothing problematic in their own reactions or mental life must be taken into account in understanding life's dilemmas.

Like the preacher who claims to be simply reading directly from the Word, eschewing the vagaries of symbolic meanings and interpretive uncertainty, Bass and Davis approach the feminine unconscious as though it speaks directly to women in an entirely literal way. This "repression" of the role of professional translators, of the multiple meanings in the "text" of memory, as well as of the influence of drugs on mental states, leaves women without any means of understanding the operations of power in the production of their own stories. For Bass and Davis, "honoring the truth" means holding the ground around a very literal interpretation of memory, while conceding, in their revised edition, that there may be a few "false positives" (p. 449). Such a vision offers an impoverished view of mental life. Much of the complexity of the mind—with its imaginative, symbolic capacities—is rendered away in a one-dimensional tale of feminine innocence lost and regained.

Collective Remembering

In her keynote address to the meetings of the American Psychological Association in 1995, Gloria Steinem (1995–1996) began with an interesting comment: "I must say, now that I am sixty-one years old myself, that I sometimes think I've reached the age when remembering something right away is as good as an orgasm" (p. 7). While she went on to review the history of the sexual survivor movement, her statement signaled an underanalyzed area of the recovered memory movement. In many of the popular and clinical reports, there is, indeed, allusion to an orgasmic release in storytelling, although the clinical term for this is *abreaction*. While most therapists in the trauma field stress the painful affects associated with remembering sexual abuse, the pleasurable aspects of remembering, whether in the reporting of women's "war stories" or in the intimacy established in the telling of them, tend to be neglected.

One need not minimize the anguish of recalling sexual abuse to recognize how such recollections may serve multiple functions for and arouse myriad responses in tellers and listeners alike. There is an interpersonal dimension—a "call and response" exchange—to the telling of an arousing story. The art of storytelling is based not merely on chronicling a sequence of facts but in the artful juxtaposition of dramatic elements. The power of the story to stir others, to communicate shared tribulations and victorious moments, depends on its felt truth and plausibility rather than on its mere facticity. Further, trauma stories, like legends of collective trauma, may have many functions. By preserving a collective memory of past injuries, they may, for example, serve as a reminder of the necessity of continual struggle. Trauma legends may also renew collective identity by re-establishing the group's entitlement—the rewards of suffering and righteousness—as well as the group's mourned losses.

Sexual Differences

Whether "recovered" or continuous, memories of childhood sexual encounters have been transformed in recent decades through insurgent social scripts—means of registering and interpreting events—that were unavailable to previous generations. Yet movements advancing new social ideals inevitably contain unresolved conflicts and dilemmas. While the right of children to resist adult authority has been one of the most progressive advances in recent times, this right has been largely won by restoring "pre-Freudian" conceptions of childhood. Cultural discomfort with childhood sexuality, and particularly with the sexuality of girls, intensifies the moral outrage in campaigns against child sexual abuse. Female chastity, as a cultural ideal, has a long, ambivalent history within feminism, no less than in reactionary politics.

One of the implicit, subtextual differences between the trauma stories of men and those of women in the sexual abuse recovery literature is in the degree of "license" to convey an admixture of horror and pleasure in the telling of the trauma story. Some of the pleasure in social remembering, in the sharing and creation of a common stock of stories, is in the sense of strength that the group provides in protecting against previously overwhelming experiences, thus making them more emotionally manageable. But the sexual abuse recovery literature tends to "repress" the erotic and voyeuristic aspects of sexual storytelling. Giving voice to the more painful feelings associated with remembering and listening to stories of sexual abuse—sadness, helplessness, and anger—is vital to recovery from abuse in that women's suffering is so habitually repressed under patriarchy. But this project of recovery may reinforce the idea that "normal" women do not have unwholesome thoughts. In much of the sexual abuse recovery literature, the voyeuristic, sexually aggressive, and incestuous currents in female mental life are admitted across the borders of collective consciousness only when they are smuggled through the more socially acceptable cargo of a sexual abuse memory.

Men, in contrast, can share their war stories with a certain nostalgic longing and can even import moments of homoerotic desire into the "buddy" story, while preserving their claims as bona fide trauma survivors (see Shay 1994). In the male sexual abuse survivor literature, sexual arousal is recognized as a feature of the experience—to such an extent that it is often framed as the source of the shame attached to the abuse (Hunter 1990a; Lisak 1994). Further, adolescent males are far more apt than are adolescent females to describe sexual contacts with older persons as predominantly positive (Rind and Harrington, forthcoming). Working through sexual abuse for male survivors often means confronting the complex currents of their own desire, including its homoerotic and "feminine" (passive, receptive) elements. For gay men, adolescent experiences with adult males are often recalled quite fondly and are understood to be integral to the experience of coming out (Arey 1995). As practitioners in the sexual abuse field so often point out, males are less likely to identify themselves as victims of sexual abuse because the position of victim is so feminized in the culture. To some extent, societal beliefs about the "durability" of boys—beliefs that are internalized in the course of male development—may protect boys from the traumatic effects of childhood sexual encounters. But the same beliefs operate repressively in reinscribing gender codes, particularly the idea of male invulnerability. The stories of male sexual abuse survivors, much like the posttraumatic stress disorder literature on the effects of combat, signify male resistance to this culture of manhood and an alliance with feminist critiques of sexual domination (see Hunter 1990b).

Nonetheless, gender differences in accessing sexual abuse memories are embedded in a cultural vocabulary that runs deeper than identification with the position of victim. Sexual victimization is a far more pervasive theme in female than in male development, from lewd comments on the part of males, "bra-snapping," and pinched bottoms through male sexual exhibitionism, rape, and incest. In other words, male intrusions into female spaces—psychological and physical–continue to be deeply normative. While males may less readily acknowledge their victimization experiences—and suffer from the effects of unacknowledged vulnerability—they also have more cultural and social scaffolding to maintain a sense of "intactness," in part because they have fewer invasive experiences to manage. Further, the mingling in "social memory" of normative, intrusive encounters and more traumatic ones makes the sexual abuse recovery narrative a potent, unifying story. For many girls and women, the concept of sexual invasion infiltrates and colors autobiographical recall, capturing the deep cultural affinity between sexual vulnerability and femininity.

We may decipher areas of "leakage" in this dominant feminine narrative. For example, one survivor in *The Courage to Heal* describes the agony and ecstasy of recovering memory of early abuse. Initially, she presents excruciating flashbacks:

> I'd be driving home from my therapist's office, and I'd start having flashes of things—just segments, like bloody sheets, or taking a bath, or throwing away my nightgown. For a long time, I remembered all the things around being raped, but not the rape itself. (Bass and Davis 1994, p. 79)

While recovered memory is typically described as having this unbidden character—the force of an external agency breaking through consciousness in a fragmented form—such imagery can result from various sources. Some women may recover memories of actual abuse in this way, as the inquiry of psychotherapy or other intensive self-exploration stimulates focused attention on the past. Yet one of the legacies of patriarchal oppression for women involves the suppression and repression of sexual and aggressive fantasies. Violent sexual imagery can be particularly frightening to women, both because it may signal actual memories of abuse and because it departs from domesticated versions of the feminine mind. In much of the clinical literature, narratives of childhood sexual abuse broaden the range of sexual imagery for women as long as this chain of mental signifiers is stabilized through the recovery of a discrete traumatic scene. The belief that a trauma memory lies behind every disturbing sexual image that surfaces in consciousness may reinforce women's fears of their own imaginations and intensify the search for memories of sexual abuse as the only available path of female redemption.

Seductive Mothers

For many survivors, the absent mother, her failure to protect her daughter from abuse, emerges as a dominant motif.[2] And for feminists, the issue of the mother's culpability has always been a thorny one (see Herman 1981). Davis addresses this issue in her own story, even though she offers no discussion of the complex verities of memories of the mother—or of the problematic interplay of real and fantasied maternal failures. Davis's story, titled "I'm Saying No, Momma," centers on "weaning" from her mother and on the rocky road of feminine exile from the family. Guilt over the daughter's struggle to separate from the mother is a palpable dilemma in contemporary feminist discourse. Davis poses the question of how she is able to keep her mother out of her life:

> I'll tell you how, Momma, I'll tell you how. Brick by careful brick, that's how. Momma, I've built this wall between us with careful, conscious precision. It is thick, my wall. Thick and nontransparent. I stand behind it and you cannot reach me. Its walls are smooth, Momma, flattened by ancient anger.
>
> (Bass and Davis 1994, p. 302)

The narrative then moves to an assertion of the freedom that this new wall permits, including the freedom to "set boundaries" and to break from the past. The de-idealization of the father in the recovered memory narratives, then, finds its parallel in the de-idealization of the mother:

> I'm not the daughter you wanted, Momma. I've always known that. But with my wall close around me, I can see you're not the mother I wanted either, all-knowing, all-giving, all-protective.
>
> (p. 302)

The recovered memory often serves as the decisive break from parental binds that are ensnaring, particularly for daughters. Daughters, more than sons, are expected to preserve intergenerational ties and to care for aging parents. Feminists, however, cannot easily equate the sins of the father and those of the mother. It is true that daughters may be let down by their mothers in irremediable ways and that women who have the freedom to sever ties with destructive or controlling mothers may feel the need to do so. It is an odd oversight, however, for a feminist text to omit commentary on recovered memory of maternal abuse while simultaneously explaining paternal abuse as a direct expression of patriarchal oppression. In other words, there is no attentiveness in the recovered memory debate to claims made by women that require more careful feminist scrutiny.

One of the liberating aspects of feminism is in its laying claim to a much larger world than that known by prior generations of women. Girls often discover firsthand their mothers' rage and disappointment, although these discoveries may not be informed by understandings of a larger social world of determinants. The daughter may encounter the mother's destructive side, as the mother takes out her own frustrated longings and aggression on a more vulnerable female counterpart. Mothers may minimize the daughter's distress, just as they minimize their own, and look the other way in order to maintain the peace.

But there are other dimensions to remembering the mother, dimensions intimately tied to infantile fantasies. Since the first object of dependency is typically the mother, the first struggles for independence also are with her. The powerful ambivalence generated by this attachment—often heightened by the social isolation of the nuclear family—infuses later imagery of the mother with infantile conflicts (see Chodorow 1994; Benjamin 1988). Memories of the real failures of the mother mingle with fantasy representations of her, infused by the rage, disappointment, and desire that are the lingering legacy of childhood. The disavowal of fantasy elements of memory removes this troubling uncertainty in defining the "boundaries" of self and (m)other in the internal world. So, too, sexual desire is dissociated from its emotional origins in developmental conflicts, including in sensual longings for the mother.

Sex for Survivors

In one of the few stories that restores some sexual agency to the survivor, Davis offers an account of her own vacillating movement in and out of sexual passion as she makes love with her partner. The story speaks to female ambivalence around sexuality, on the part of both abuse survivors and nonsurvivors, both lesbians and straights. In this modern narrative, Davis retreats from a moment of sexual awakening—from "the sudden jolt of passion"—as genital desire vanishes inexplicably. In a reversal of the traditional story, this modern Sleeping Beauty is awakened by the kiss only to fall back into a somnambulant state. While Davis's story reverberates with female ambivalence over sexuality, it also registers the complexity of what is awakened through sexual desire. The dread of abandonment and the confusing merger of aggression and pleasure that comes with the mingling of body parts make sexual desire the realm of both the imaginary and the real.

Davis's story reaches its denouement in a final explanation for the torturous ambivalence of this sexual encounter: "I was molested," she utters in a "tiny child's voice" (p. 87). And while we may recognize in this revelation an expression of self-understanding and intimacy, this narrative, like the others in *The Courage to Heal*, tends inexorably to narrow the explanation down to a woman-child with no history or sexual knowledge to draw on beyond that of the trauma memory. This pervasive infantilizing of female sexuality seems to waver uneasily at the threshold of its own erotic subject matter.

In discussing survivors' efforts to come to terms with sex, *The Courage to Heal* maps out the minefield that many women—whether abuse victims or not—encounter in discovering their own active desires and separating them from the invasions of past abusers. Bass and Davis introduce their chapter on "Sex" by noting the formidable obstacles women face in achieving sexual agency in a patriarchal and phallocentric society such as ours. And they affirm the right of survivors to assert control in the area of sexuality and to reclaim their sense of their bodies as their own. While women may feel "damaged beyond repair" (p. 250), the message is one of hope and encouragement. Women are advised to masturbate as a means of relearning what feels good, and to "start slowly and with awareness" (p. 251). Lesbian relationships are affirmed, and examples of sexual explorations in the course of women's healing are equally divided between female and male lovers.

While Bass and Davis advance a conception of liberated sexuality based on women's own self-conscious explorations, their views also understate the complex, conflicting currents of sexuality. Much of their advice is standard 1990s liberal fare: sex in moderation is "fun" and important, but it can also be "addictive" or a "re-enactment" of childhood abuse. Women are cautioned that one result of incest or other childhood sexual abuse may be an "excessive" use of sex, an ambiguous category that seems to include sexual encounters outside committed relationships.

Being a sexual abuse survivor also permits women to account for feelings of revulsion toward male genitals without having to explore too fully the various implications of such feelings. Gizelle's story, discussed earlier, includes this theme:

> You know, in my fantasies, when I imagine having a lover, I'm making love to him and everything is going along beautifully until he takes out his penis. And then I vomit all over the floor. Literally, in my fantasy, I vomit all over the floor! (Bass and Davis 1994, p. 266)

This admixture of interest in and revulsion toward male genitals is normalized through the sexual survivor narrative, and the source of these feelings is located in an abuse scene in the past. While some women may have difficulty separating their current lover's genitals from "the genitals that violated you as a child" (p. 266), the framework of sexual abuse survivorship excludes a range of conflicts not inevitably attributable to abuse. More pervasive sources of female ambivalence toward heterosexuality, including the impulse to orally "ejaculate" on the man, are overlooked by the singular focus on sexual abuse.

Sexual abuse survivors, we learn, should educate their partners about their special needs and ensure that the partner is responsive to the survivor's need to "take it slow." Implicitly, nonabused women have fewer claims in this area—fewer rights to insist on a partner's adaptations to their special needs. When all ambiguity and disturbing sexual material are constructed as a sign of a wounded femininity in need of "healing," women are able to make claims on lovers only within a discourse of illness.

Such a "journey to recovery" takes women on a narrow, constricted path of discovery, where disturbing sexual images are understood preemptively as flashbacks of the abuse. One survivor, who describes her intense shame and terror over sadomasochistic fantasies, is offered the recuperative power of the abuse narrative: "If abuse and sadism turn you on, you aren't to blame. You did not create these fantasies out of nothing. They were forced on you just as intrusively as those hands, penises, and leers were forced on you during the original abuse" (Bass and Davis 1994, pp. 272–273).

It is true that sadistic sexual fantasies can result from abuse and that perpetrators invade the imaginations as well as the bodies of their victims. But such fantasies also can have other sources. Just as small children may squeal with delight in being "captured" by their parents as they playfully flee, images of being tied up or forcefully held during sex may be infused with infantile forms of pleasure. The sexual excitement associated with the fantasy of rape must be distinguished from the experience of actual rape. Rape fantasies may draw on motifs that predominate in our "rape culture," providing a sense of mastery over threatening aspects of the social world, and simultaneously may draw on a range of aggressive sensations and impulses that mingle with sexual ones.

Arousing Memories

One of the subtextual themes in Bass and Davis's account of sexual healing concerns the sexualizing of memory itself. One survivor describes the admixture of pleasure and pain that emerges in the course of recovering abuse memories: "It seems to me that the memories are stored at the same level the passion is. If I don't make love, I don't connect with them. But whenever I open myself to feelings of passion, the memories are right there. It's a little like opening Pandora's box" (Bass and Davis 1994, p. 265).

When disturbing mental imagery is defined as literal memory, women are permitted to experience it as a normal upsurge of traumatic material and as part of the healing process. When this same imagery is identified as fantasy—that is, as internally generated material—its fate is less certain. In *The Courage to Heal*, women describe aggressive sexual fantasies, but these are assumed to be merely echoes of a past abuse. There is even one reference, exceedingly rare in the survivor literature, to how sexually stimulating reading about sexual abuse may be for women. As one survivor confesses: "For weeks on end I compulsively read about incest—*If I Should Die before I Wake* in one hand and my vibrator in the other" (p. 272).

While such experiences are recognized to be unusual—and most likely are—they are embraced in the welcoming arms of the sexual survivor movement as part of the recovery process. Bass and Davis display no recognition that some incestuous fantasies may not derive from explicit abuse and that they may be a part of normal female experience. It is only the survivor who is "allowed" such imagery, and this same survivor is instructed to understand her forbidden memories as an essential part of the healing process.

Storytelling and Solidarity

In the sexual abuse survivor literature, incest both stands as one among myriad sexual violations and serves as archetype of abuses of patriarchal power. Just as stories of clerical abuse of children galvanized rebellion in the Roman Catholic Church in the 1980s, recovered memories of father-daughter incest recount unambiguous breaches of authority. And in both the religious and familial contexts of these illuminations of fatherly sins, sexual abuse of children comes to stand for something beyond itself. (See Burkett and Bruni 1993.)

While exposure of men's dirty sexual secrets signifies a crisis in their ability to exercise absolute power, it may also represent cultural ambivalence of a more complex sort. Historically, when progressive movements are losing ground to conservative forces, the sexual violation of children stands in for other, unspoken transgressions. Losing ground in the movement to overturn papal proscriptions against abortion and against women and gays in the clergy may lead to a transfer of these political energies to a more unifying moral terrain. It is more possible to arouse moral outrage over a priest's sexual abuse of an innocent child than it is to mobilize moral outrage against the same priest's repressive doctrines on women and homosexuality. Exposing the hypocrisy of the holy fathers—how they violate their own moral codes—can be a means of establishing a chink in the wall. At the same time, creating a chink in the wall can easily become a substitute for tearing it down and building a new structure.

Since sexual violation of the body of a child evokes public revulsion and horror and signifies as well the corruption and degradation of protective institutions, the allegation of paternal incest conveys the sense of a profound cultural crisis. Statistics circulated widely in the late 1970s and 1980s estimated that one in three women was the victim of child sexual abuse and one in four was the victim of incest. (See Armstrong 1994.) Even though these numbers have been more recently challenged, on the basis that definitions were either too broad or vague, almost no one has returned to the prefeminist claim that incest is "rare, perhaps one in a million" (Armstrong 1994, p. 24). Even critics of the incest recovery movement feel compelled to pay homage to the gains of feminism in raising awareness of the widespread occurrence of child sexual abuse and to affirm that it is, indeed, a tragic social problem.

Yet exaggerated claims of sexual abuse and incest did unify women around a pervasively felt reality: the invasion of female boundaries, either bodily or emotionally, was discovered to be deeply normative, and moving from childhood to adulthood meant more relinquishing of boundaries than consolidation of them. Women could speak up about violations from the perspective of the innocent child—either their own children or the "child within"—more easily than in the thicket of morally suspect, mature sexual encounters. Demonstrating the absolute innocence and nonculpability of women in cases of date rape, sexual harassment, and domestic violence was an onerous challenge. Winning sympathy for child victims—particularly victims of incest—was far less daunting.

Given the diffuse and pervasive effects of gender, as well as other determinative life events, locating the source of feminine troubles can be similarly daunting. Identifying a moment in time, a momentous rupture of innocence when the girl was cast out of the kingdom, provides a means of both containing and transforming a diffuse and pervasively gendered past. The troubles of growing up female are located in an identifiable source and a time when virtue and villainy could be decisively uncoupled, setting the stage for a subsequent rebellion.

Diversity in Storytelling

In his analysis of how history reworks memory through literary representations, Richard Terdiman (1993) argues that nowhere is memory more fraught with emotional conflict than in intergenerational relations—in the tributes children owe to their parents: "The stories a culture tells about parents and children frame, as if in microcosm, the culture's conception of the inevitably problematic inheritance, of the present's perplexing relation to the past" (p. 214).

Once familial sexual abuse emerges as a political category and assumes a central place as a leitmotiv in female collective resistance, it may be employed in various contestations over authority. Since sexuality often evokes forbidden longings, female struggles to emancipate from patriarchal control may be symbolically expressed through an eroticized familial story. Sexual abuse allegations may acquire social symbolic meaning over time, as they gravitate from their original entry point in public consciousness.

But sexual motifs in women's storytelling also are shaped by other aspects of cultural history. The project of emancipation from familial constraints is a more ambivalent one for many women of color, who experience acutely the illusory aspects of feminine "autonomy," than for white women. Confronting the powerful fathers may be more problematic when father and daughter share a common history of oppression, including racist stereotypes of "oversexed" dark-skinned people. Sexual violations may be difficult to disentangle from the larger web of social forces that crush the spirits of parents and children alike. (See Collins 1990.) In describing the dilemmas of black women incest survivors, Melba Wilson (1994) suggests that the taboo against "putting our business out in the street" is stronger than the incest taboo.

The social sciences provide sparse findings and even sparser insights into the particular abuses black women have endured. But although the voices of women of color in the survivors' movement and literature are few, incest and sexual abuse are powerful themes in literary explorations of black women's lives. Fictional storytelling allows for denser, richer experiences than those representations that circulate in the social science literature. The social science and mental health literature tends to decontextualize abuse, often reducing it to psychological variables. Black women writers, however, are likely to place private enactments of violence within a broader, dehumanizing context. (See Butler-Evans 1989.) In Toni Morrison's *The Bluest Eye*, for example, the rape of Pecola by her father, Cholly, dramatizes a violence that neither begins nor ends with the broken body of the young girl. While the narrative forcefully conveys the horror of the rape, trauma emerges out of a larger constellation of destructive experiences and unbearable losses that grip both father and daughter. The designation of perpetrator—the one who is responsible for destroying the spirit of this black girl—never settles resolutely on the shoulders of the defeated father but shifts and turns within a broader drama of racist brutality.

In addition to Morrison's novel, there is by now an entire genre of novels—including Maya Angelou's *I Know Why the Caged Bird Sings*, Alice Walker's *The Color Purple*, Joan Riley's *The Unbelonging*, Opal Palmer Adisa's *Bake Face and Other Guava Stories*—where incest emerges as an important, but not the singular, source of black women's pain. Through these novels, Wilson (1994) writes,

> I began to think of myself in a whole new way—as someone, if you will, whose experience counted for something. Began to feel that those everyday, ordinary things—which help to make up mine and the collective fabric of all black women's lives—were important to remember, record and pass on to those who came after. But even more importantly, here too was my experience of incest. (p. 41)

The candid portrayal of sexual abuse in *The Color Purple*, including father-daughter incest, stirred intense controversy in black communities
when the film was released in the early 1980s. In interpreting Walker's novel
and in reframing the controversy, the Brixton Black Women's Group in
London writes: "It is not like a story because you instinctively feel the truth
of it. . . . But like most stories you know it is derived from Every Black
Woman" (Wilson 1994, p. 41). Walker's novel probes the cultural dynamics
and contingencies of existence that set the drama of women's lives in motion, closing off some avenues of possibilities while opening up others. In
this context, incest is Every Woman's story, not because every woman has
experienced it but because it occurs within a common matrix of binding
situations. Sexual abuse is deeply wounding, in part because other destructive forces are at work that undermine efforts at self-restoration.

Solidarity and Sexual Stories

Sexual tale-telling is an inhibited affair for most women. (See Thompson
1994; Tolman 1991; Vance 1989.) Men tell tales of sexual prowess and con-
quests, and these tales have often been the basis of male solidarity against
the frightful power of the "feminine." Conventional narratives do grant
women some authority as domesticators of male sexuality—as representa-
tives of familial obligations, binding commitments, and the necessity of
sexual constraint. This female socialization project, like Beauty's task, centers on the taming of unruly masculine desires.

If men establish social bonds through tales of sexual potency and conquest, how do the sexual tales of women build solidarity? Further, since
women have had less cultural license to tell sexual stories than have men, how
does this legacy of inhibitions operate in the storytelling that emerges? Part
of the answer is that women, and particularly middle-class women, have had
fewer stories to tell, being granted less social freedom and mobility than men.
Traditionally in Western, industrial societies, injunctions against female sexual experimentation were based on the necessity of protecting and maximiz-
ing feminine sexual capital. Protecting inner spaces against phallic intrusions
has been a condition of feminine virtue and the currency of upward mobility. Selling too soon or too cheap could mean a precipitous depreciation of
value in the marriage market. As authority over women was transferred from
fathers to husbands, the negotiation of sexual rights and obligations gave
wives far fewer degrees of freedom than husbands.

The double standard has always implied a further cultural split between the "good" and the "bad" female object of desire. If women were "good"— sexually circumspect—patriarchy would protect them. Women who ventured across the sexual boundary became the objects of masculine ambivalence. The female sexual rebel was simultaneously exciting and dangerous. Outside the protective arms of patriarchal codes, "fallen women" became receptacles for primitive masculine reactions and conflicts concerning women. As "damaged goods," female sexual outlaws, whether labeled "sluts," "prostitutes," or "lesbians," shared a common fate as socially condoned objects of male rage.

While white women may suffer severe penalties for violating moral and sexual codes, black women never were as protected by the embracing arms of patriarchy. But the rage of black women extends beyond this differential treatment—their more fundamental lack of protection—to the complicity of white women in racist storytelling. White women's outrage over sexual abuses, their conviction that this is the worst of crimes against humanity, may easily overlook the racist history of sexual allegations. When Susan Brownmiller's (1975) groundbreaking book on rape was taken up by feminists, with rape emerging as the prototype of women's oppression generally, some feminists criticized her ahistorical understanding of sexual violence and her failure to address the racist history behind allegations of rape. Black women were less readily inclined than white women to reflexively "believe the victim," given their own cultural history strewn with lynchings and castrations of "oversexed" black men. (See Walker 1982.)

Jacquelyn Dowd Hall (1983) responded to this controversy of the late 1970s by recovering this forgotten memory in feminism, probing the complex interpenetration of sexual and racial imagery in American history. Hall chronicles this gruesome history, with the 1955 lynching of Emmett Till for whistling at a white woman serving as reminder of the persisting expressions of racist sexual violence. She explores the use of sexual allegations as a tool in racial oppression, a violent psychodrama enacted to fortify the control of white men on two fronts: the post-Reconstruction mobility of blacks and the perceived threats of turn-of-the-century feminism. By presenting themselves as the defenders of female chastity, white men were able to control daughters and wives by inscribing the world outside the family as rife with rampant sexual violence. This racist portrait of sexual violence served to displace tensions within the bourgeois family, as wives and daughters chafed under the rule of powerful husbands and fathers. Similarly, the sexual double standard, including sexual assaults of property-owning men against black women, could be projected outward, as black men were targeted as the threat to the sanctity of the family.

In the 1980s, there was a decisive shift from rape to incest as paradigmatic of women's sexual oppression. In reviewing this history, Louise Armstrong (1994) suggests that incest, even in its early entry into popular consciousness, tended to be more psychologized than rape, ushering in armies of mental health professionals who influenced the contours of the sexual abuse survivor movement. Armstrong laments the depoliticizing of sexual abuse that followed from the movement to treat incest as a "special case"— as more psychologically rooted than other forms of family violence.

But there may be a deep affinity between incestuous abuse and the anxieties of many middle-class women who shaped feminist politics in the 1980s. The prototypical rapist had always been associated in the popular imagination with the dark terrors of public life, and folktales of rape often operated as a cautionary tale against female ventures across social boundaries. The idea that female protection within the family was often illusory took hold as a unifying motif early on in feminism, fortified by findings that more women are harmed or killed in their homes than on the streets (Walker 1984). Shifting the ideological ground from stranger rape to date rape, marital rape, and other violations in the context of intimate relationships was part of a broader struggle to achieve emancipation from domestic confinement and to dismantle psychological and social barriers for women in entering public life. Since child sexual abuse, and particularly incest, is considered the most egregious of violations, it served as the one moral justification for adult daughters to sever family ties without suffering the debilitating guilt so often inflicted on prodigal daughters.

Incestuous abuse—whether at the hands of fathers or of various father surrogates—also captured more of the intimate side of the operations of power than did rape. Incest acquired a powerful social symbolic function in feminism, not only as a means of legitimizing the passage out of the suffocating constraints of the family but also as a potent signifier of seductive, patriarchal authority. As women entered the paid workforce in greater numbers in the 1980s, the prototypical cautionary tales of the past, including those offered by earlier periods of feminist struggle, confronted more complex social realities. The borders between private and public domains for women were blurred as women wrestled with new freedoms in a world of abiding constraints.

Yet the conflicts and complexities of eroticized power relations were anxiously re-repressed in much of the storytelling that took place in the sexual abuse survivor movement. Nonetheless, the latent meanings and expressive possibilities in storytelling may be at least as compelling as the more overt plot line. Stories of father-daughter incest emerged as more captivating than accounts of rape because they arise out of a context of intimacy. Just as Freud's early trauma model, seduction theory, suggested a confusing, guilty state of arousal associated with a premature sexual experience, contemporary trauma narratives center on the father's betrayal of the daughter's trust. The dilemmas women faced in the 1980s in responding to a more complex cultural terrain, where women were no longer entirely relegated to the private domain, may have created anxieties over how to manage effectively the conflictual, erotic aspects of power. As a symbolic tale, the contemporary incest story feels universal to many women, both because it is all too common and because it evokes the sense of complicity, of feeling entranced by oppressive encounters.

Sexual abuse survivorship extended beyond childhood incest, of course, even though the fuzzy borders of the concept of sexual abuse may have precipitated the emphasis on incest as prototype. As sexual abuse enlarged in the 1980s to include a broadening array of experiences—from various degrees and forms of incest (and other childhood sexual contacts with older persons) through date rape, marital rape, and sexual harassment in adolescence and adulthood—the precise and differing meanings of these experiences were collapsed in the unifying appeal of survivorship. A leading figure in the survivor movement, Wendy Maltz (1992), includes in her own version of this lengthening list "disparaging remarks about one's gender." In the welcoming arms of the sexual survivor movement, estimates that 30 to 40 percent of women are victims of child sexual abuse are grossly conservative. Since sexual abuse has become emblematic of the oppression of women generally, more "realistic" estimates should hover just under 100 percent.

What is gained and what is lost in this enlarging category of bodily located harm? This expanded lens advances understanding of the pervasiveness of sexually coded forms of oppression and the various ways in which women come to experience their bodies as objects of male domination, in private and public life. Since the more subtle or ambiguous forms of bad treatment girls and women endure so readily fall below the threshold of cultural awareness—indeed, they hardly register—dramatizing abuse may be the strategy of resistance most readily available. The downside of this unity, however, is that it may be more difficult to remember collectively other painful or difficult experiences that shape female selfhood and social identity. In contemporary literature on child abuse and trauma, incidents of inappropriate touching overshadow in importance other childhood assaults, such as whippings and emotional cruelty. Chronic neglect—which is the most common form of maltreatment that children, and particularly girls, endure—is particularly difficult to represent in the collective narratives of memory. (See Edwards and Alexander 1992.) In the project of remembering, it may be easier to struggle against a demonic presence than a perniciously absent one. This area of relative silence is not surprising, given that there is far less agreement in the culture that physical discipline—spankings, whippings, slaps—is harmful to children than is the case with sexual abuse. Further, because physical assaults of children are apt to be understood as "for your own good," it may be more difficult to claim these incidents as abusive. The memory of this same "for your own good" whispered in a girl's ear as her stepfather fondles her breast may be more readily detected as a lie, particularly after this girl grows up and moves beyond his reach.

Unlike other harms of childhood, secret sexual alliances may acquire a unique destructiveness because they are more bound up in complex emotional needs, including the desire for physical contact and pleasure. Even "minor" incidences of sexual abuse may be distressing because they may arouse confusing distinctions between "good touch" and "bad touch," between loving and harmful attention. Creating and sharing stories transforms these disturbing private recollections, as does the enlistment of others in emotionally managing them.

Conclusions

The very historical reality of incest and sexual trauma has given rise to its generative possibilities in women's storytelling practices. The contemporary incest survivors' movement turned private remembrances into social testimonials, as women refused to remain the guardians of the fathers' secrets. Exposing the fathers' secrets, however, opened up a Pandora's box of possibilities in the late 1980s and early 1990s as the incest narrator emerged as Every Woman in feminism and popular culture. *The Courage to Heal* became the heretical text of this movement—and a lightning rod for the growing cultural confusion and turbulence over women's recollections of childhood abuses.

My own exegesis of this feminist text stresses three main points. First,

The Courage to Heal is based on the idea that women's difficulties have a common origin in sexually invasive experiences in childhood. Given the pervasiveness of sexual intrusions in female development—ranging from the "sexual gaze," disparaging remarks, unwelcome touching, to overt rape and incest—it is not surprising that women find common cause in the identity of sexual abuse survivor. Second, Bass and Davis offer a "fundamentalist" version of feminism, an inspirational and comforting treatise that carries some of the same costs as religious fundamentalism. By ignoring the social context of memory retrieval and by treating memory as a sacral function that "reveals" itself in an unmediated fashion, the authors suspend critical awareness of the various influences shaping how women's stories get told. Third, the conflictual aspects of female sexual desire are too wedded to a model of trauma and injury. While the identity of sexual abuse survivor does permit women to express a broad range of sexual imagery and rebellious impulses, their "redemption" requires the recovery of a childhood sexual abuse scene. There is little recognition of sexuality as an area of inhibition or conflict for women, short of overt sexual abuse; nor is there recognition of alternative interpretations of ambiguous sexual imagery.

In approaching the incest survivor literature as feminist mythology, I am not reducing it to "untruth" but, rather, suggesting that the evocative power of these narratives extends beyond their factual content. From a feminist perspective, we can recognize the deep importance of women's struggle to achieve memory—to recover more authentic representations of the past—and the vital place of reclaiming, specifically, forgotten or minimized sexual injuries. At the same time, we must recognize how feminist memorial projects mobilize a wide range of psychological and social meanings, some of which are woven unconsciously into the fabric of memory. We need not be embarrassed to acknowledge this deeply social aspect of remembering or the mind's tendency to transform mental images and imprints of events, imaginatively embroidering on their narrative content. Indeed, if we are to achieve full equality, we need more than the courage to remember or to heal. We also need the courage to imagine.

NOTES

1. Unless otherwise specified, I refer throughout to the third edition of *The Courage to Heal.*

2. For a discussion of mother-blaming in the incest literature, see Herman (1992) and Armstrong (1994).

REFERENCES

Arey, D. 1995. Gay males and sexual child abuse. In L. A. Fontes (ed.), *Sexual abuse in nine North American cultures: Treatment and prevention.* Thousand Oaks, Calif.: Sage Publications, 200–235.

Armstrong, L. 1994. *Rocking the cradle of sexual politics: What happened when women said incest.* New York: Addison Wesley.

Bass, E. March 1993. The courage to heal: A five year retrospective with Ellen Bass. Paper presented at "Advances in Treating Survivors of Sexual Abuse: Empowering the Health Process II," Institute for Advanced Clinical Training, San Diego, Calif.

Bass, E., and Davis, L. 1994. *The courage to heal: A guide for women survivors of child sexual abuse.* 3d ed. New York: HarperCollins.

Beattie, M. 1987. *Co-dependent no more.* New York: Harper & Row.

Benjamin, J. 1988. *The bonds of love: Psychoanalysis, feminism, and the problem of domination.* New York: Pantheon Books.

Brownmiller, S. 1975. *Against our will: Men, women, and rape.* New York: Simon & Schuster.

Burkett, E., and Bruni, F. 1993. *Gospel of shame: Children, sexual abuse, and the Catholic Church.* New Haven, Conn.: Viking.

Butler-Evans, E. 1989. *Race, gender, and desire.* Philadelphia: Temple University Press.

Chodorow, N. 1994. *The reproduction of mothering: Psychoanalysis and the sociology of gender.* Berkeley: University of California Press.

Collins, P. H. 1990. *Black feminist thought.* New York: Routledge.

Edwards, J. J., and Alexander, P. C. 1992. The contribution of family background to the long term adjustment of women sexually abused. *Journal of Interpersonal Violence* 7, 306–320.

Goldstein, E., and Farmer, K. 1992. *Confabulations: Creating false memories, destroying families.* Boca Raton, Fla.: SIRS Books.

Haaken, J. 1993. From Al-ANON to ACOA: Co-dependence and the historical transformation of caregiving. *Signs* 18, 321–345.

———. 1998. *Pillar of salt: Gender, memory and the perils of looking back.* New Brunswick, N.J.: Rutgers University Press.

Hall, J. D. 1983. "The mind that burns in each body": Women, rape, and racial violence. In A. Snitow, C. Stanswell, and S. Thompson (eds.), *Powers of desire.* New York: Monthly Review Press, 328–349.

Herman, J. L. 1992. *Trauma and recovery.* New York: Basic Books.

————, with Hirschman, L. 1981. *Father-daughter incest*. Cambridge, Mass.: Harvard University Press.

Hunter, M. 1990a. *Sexually abused boys: The neglected victims of sexual abuse*. New York: Fawcett Columbine.

———— (ed.). 1990b. *The sexually abused male*. Vol. 1. Boston: Lexington Books.

Lisak, D. 1994. The psychological impact of sexual abuse: Content analysis of interviews with male survivors. *Journal of Traumatic Stress* 7, 525–548.

Loftus, E., and Ketcham, K. 1994. *The myth of repressed memory: False memories and allegations of sexual abuse*. New York: St. Martin's Press.

Maltz, W. 1992. *The sexual healing journey: A guide for survivors of sexual abuse*. New York: Harper Perennial.

Merskey, H. June 1995. What is a syndrome? *FMS Foundation Newsletter* 6.

Pendergrast, M. 1996. *Victims of memory: Sex abuse allegations and shattered lives*. Hinesburg, Vt.: Upper Access.

Rind, B., and Harrington, E. Forthcoming. A critical examination of the role of child sex abuse in causing psychological maladjustment: A review of the literature. In D. Halperin (ed.), *False memory syndrome: Therapeutic and forensic perspectives*. Washington, D.C.: American Psychiatric Press.

Russell, D. E. H. 1986. *The secret trauma: Incest in the lives of girls and women*. New York: Basic Books.

Schaef, A. W. 1986. *Co-dependence: Misunderstood and mistreated*. New York: Harper & Row.

Shay, J. 1994. *Achilles in Vietnam: Combat trauma and the undoing of character*. New York: Simon & Schuster.

Steiger, H., and Zanko, M. 1990. Sexual trauma among eating-disordered, psychiatric and normal female groups. *Journal of Interpersonal Violence*, 5, 74–86.

Steinem, G. Nov./Dec. 1995–Jan./Feb. 1996. Making connections. *Treating Abuse Today* 5, 7–11.

Terdiman, R. 1993. *Present past: Modernity and the memory crisis*. Ithaca, N.Y.: Cornell University Press.

Thompson, S. 1994. *Going all the way*. New York: Hill & Wang.

Tolman, D. L. 1991. Adolescent girls, women and sexuality: Discerning dilemmas of desire. In C. Gilligan, A. Rogers, and D. L. Tolman (eds.), *Women, girls and psychotherapy: Reframing resistance*. New York: Hawthorne Press, 55–67.

Vance, C. (ed.). 1989. *Pleasure and danger: Exploring female sexuality*. London: Pandora.

Walker, A. 1982. *Advancing Luna—and Ida B. Wells, You can't keep a good woman down*. New York: Harcourt Brace Jovanovich, 85–104.

Walker, L. E. 1984. *The battered woman syndrome*. New York: Springer.

Wilson, M. 1994. *Crossing the boundary: Black women survive incest*. Seattle: Seal Press.

Chapter Two

The Challenge to Feminism Posed by Women's Use of Violence in Intimate Relationships

Claire Renzetti

In her best-selling book *Fire with Fire: The New Female Power and How to Use It*, writer Naomi Wolf (1993) rails against what she calls "victim feminism." Among other things, victim feminism idealizes the notion of the "good" woman as helpless victim and "projects aggression, competitiveness, and violence onto 'men' or 'patriarchy,'" while ignoring those qualities in women (Wolf 1993, 137). Although there is much to fault in Wolf's often polemical anti-polemic, a good deal of what she says has a ring of truth for many readers. Recent research, for example, indicates that although a substantial segment of the general public, including a significant percentage of young women, support the feminist goal of gender equality, they nonetheless view *feminism* and *feminists* negatively, equating the terms with "man hating" and "male bashing" while simultaneously putting women on a pedestal of moral and social superiority (Denfeld 1995; Faludi 1991; Miller-Bernal 1992; Roiphe 1993). Those who share this view typically argue that if women want to be equals with men, they must take responsibility for their behavior just as they want men to do.

One manifestation of this anti-feminism is the widespread belief that women are as violent as men but are not held accountable for their violence. Such a view has been popularized in journalistic discussions of intimate violence (see, for example, Pearson 1997), but it can also be found in academic works (e.g., McNeely and Robinson-Simpson 1987; Steinmetz and Lucca 1988; Stitts and Macklin 1997; Straus 1993). Indeed, feminist researchers of intimate violence have sometimes been accused of hiding or suppressing data on female-to-male violence (see, for example, DeKe-seredy 1998).

In this chapter, I first review the empirical data on gender symmetry in intimate violence, discussing both the feminist and anti-feminist interpretations of those data. I give special attention to the ways in which the data are typically collected, since research methodologies often place constraints on precisely what the data can tell us. I think this discussion will illuminate the need for feminists to develop a comprehensive analysis of women's use of violence in intimate relationships. I conclude by identifying what I consider to be some of the key issues that feminists must address in developing such an analysis.

Are Women as Violent as Men?
What the Data Do and Do Not Tell Us

Intimate violence continues to be a serious and widespread problem in U.S. households, despite recent legal reforms and enhanced social service and law enforcement efforts to address it. Traditionally, the orientation of social scientists has been to view women as the victims of intimate violence and men as the perpetrators. However, since the 1980s, various researchers have been calling attention to women's perpetration of intimate violence. Murray Straus (1993), for example, reports results from the 1985 National Family Violence Survey, with a sample of 6,002 couples, showing that the overall rate of assaults by wives was 124 per 1,000 couples, compared with an overall rate of assaults by husbands of 122 per 1,000 couples. The rate of minor assaults by wives was 78 per 1,000 couples, whereas the rate of minor assaults by husbands was 72 per 1,000 couples. The rate of severe assaults by wives was 46 per 1,000 couples, and the rate of severe assaults by husbands was 50 per 1,000 couples. These differences were not statistically significant. Other researchers have obtained similar findings for married couples, as well as for cohabiting and dating partners (Brush 1990; DeKeseredy, Saunders, Schwartz, and Alvi 1997; Sorenson and Telles 1991; Sugarman and Hotaling 1989).

Some interpret these data as evidence of gender symmetry in intimate violence and argue that if women are as violent as men, feminist explanations of intimate violence that rely on patriarchy are inadequate at best (e.g., McNeely and Robinson-Simpson 1987; Stitts and Macklin 1997; Steinmetz and Lucca 1988; Straus 1993). Michael Dutton (1994), for example, claims that direct empirical tests of the feminist hypothesis that patriarchal ideology is a cause of intimate violence are few, and those that exist provide only qualified support for the hypothesis. Instead, Dutton argues, the data on both male and female violence in intimate relationships point strongly to the psychopathology of batterers as a primary causal factor. Other researchers, however, have challenged the gender symmetry research on various grounds. Most of these challenges center on the methodological constraints inherent in relying on a single measure of relationship violence. More specifically, the majority of studies that report gender symmetry in intimate violence use the Conflict Tactics Scales (CTS), developed by Murray Straus (1979), or some "modified" version of the CTS.[1] The CTS asks respondents to report the number of times in the previous twelve months that they have used and/or been the victims of various acts when attempting to resolve conflicts with their intimate partners. The acts range from "tried to discuss the issue calmly" to "yelled and/or insulted" to "hit with something hard."

One difficulty with relying solely on such a measure is that it fails to take into account the potentially different outcomes of each act when engaged in by men and women. Given average sex differences in physical strength and size, for instance, a woman who pushes a man is not likely to injure him, whereas a man who pushes a woman might do her serious harm. Consequently, several researchers (e.g., Brush 1990; Saunders 1989) argue that the claim that women are as violent as men is overstated if one factors in injurious outcomes. Domestic assaults by men are six times more likely to cause injury than domestic assaults by women. (See also Dobash, Dobash, Cavanagh, and Lewis 1998; Vivian and Langhinrichsen-Rohling 1994.)

A second serious problem with relying exclusively on the CTS is that it does not allow us to determine the "context" in which the violence occurred, the "motivations" underlying the use of violence in a specific situation, and the "meanings" that the actors give to specific actions (i.e., the social actors' subjective interpretations of an action and how these interpretations vary from individual to individual). The focus on comparative rates of violence by men and women rests on the faulty assumption that all violence is the same, when, in fact, there are important differences between initiating violence to punish or control one's partner, using violence in self-defense, and retaliating against a violent partner. As Daniel Saunders (1989) has pointed out, this is not simply an issue of who hits first, since individuals may be motivated to strike first because they believe violence against them is imminent.[2]

Unfortunately, research on gender differences in context, motivation, and meaning of intimate violence is limited. Studies that have examined these variables have typically collected data from small, nonrandom samples of battered women or battering men or, less often, from both partners. (See, for example, Barnett, Cheok, and Thelan 1997; Cascardi and Vivian 1995; Das Dasgupta, forthcoming; Dobash et al. 1998; Stets 1988.)[3] Although these studies have also sometimes used the CTS or a derivative of it, most use in-depth interviewing to collect data. The studies suggest that men's and women's motives for using violence and their experiences of violence are quite different. Men, it appears, are more likely to use violence against an intimate partner when they perceive themselves losing control of the relationship or when they interpret their partner's words or behavior as a challenge to their authority. Women are more likely to use violence against an intimate partner in self-defense or to fight back when attacked. Indeed, Michelle Cascardi and Dina Vivian (1995) report that women are more likely than men to use severe physical aggression in self-defense.

In sum, there are those who feel that the data, despite methodological problems, indicate that feminist theory, by focusing solely on men's violence against women, is inadequate at best because it cannot account for women's use of violence in intimate relationships. They therefore are calling for researchers to "move beyond" feminism to the development of an analysis that sees intimate violence as a "human" problem rather than a "gender" problem and that holds women responsible for their violent behavior. (See, for example, Dutton 1994; Pearson 1997; Wolf 1993.)

But my interpretation of the data is just the opposite: For me, feminist perspectives—regardless of the differences among them—are the only perspectives that collectively use gender as a central organizing variable for understanding human behavior and social organization. And despite all we do not know about intimate violence, we do know that it is *gendered*. When I look at the data that have been collected by both feminist and nonfeminist researchers, I see strong evidence that women's and men's violence are both quantitatively and qualitatively different. That women are sometimes violent in intimate relationships does not diminish the importance of discerning the role that gender plays in the etiology and perpetration of intimate violence.

If women use violence in intimate relationships, we should not assume that they are "acting like men." It has been feminists who have pointed out the error of applying male behavior as normative and evaluating female behavior in terms of this male standard. Consider, for example, that many men exhibit proficiency in violence (Albert Cardarelli, quoted in Ptacek, forthcoming). In other words, their violence is a routinized method of controlling others; they are prepared, both physically and emotionally, to behave violently. Most women do not exhibit such proficiency, but they are well aware of their male partners' proficiency in violence and this, in itself, intimidates them. Few women can intimidate others the way men can. Because feminists take such differences into account—indeed, many feminist theorists make gender differences the centerpiece of their theorizing—I believe it is feminists who can best develop a solid, empirically grounded understanding of women's use of violence, with gender as a primary explanatory variable.

As I have pointed out elsewhere (Renzetti 1994), however, feminist researchers and theorists have not focused unidimensionally on gender. A substantial amount of feminist research documents the historical and cultural specificity of particular behaviors and social structures. In addition, an examination of how gender intersects with other status variables, including race, social class, age, and sexual orientation, has become a critical component of most feminist research and theorizing. It is these building blocks of feminist theory that we must bring to bear in an analysis of women's use of violence in intimate relationships. In fact, it is for these very reasons that I will not "move beyond" feminism—a call that I see as asking me to abandon feminism—for feminism, it seems to me, offers the most fertile ground for the development of a gendered, multidimensional theory of intimate violence.

But Don't We Already Have a Feminist Theory of Women's Use of Violence?

There are some readers, I suspect, who are puzzled by my call for a feminist analysis of women's use of violence. "What's she getting so worked up about?" they're likely thinking. "Don't we already have such an analysis?" I would argue that what we have is only partial and fragmented; it is incomplete and, at times, disjointed.

We have already seen, for instance, that we have a good deal of research which tells us that in abusive heterosexual relationships, husbands and boyfriends initiate the violence in the "majority" of cases; in instances in which wives or girlfriends initiate the violence, it is "usually" because they believe violence against them is imminent. When women assault men with whom they are intimate, it is "typically" in self-defense (Das Dasgupta, forthcoming; Saunders 1989). Women are "more likely" than men to be injured during domestic confrontations, and when men kill their intimate partners, they are significantly "less likely" to do so in self-defense (Bachman and Saltzman 1995; Daly and Wilson 1988). The little research that is available on violence in lesbian relationships tells us that, as in abusive heterosexual relationships, the violence is "rarely" mutual abuse; if violence is used by both partners, one is "typically" acting in self-defense (Renzetti 1992).

We "know" all these things about these types of situations, but we do not know much about other, "atypical" situations. The fact is that women use violence in a variety of contexts and relationships: Women may abuse their children, their parents, and, yes, their intimate partners, heterosexual or lesbian. Are all female perpetrators the same? I doubt it. Is all violence perpetrated by women the same? Of course not. Is it caused by the same factors? That's highly unlikely. *But what kinds of answers are these to such important questions?* Feminist researchers have spent an incredible amount of time studying men's violence against women, demonstrating that women are not to blame for the violence, that they don't ask for it, that they can't easily escape it. And I emphasize that I am not arguing that these efforts have been misplaced. To the contrary, they were and are— perhaps especially in this time of backlash—fundamentally necessary. However, what is also necessary is careful attention to those situations in which women use violence in intimate relationships as perpetrators, not in self-defense or even in retaliation. It is feminists who must undertake this work.

Why the urgency in my call? Research *frames* a problem in the political and public consciousness. Researchers create the language with which a problem is described and assessed. As criminologists Martin Schwartz and Walter DeKeseredy (1993, 249) have pointed out, "There is an important battle being waged right now over the nature of women's behavior and its role in woman abuse." In this battle, it is the voices of anti-feminists, such as Patricia Pearson, that are shaping the public consciousness about—as well as many clinical and criminal justice responses to— women's use of violence, and this has serious consequences for many women.

For example, abused women who fight back against their attackers are increasingly being ordered to batterer treatment programs under mandatory arrest policies (Hamberger and Potente 1994). Some judges are also now in the habit of issuing mutual restraining orders, requiring abusive husbands/boyfriends and their abused wives/girlfriends who have fought back to stay away from each other. James Ptacek (forthcoming) argues that such mutual orders, besides going against the guidelines of the law, attest to the backlash against feminist efforts to transform the legal system's response to battered women and to the anger being directed at battered women. In short, battered women are being forced to pass an increasing number of "tests" to prove that they are "true" or "worthy" victims, and their survival strategies are being criminalized.

A worthy victim is innocent of wrongdoing. The notion of "wrongdoing" here rests on certain assumptions about femininity—in particular, *respectable* femininity. A woman may deviate from the standards of respectable femininity in at least two ways. One is by not behaving as a lady should—for example, drinking or using drugs, dressing "seductively," having an extramarital affair. I am reminded of a 1994 case in which a Maryland judge sentenced the defendant, a man who had killed his wife after he found her in bed with another man, to just eighteen months probation, reasoning that most men would have felt compelled to punish their wives under such circumstances ("Punishment Is Eighteen Months" 1994). Similarly, a woman who has been abused may be deemed a worthy victim, but when she uses violence against her intimate partner, she is no longer innocent. Her "unladylike" behavior discloses her culpability in her own victimization. Even the successes of the battered women's movement can be turned against women who have fought back or retaliated against an abusive partner: With more hotlines and shelters available than ever before, battered women now have far fewer "excuses" for staying in an abusive relationship.

A second, not unrelated way in which women can violate social standards of femininity is by being too much like a man. Women who engage in behavior stereotyped as masculine are deemed abnormal and certainly ineligible for worthy victim status. Consider, for example, lesbians who have been abused by their intimate partners. I found, when conducting my research on lesbian battering, that many heterosexuals were not at all surprised by the abuse itself. After all, they said, lesbians really want to be men, and men are often violent. Not surprisingly, then, many struggled with applying the label "victim" to the abused partner, since lesbians, by this definition, were masculine and could successfully repel an attacker. Consequently, lesbian abuse victims who had a masculine appearance, whose abusers appeared more feminine, and who did fight back faced tremendous obstacles when they sought help. When asked what kind of help would have been most beneficial to them as victims, many replied that they simply want to be listened to and believed. As one respondent said, "Treat me as you would treat any woman who has been the victim of a violent crime" (Renzetti 1992, 131).

The typification of battered women, lesbian or heterosexual, as culpable underlies the belief that their violence is the same as men's violence, unless they can prove otherwise. When men are violent, it may be explained away as "boys just being boys"; men are aggressive by nature (Newburn and Stanko 1994). Since we construct sex and gender in oppositional terms— what men are, women are not, and vice versa—it is women's "nature" to be passive; the respectable woman, the feminine woman, is socially constructed as a natural victim. Thus, the woman who uses violence is inherently a "bad" woman. To paraphrase Elizabeth Stanko (forthcoming), she is dangerous because her violence is proof of her ability to transgress the control of normative femininity.

The police, attorneys, and judges, like the backlash writers, argue that women, like men, must be held accountable for their behavior. To them, prosecuting women who have used violence against an intimate partner represents a gender-neutral application of the law.[4] However, by decontextualizing women's violence and scrutinizing it in terms of a male normative standard juxtaposed against stereotypes of respectable femininity, the justice system thereby treats unjustly many women who have used violence. The outcome will be—indeed, it already is—"gendered injustice." Women are increasingly being treated like men by the legal system, even though their circumstances typically are quite different. If these differential circumstances are not taken into account, the outcomes can hardly be fair. But let me underline a point I made earlier: I am not arguing that women are never willfully violent or that all women who use violence are responding to violent men and therefore should not be held accountable for their behavior. Rather, I am arguing that contemporary criminal justice policies that claim to be gender neutral are producing unjust and harmful legal outcomes for women by not taking into account the complex circumstances surrounding both female violent offending and violent victimization and by not examining the diversity of women's lives. In developing a feminist theory of women's use of violence, which places gender at the center of the analysis, feminist researchers will take an important step in redressing this injustice.

What Will a Feminist Theory of Women's Violence Look Like?

Unfortunately, I cannot outline with more than the broadest strokes what I think the content of a feminist theory of women's use of violence will be. That content will emerge more clearly as feminists undertake their research on all the various types of violence used by women. What I do here in conclusion, however, is state briefly what I think is necessary as a foundation for a fully feminist theory of women's use of violence.

First, as I have already emphasized, we need to *contextualize* women's use of violence by considering its meanings to women, their motives for using violence, and the outcomes of their violence. At the same time, this contextualization must recognize that women's use of violence is culturally mediated. The meanings and motives attached to violence by White, middle-class women are not likely to be the same as those of women from cultures that ascribe greater or lesser power to women in the use of physical force or psychological manipulation. For example, Shamita Das Dasgupta, director of Manavi, an advocacy organization for East Asian immigrant women, recently discussed Indian wives' responses to their husbands' violent behavior towards them (Das Dasgupta 1995). She pointed out that in the face of severe and prolonged abuse, Indian women are more likely to kill themselves than to kill their abusers. They may also kill their children before committing suicide, because they are responsible for the children and to leave the children with the abuser would be unconscionable. The role of abusive husbands in such cases is rarely, if ever, investigated by the police. Thus, the batterer is not held responsible for his role in the murder-suicide.

In contrast, consider Australian Aboriginal women. Although the incidence of wife abuse is high in Australian Aboriginal communities, researchers report that women typically fight back. According to anthropologist Victoria Burbank (1994), these women experience aggression as *aggressors*, which is different from women who experience aggression primarily as *victims*. Burbank clearly associates victim status with helplessness, loss, and disempowerment. She identifies, as legal scholar Nan Hunter does, woman-as-victim as "a cultural script that evokes sympathy without challenging the hierarchical structure" (quoted in Lewin 1992, E6). In Burbank's view, the cultural norms that prescribe fighting back by Aboriginal women better prepare them to combat the potentially traumatizing effects of men's violence against them. This is not to say that these women are unharmed physically or psychologically, but Burbank reports that to the women themselves, their aggression is an important source of self-esteem, a marker of their independence from men. "These are not women deviating from societal norms, 'rejecting their proper sex role,' or 'having identity problems.' Rather, they are women who are displeased with a turn of events and express their displeasure in culturally prescribed, culturally expected ways" (Burbank 1994, 184).

Similarly, criminologists Rodney Brunson and Jody Miller (forthcoming) have criticized both feminist and nonfeminist scholarship on girls' violent behavior in gangs because it depicts girls' physical aggression as purely defensive, as a response to threat, as resistance to victimization by men. While such a depiction is certainly an improvement over portrayals of violent females as pathological or "crazy," it nevertheless denies female agency. The question must be raised, "What does the behavior mean to the women themselves in this specific context?" The answers to this question, no doubt, will vary widely.

In addition to contextualizing women's use of violence, feminist analyses of this violence must be *collaborative.* Academics, practitioners, advocates, women survivors and offenders—the last of these sometimes being one and the same—must develop a feminist theory of women's use of violence together. Too often the voices of advocates, and especially those of survivors and offenders, get drowned out by academics and clinicians, who are regarded—and who regard themselves—as the "experts." Those of us who are academics or clinicians need to learn to listen to these voices and, more important, *to trust what they say to us,* rather than imposing our own preconceived analytic categories on their accounts, dismissing their explanations of the meanings and motives underlying their behavior as simply false consciousness. Jill Davies and her colleagues (1998) take this approach to improving services for battered women; they call it *woman-defined advocacy.* We can apply their model to the task of theory building: This means theory building that starts from the perspective of women who have used violence and "integrates the [theorist's] knowledge and resources into the woman's framework, and ultimately values her thoughts, feelings, opinions, and dreams—that she is the decision maker, the one who knows best, the one with the power" (Davies, Lyon, and Monti-Catania 1998, 3–4).

Finally, and perhaps most difficult, feminists must *own* the problem of women's use of violence. I must admit that I, like many feminists, have been reluctant to delve into this issue for fear that my work will be used against women. However, as the media attention that has greeted books like Pearson's (1997) indicates, the issue is already being used against us. I urge feminists, therefore, to seize this issue and make it our own. Moreover, in so doing, we must not succumb, as Jane Flax (1990) has warned, to victim status:

> We need to avoid seeing women as totally innocent, acted upon beings. Such a view prevents us from seeing the areas of life in which women have had an effect, are not totally determined by the will of the other, and the ways in which some women have and do exert power over others.   (Flax 1990, 181–182)

The labels "victim" and "battered woman" are stigmatized identities. "They are often applied to people in order to rob them of the full range of their humanness" (Ptacek, forthcoming). Documenting, denouncing, and acting to prevent men's violence against women does not require us to deny women's agency.

Angela Browne (1995) points out that the primary focus of our research and clinical interventions has traditionally been on the traumatic outcomes of victimization and obstacles to recovery for victims. Browne advocates instead the adoption of a "strengths model" that, among other things, centers research and intervention on building on victims' strengths and effective survival strategies. This is not to say that we neglect victims' suffering. Rather, Browne argues that the emphasis on the negative aspects of victimization has obscured the fact that victims possess tremendous internal strengths that help see them through the trauma. If we look at victimization through the lens of the strengths model, we get a more complete and accurate picture of victims while simultaneously promoting more effective and long-term healing (Browne 1995). Or as Ptacek (forthcoming) puts it, if social stigma represents the reduction of one identity to a single discredited characteristic, then the antithesis of a stigmatizing interaction is one that recognizes the full humanity of an individual.

One of Naomi Wolf's (1993) chief complaints about feminism is that it dwells on women's weaknesses and not on women's strengths. "In short," she writes, "we never let ourselves enjoy feeling strong" (Wolf 1993, 156). I urge feminists, therefore, to build a theory of women's use of violence that is not only woman defined but also firmly grounded in the strengths model. By taking ownership of the tasks of researching and theorizing women's use of violence, feminists can at once lay bare women's strengths and women's suffering, a process that I think will both empower women and harness the backlash.

NOTES

1. Recently, Straus and his colleagues (1995) introduced the Revised Conflict Tactics Scales (CTS2), an expanded version of the CTS. It consists of three scales that were part of the original CTS, plus two new scales that purport to measure sexual coercion and physical injury. The CTS2 was developed in response to some of the criticisms of the original CTS, but the reliability and validity of the new measure has yet to be established.

2. For a more detailed critique of the CTS, see DeKeseredy and Schwartz 1998.

3. The samples are typically drawn from clinic or shelter populations. The individuals who make up the samples have usually been mandated for treatment (e.g., by the courts) or have sought help for the problem of intimate violence or for general marital problems. Consequently, these samples are not likely to be representative of all individuals who have used violence against an intimate partner.

4. There is evidence that social controls over women are increasing, particularly formal legal controls. Elsewhere (Renzetti 1998), I ask whether it is purely coincidental that efforts to impose more far-reaching controls over women have followed a period during which women as a group struggled successfully for greater autonomy and self-determination. Likewise, Susan Miller (1998) points out that many of the proponents of recent get-tough crime control policies are also outspoken leaders of the anti-feminist backlash.

REFERENCES

Bachman, R., and Saltzman, L. E. 1995. *Violence against women: Estimates from the redesigned survey.* Bureau of Justice Statistics Special Report, NCJ-154348. Rockville, MD: U.S. Department of Justice.

Barnett, O. W.; Cheok, Y. L.; and Thelan, R. E. 1997. Gender differences in attributions of self-defense and control in interpartner aggression. *Violence against Women* 3, 462–81.

Browne, A. 1995. Returning women's strengths into the domestic violence discourse. Paper presented at the Wheaton College Conference on Feminism and Domestic Violence, Wheaton, MA.

Brunson, R. K., and Miller, J. Forthcoming. Girls and gangs. In Renzetti, C. M., and Goodstein, L. (eds.), *Women, crime, and justice: Contemporary perspectives.* Los Angeles: Roxbury.

Brush, L. D. 1990. Violent acts and injurious outcomes in married couples: Methodological issues in the National Survey of Families and Households. *Gender and Society* 4, 56–67.

Burbank, V. K. 1994. *Fighting women.* Berkeley: University of California Press.

Cascardi, M., and Vivian, D. 1995. Context for specific episodes of marital violence: Gender and severity of violence differences. *Journal of Family Violence* 10, 265–93.

Daly, M., and Wilson, M. 1988. *Homicide*. Hawthorne, NY: Aldine de Gruyter.

Das Dasgupta, S. Forthcoming. Violence by women—A critical view. In Shepard, M., and Pence, E. (eds.), *Coordinating community response to domestic violence: Lessons from the Duluth model*. Thousand Oaks, CA: Sage.

————. 1995. Women who kill: A challenge for inclusion. Paper presented at the Conference on Women, Sexuality and Violence: Re-visioning Public Policy, Philadelphia, PA.

Davies, J.; Lyon, E.; and Monti-Catania, D. 1998. *Safety planning with battered women*. Thousand Oaks, CA: Sage.

DeKeseredy, W. S. 1998. The anti-feminist backlash against woman, abuse surveys: Some Canadian examples. Paper presented at the Annual Meeting of the Academy of Criminal Justice Sciences, Albuquerque, NM.

DeKeseredy, W. S.; Saunders, D. G.; Schwartz, M. D.; and Alvi, S. 1997. The meanings and motives for women's use of violence in Canadian college dating relationships: Results from a national survey. *Sociological Spectrum* 17, 199–222.

DeKeseredy, W. S., and Schwartz, M. D. 1998. Measuring the extent of woman abuse in intimate heterosexual relationships: A critique of the Conflict Tactics Scales. U.S. Department of Justice, Violence against Women Grants Office Electronic Resources (http://www.vaw.umn.edu/research.asp).

Denfeld, R. 1995. *The new Victorians: A young woman's challenge to the old feminist order*. New York: Warner Books.

Dobash, R. P.; Dobash, R. E.; Cavanagh, K.; and Lewis, R. 1998. Separate and intersection realities: A comparison of men's and women's accounts of violence against women. *Violence against Women* 4, 382–414.

Dutton, D. G. 1994. Patriarchy and wife assault: The ecological fallacy. *Violence and Victims* 9, 167–82.

Faludi, S. 1991. *Backlash: The undeclared war against American women*. New York: Crown Publishers.

Flax, J. 1990. *Thinking fragments*. Berkeley, CA: University of California Press.

Hamberger, L. K., and Potente, T. 1994. Counseling heterosexual women arrested for domestic violence: Implications for theory and practice. *Violence and Victims* 9, 125–38.

Lewin, T. 1992. Feminists wonder if it was progress to become victims. *New York Times*, May 10, E6.

McNeely, R. L., and Robinson-Simpson, G. 1987. The truth about domestic violence: A falsely framed issue. *Social Work* 32 485–90.

Miller, S. L. 1998. Introduction. In Miller, S. L. (ed.), *Crime control and women* (pp. xv–xxiv). Thousand Oaks, CA: Sage.

Miller-Bernal, L. 1992. To be or not to be a feminist: Students' views of feminism.

Paper presented at the Annual Meeting of the American Sociological Association, Pittsburgh, PA.

Newburn, T., and Stanko, E. (eds.). 1994. Just boys doing business: Men, masculinity and crime. London: Routledge.

Pearson, P. 1997. *When she was bad: Violent women and the myth of innocence.* Toronto: Random House.

Ptacek, J. Forthcoming. *Disorder in the courts: Women, battering, and judicial responses.* Boston: Northeastern University Press.

Punishment is eighteen months for killing cheating wife. 1994. *New York Times*, October 19, A20.

Renzetti, C. M. 1998. Connecting the dots: Women, public policy, and social control. In Miller, S. L. (ed.), *Crime control and women* (pp. 181–89). Thousand Oaks, CA: Sage.

———. 1994. On dancing with a bear: Reflections on some of the current debates among domestic violence theorists. *Violence and Victims* 9, 195–200.

———. 1992. *Violent betrayal: Partner abuse in lesbian relationships.* Newbury Park, CA: Sage.

Roiphe, K. 1993. *The morning after.* Boston: Little, Brown.

Saunders, D. G. 1989. Who hits first and who hurts most? Evidence for greater victimization of women in intimate relationships. Paper presented at the Annual Meeting of the American Society of Criminology, Reno, NV.

Schwartz, M. D., and DeKeseredy, W. S. 1993. The return of the battered husband syndrome through the typification of women as violent. *Crime, Law and Social Change* 20, 249–65.

Sorenson, S. B., and Telles, C. A. 1991. Self-reports of spousal violence in a Mexican-American and non-Hispanic white population. *Violence and Victims* 6, 31–15.

Stanko, E. A. Forthcoming. Women, danger and criminology. In Renzetti, C. M., and Goodstein, L. (eds.), *Women, crime, and justice: Contemporary perspectives.* Los Angeles: Roxbury.

Steinmetz, S. K., and Lucca, J. S. 1988. Husband battering. In Van Hasselt, V. B.; Morrison, R. L.; Bellack, A. S.; and Hersen, M. (eds.), *Handbook of family violence* (pp. 233–46). New York: Plenum.

Stets, J. E. 1988. *Domestic violence and control.* New York: Springer-Verlag.

Stitts, S., and Macklin, A. 1997. Battered men: The hidden victims of domestic violence. Paper presented at the World Congress on Violence, Dublin, Ireland.

Straus, M. A. 1993. Physical assault by wives: A major social problem. In Gelles, R. J., and Loseke, D. R. (eds.), *Current controversies on family violence* (pp. 67–97). Newbury Park, CA: Sage.

———. 1979. Measuring intrafamily conflict and violence: The conflict tactics (CT) scales. *Journal of Marriage and the Family* 41, 75–88.

Straus, M. A.; Hamby, S. L.; Boney-McCoy, S.; and Sugarman, D. B. 1995. The personal and relationship profile: A package of instruments for research and clinical screening of couple violence. Paper presented at the Fourth International Conference on Family Violence Research, Durham, NH.

Sugarman, D. B., and Hotaling, G. T. 1989. Dating violence: Prevalence, context and risk markers. In Pirog-Good, M. A., and Stets, J. E. (eds.), *Violence in dating relationships: Emerging issues* (pp. 3–32). New York: Praeger.

Vivian, D., and Langhinrichsen-Rohling, J. 1994. Are bi-directionally violent couples mutually victimized? A gender-sensitive comparison. *Violence and Victims* 9, 107–24.

Wolf, N. 1993. *Fire with fire: The new female power and how to use it.* New York: Ballantine Books.

Chapter Three

"I Wasn't Raped, but … "

Revisiting Definitional Problems in Sexual Victimization

Nicola Gavey

> Feminist theory [must] … not leave a wide open space in
> which a backlash can become established.
> —(Hollway 1995, p. 129)

When a woman says she wasn't raped but describes an experience of forced, unwanted sexual intercourse, what are we to think? Was she "really" raped, despite disowning that label for her experience? Or does her refusal of the label suggest that her interpretation of the experience as other than rape makes it so? And what does it say about our culture(s) that there can be so much ambiguity over the differential diagnosis of rape versus sex? How should we conceptualize and judge the myriad coercive sexual acts that lie somewhere between rape and consensual sex? Finally, is being the object of violence or coercion always the same thing being the *victim* of such violence or coercion?

In this chapter I begin to explore some of the convoluted layers of issues in which such questions are embedded. My position on these issues is a very unstable one. In thinking through and around these questions, I find I can't settle comfortably into a straightforward, unitary position from which to craft an argument. Consequently, I try to be faithful to this confusion and ambivalence, because the one thing I have concluded is that there are indeed murky issues at the interface between (hetero)sex and sexual victimization. Even at the most basic level, I want to talk about and against rape and sexual victimization (as though these are straightforward terms) at the same time as I destabilize these categories, in the belief that this is an important part of the same fight at a different level.

I trace some of the changes in research on rape and sexual victimization over the past two decades and consider some of the implications of the new feminist social science approach. In particular, I consider three points that raise the need to revisit current conventions for conceptualizing sexual victimization. These points concern the concept of the unacknowledged rape victim, the loose distinction between rape and attempted rape, and the use of the term *sexual victimization* to refer to a broad range of arguably normative coercive heterosexual practices. In working from the assemblage of my shifting positions, I simultaneously tell at least two, potentially opposing stories about feminism and sexual victimization. When either of these stories is told on its own as an unproblematic account, I fear either that we may leave open a fertile space for backlash to take hold, as Wendy Hollway (1995) warns, or that we may unintentionally become part of the backlash ourselves.

A Starting Point

In the title of this chapter, I refer back to Martha Burt and Rhoda Estep's 1981 paper "Who Is a Victim? Definitional Problems in Sexual Victimization." In their timely and convincing article, Burt and Estep mapped the nascent influence of 1970s feminism on a redefinition and reconceptualization of sexual assault. They endorsed the more inclusive definition of sexual assault that was emerging from feminism at the time, drawing attention to the similarity between rape and other coercive sexual practices. Moreover, they argued strongly for the benefits for all women who have been sexually assaulted to claim the victim role. Although aware of what they called the "negative social value" and the "obligations" of the victim role, they proposed that the benefits would include "the right to claim assistance, sympathy, temporary relief from other role responsibilities, legal recourse, and other similar advantages" (p. 16).

Burt and Estep (1981) suggested that the analysis of the feminist movement increased the visibility of all forms of harassment, brutality, and violence toward women by men. They further claimed:

> In each instance, that analysis leads to challenges to the ways in which the dominant ideology has privatized, psychologized, and denied the victimiza-

tion of women. "Victimization" is political. Power dictates who victimizes and who gets victimized, and power dictates what will be viewed as victimization. A person recognized, legitimated, as a victim is recognized as someone who has received a wrong, who has been treated unfairly and unjustly.   (p. 25)

In this way, the language of victimization was proposed as a way of making sense of and opposing the moral injustice of women's oppression in the forms of violence and harassment.

The "New" Feminist Research on Sexual Victimization

Since 1981, quite a bit has changed on the landscape of sexual politics and cultural politics more generally. Both feminist activism and feminist social science have been instrumental in promoting a major rethinking of rape and sexual victimization in many western societies. Many of the sentiments expressed by Burt and Estep have been echoed and developed in feminist-influenced[1] social science research, which has itself become one of the most dominant paradigms in psychology for researching rape and sexual coercion. In a very short time we moved from a climate in which rape was widely regarded as rare to one in which rape is regarded as a widespread social problem. For example, in 1981, Mary Beard Deming and Ali Eppy referred to rape as "a statistically rare event" (p. 374), and in 1977, Edward Shorter surmised that "the average woman's chances of actually being raped in her lifetime are still minimal" (p. 481). However, in the 1980s, new research was being published which suggested that up to 15 percent (Koss, Gidycz, and Wisniewski 1987) or even 24 percent (Russell 1984) of women have experienced rape at some point in their lives. Moreover, these estimates of rape prevalence have been regarded by some researchers as likely underestimates of the extent of the problem, due to the unwillingness of some women to disclose their experiences to a researcher (e.g., Russell 1982; 1984).

This new feminist empirical research was specifically designed to overcome the limitations of previous estimates of rape prevalence (which relied on reports of rape to the police or reports in national crime surveys). Thus, this work introduced an important methodological point of departure from any previous attempts to measure the scope of rape. Women were asked not whether they had been raped[2] but rather whether they had had any experiences that matched behavioral descriptions of rape. For example, they were asked whether they had ever had sexual intercourse when they didn't want to because a man threatened or used some degree of physical force to make them do so (e.g., Koss et al. 1987). Moreover, this question was one among many such specific questions that women would be asked about a range of coercive sexual experiences. Such methodological refinements were designed to be sensitive to women's reluctance to report rape. They were seemingly successful, and the body of research produced shocking new data showing widespread rape and sexual victimization.

At the same time, two other important changes to the picture of rape emerged from this research. First, Diana Russell (1982; 1984)—and later, others—showed that women were far more likely to be raped by husbands, lovers, boyfriends, and dates than by strangers. Not only were the cultural blinkers that had enabled this to be regarded as "just sex" lifted, but it was found that such rapes were far more common than the stereotypical rape by a stranger. Second, a dimensional view of rape and sexual victimization replaced a typological view in much of the research: That is, while rape is the extreme act, it is regarded as being on a continuum with more subtle forms of coercion, from an unwanted kiss to unwanted sexual intercourse submitted to as a result of continual verbal pressure. The research by Koss and others (myself included—e.g., Gavey 1991a; 1991b) claimed that over 50 percent of women have experienced some form of sexual victimization on this continuum.

The dimensional view of rape combined with data on the high prevalence of all forms of sexual victimization, especially within legitimate heterosexual relationships, have two important effects: (1) They construe experiences that would have previously fallen within the realm of sex as forms of sexual *victimization*; and (2) they implicitly invite a critical examination of the whole realm of normative heterosexual practice (although this tends not to be explicitly discussed in the empirical literature).

It is perhaps not surprising that these feminist-influenced shifts in the meaning of rape and sexual victimization have been resisted on many fronts. In drawing attention to some of the more subtle forms of sexual coercion and theorizing their relationship to rape, this work has provided a troubling framework for making sense of what previously could be considered "just sex." In representations of normative heterosexuality, women are portrayed as the passive recipients of an active male desire; moreover, they are assumed to have the dual roles of responding to men's (appropriate) sexual initiatives and restricting inappropriate male "access."[3] Although traditional ideals of heterosexual romance suggest a woman's quiet desire waiting to be awakened by a man's expert seduction, this sort of representation of heterosexuality nevertheless *permits* forms of heterosexual relating in which a woman's desire and interest are absent. Male seduction can be enacted on a woman whose willingness is always in question.

Against a backdrop where rape was considered to be rare—and where complaints of rape were commonly regarded to be lies, distortions of normal sex, harmless, or provoked by the victim—the call to broaden the definition of sexual assault and victimization has been an important feminist move. Similarly, the way in which we have elaborated on the understanding of rape as a form of *victimization* has arguably contributed to more widespread concern about rape as a serious social problem. These moves have been one part of increased focus during the 1980s on many forms of victimization, and of widespread social concern for understanding their extent and dynamics and for ameliorating and preventing their harm.

"Victimization" in Crisis

At this point in the late 1990s, the concept of victimization is arguably in crisis. Joel Best (1997) opened a recent *Society* commentary with the unfavorable verdict that "victimization has become fashionable" (p. 9). As Richard Feldstein (1997) has observed, the term *victim* is just part of the "lexical string" (p. 10), along with *political correctness,* that has been targeted for critique by neoconservatives in the United States. A similar, if not identical, trend of backlash derision of the whole concept of victimization is also evident now in New Zealand. As part of more general conservative campaigns against research and services relating to victimization, there has been critical dispute over the new feminist research on rape—especially that on "date rape." It has been claimed that the issue has been exaggerated or that it has no validity as a concept (e.g., Gilbert 1994; Paglia 1992; Roiphe 1993; see also Denfeld 1995; Sommers 1994; Newbold 1996).

It is difficult to predict how such trends will be captured by the evolving public discourse about victimization. Representations of victims have always been double-edged, and there is some danger that understandings that invoke sympathy and support may again be overshadowed by those that invite disbelief and derision. As this happens, the concept of victimization will lose some of its explanatory and political efficacy. These social changes sharpen the need to reassess contemporary feminist conceptualizations of sexual victimization—if only to consider them in light of their ongoing strategic value.

Are Victims Created by a Victimization Framework?

> There are many ways to victimize people. One way is to convince them that
> they are victims.   (Hwang 1997, p. 41)

One strand of public concern at the moment is the fear that talk about victimization is needlessly creating victims. Moreover, critics of the movement against date rape have implied that it violates "assumptions of [women's] basic competence, free will, and strength of character" (Roiphe 1993, p. 69; see also Paglia 1992).

Burt and Estep (1981) were not unaware of the potentially negative aspects of the victim role, such as its denotation of dependency. Similarly, Charlene Muehlenhard and her colleagues (1992) acknowledged the connotation of powerlessness associated with using the word *victim* to refer to someone who has been sexually coerced. However, within a positivist mode of social science, these potential reservations almost have to be overlooked. But from the perspective of a poststructuralist feminism, the connotations of powerlessness and dependency of words such as *victim* and *victimization* are not so easy to overlook, because language and discourse are held to be "constitutive" of meaning. Culturally shared linguistic resources (and social practices and procedures) constrain and enable particular ways of seeing and experiencing the world. In this way, meaning is socially constructed.

There are various ways in which the language of sexual victimization can have material cultural effects. It may work at the broad cultural level to actively uphold discursive support for ways of being and acting that make sexual coercion and rape more possible. For example, it may reinforce and perpetuate images of women as weak, passive, and asexual and images of men as sexually driven, unstoppable, and potentially dangerous. These gendered ways of being may be further enhanced by the exacerbation of women's fears about rape through media reportage and through warnings about violent sexual attacks that emphasize women's vulnerability to rape over their potential for resistance. Moreover, the hegemonic interpretation of *sexual violence* (it is difficult to find a term that doesn't already contain metonymic associations with victimization) as a form of victimization specifies identities for those who are subjected to these kinds of acts. A rapist's moral infringement prescribes an experience of victimization for the rape *victim*. And the ever-present tentacles of the "psy-complex" ensure that we currently understand victimization as a process that acts on and changes individual psychology. A particular psychological outcome is preconfigured by calling the violence "victimization."

While these sorts of constitutive effects of the language of victimization need to be addressed, how valid is the sort of seductive public warning in Karen Hwang's point? Are victims really created out of thin air? When feminists and other social critics name certain practices as victimization, they are drawing attention to relationships of power that systematically privilege the experiences of some groups of people over those of others. Is the hysterical anxiety behind the suggestion that talking about victimization creates victimization a sort of head-in-the-sand approach to unpleasant social conditions—a naive hope that if a phenomenon is not seen and not heard, then it does not exist? As Linda Martin Alcoff (1997) notes, commentators such as Katie Roiphe suggest that "prior to the discourse of date rape, the experience itself did not occur, or at least not with such traumatizing aftereffects as we now associate with rape" (p. 16). Although there could seem to be superficial affinities between poststructuralist feminism and the simple determinism offered in this argument, there are important differences. While poststructuralism problematizes notions of essential, fixed identities, it does not leave us tabula rasa; at any one point in time we are some complex and fluid product of embodied-biography-in-cultural-history. We may be socially determined in some sense, but this does not imply we are blank spaces, able to be totally shaped by discrete discourses. The legacy of our positioning in the sorts of multiple and competing discourses that are currently circulating is a moral subject who is likely to experience the "wrongness" of rape in some way. This is because the late-twentieth-century cocktail of moral values—which still includes Judeo-Christian and humanist values of equality, of love and respect, of not harming others, and so on—provides a discursive context for interpreting many acts of sexual coercion and assault as morally wrong and potentially harmful. Thus, even from a discursive perspective, which emphasizes the constitutive power of language, we need not have access to a specific language of victimization or the particular notion of date rape, for example, for the sorts of practices described by these terms to have similar cultural meanings.

In light of the backlash crisis of representation of victimization and the different insights of poststructuralist feminism, it is perhaps time to revisit Martha Burt and Rhoda Estep's (1981) contention that it is in a woman's best interests to be perceived as a victim when she has experienced sexual coercion or violence. It is difficult to know how to evaluate this claim, and our attempts may benefit from some empirical analysis of women's accounts of their experiences of coercion, abuse, and violence. Few would deny that what we refer to as rape, sexual assault, sexual coercion, and sexual abuse can be victimizing. That is, they can be horrific events that traumatize women[4] and produce victims. Moreover, abusive and coercive practices can produce victims in more subtle and less horrific ways, through undermining a woman's confidence and eroding her agency over time. In the fight against rape, public feminist rhetoric has tended to privilege one of the many contradictory broader cultural meanings of rape—that is, its power to cause severe and irrevocable psychological harm to the victim. Those of us drawn to activism against rape often have firsthand knowledge of the effects of rape on friends, family members, women we have worked with, or ourselves. The potential trauma and devastating harm of rape, silenced and hidden for so many years, has now come to be almost automatically signified by the term *rape* (although not without exceptions).

There are three conventions that have developed in the sexual victimization research that, in light of the above discussion, deserve further consideration: (1) Women are classified as "rape victims" when they have experienced events that meet researchers' (and often legal) definitions of rape or sexual assault, irrespective of how they themselves identify their experiences. (2) The categories of "rape" and "attempted rape" are sometimes presented in an unproblematic conjunction as the most serious forms of sexual victimization. (3) The term *victimization* is used to refer to a broad range of coercive sexual practices. In the next sections I critically revisit the first two of these current conventions and briefly consider the third.

Unacknowledged Rape Victims

As discussed earlier, the new research on rape has tended not to rely on asking women whether or not they have ever experienced "rape." Some studies have included this direct question along with the more specific behavioral questions about forced, unwanted sex. It has been found that only around 30 to 50 percent of women who affirm they have had an experience that meets a narrow definition of rape identify that they have experienced "rape" (e.g., Koss 1988; Gavey 1991a; 1991b). The protocol in this research paradigm has been to categorize women as victims of rape if they report having had an experience consistent with the predetermined behavioral description that researchers define as rape when the questionnaires or structured interview data are analyzed. If these women do not report that they have experienced "rape" (when asked directly), then they are considered "unacknowledged" rape victims by the researchers (e.g., Koss 1985).

There are very good reasons for this method of detecting rape. The strategy recognizes the power of what Martha Burt (1980) has termed "rape myths" to cause even women who have had an experience consistent with narrow legal definitions of rape not to view what happened as rape. These myths are part of dominant discourses about women, men, power, and sexuality that help construct views about the likelihood of rape in particular situations, about the sorts of women who get raped, and about men who rape. From a feminist perspective, they were referred to as myths in recognition of the ways in which they worked to obscure rape and to minimize and justify forced sex by men who are white, "normal," and "respectable." These myths are part of discourses about normal heterosexuality as much as they are about rape. For instance, the saying "When a woman says no she means yes" embodies and inscribes traditional cultural norms for heterosex that make it difficult to perceive rape within legitimate heterosexual relationships. In this way, rape myths obscured much rape in marriage and other intimate heterosexual relationships, as well as in more casual heterosexual encounters (such as dates).

Despite the methodological rationale for not relying on women's own adoption of the label "rape," social critics have targeted this feature of the feminist empirical work on rape prevalence as a major weakness of the whole body of research.[5] Neil Gilbert (1994), for example, cites as a problem of Koss's rape prevalence estimates that "almost three-quarters of the students whom Koss defined as victims of rape did not think they had been raped" (p. 23). Following Gilbert, Katie Roiphe (1993) is similarly unimpressed with Koss's categorization of women who were "not self-proclaimed victims" (p. 52) as victims of rape. Ironically, this methodological approach is totally consistent with the positivist conventions of social and behavioral psychology more generally, where it is considered good research practice to use operational definitions for specifying precise categories of behavior that can be reliably measured. Similarly, in most areas of psychology where attitudes, experiences, and so on are classified, this is done in indirect ways not dissimilar to those used in the feminist empirical rape research. For instance, it would be considered valid to classify a person as "depressed" if he or she answered a range of questions on a depression inventory in the predicted ways, even if the individual did not affirm the statement "I am depressed."

Let us consider an example of the sort of experience that could be described as an unacknowledged rape. One woman I interviewed described an experience, which occurred when she was nineteen, of waking to find her thirty-year-old male apartment mate in her bed, "groping" her (Gavey

1990; 1992). She had no prior sexual or romantic relationship with this man, but on this night he got into her bed while she was asleep and had intercourse with her, with no apparent consideration of her lack of interest. She explained:

> *Ann:* . . . it all happened quite quickly really, but I remember thinking quite clearly, "Well if I don't—If I try and get out of the bed, perhaps if I run away or something . . . he might rape me [pause] so I had better just . . ."
> *Nicola:* If you try and run away you mean?
> *Ann:* If I tried it, if I'd resisted, then he might rape me, you know. So he did anyway, sort of thing, really, when you think about it, when I look back.

This man was rough and left her bleeding. Later, she was frightened, "confused," "nervous within the house," and hypervigilant about making sure she was never asleep before he'd gone to bed. Moreover, she felt she got a reputation in the apartment as an "uptight bitch" because she wouldn't take up the same man's offers on subsequent nights to "come and sleep with me." Nevertheless, Ann did not conceptualize this event as rape at the time.

Technically, this encounter may not count as rape in a narrow legal sense, because it is unclear how explicitly Ann communicated her nonconsent. Most feminist analyses, however, would point out the restraints on her being able to do this, such as being only just awake and fearing that her resistance might lead to worse treatment. Feminists would also highlight the absence of reasonable grounds for this man assuming consent (e.g., Pineau 1989). That is, even the most androcentric norms of heterosex would not hold it reasonable for a man to assume that a woman approached when she is asleep in her own bed by a man with whom she had no prior sexual or romantic relationship would be consenting to sex, in the absence of some active communication of this consent. Consequently, many feminists would describe this incident as rape or, at the very least, sexual assault. Clearly, in spite of Ann's resistance to the identity of rape victim, the experience had a negative psychological impact on her. It is impossible to know how, if at all, the effects would have been different had she viewed what happened as rape. There is some indication in her account that to have had an experience she would have called "rape" would have been worse—"if I'd resisted, then he might rape me." Indeed, it would have been a different experience and one that may have more powerfully signaled her lack of control and her vulnerability. Psychologically, she perhaps maintained more control (a meager but significant amount) and risked losing less by choosing not to "run away or something" than if she had resisted as hard as she could and been raped anyway.

During our interview several years after this incident, Ann moved toward retrospectively understanding it as rape—after explaining that she did not resist because "he might rape me," she said, "So he did anyway, sort of thing . . . when I look back." Nevertheless, from the point of view of a feminist research ethic, I would struggle with the validity and ethics of labeling Ann a "rape victim" at the time when she did not choose this label herself. However, the ambiguity that arises in talking about Ann's experience and how to make sense of it in the research context itself invites cultural critique of the realm of heterosexual possibility that can contain such offensive, disrespectful, and, in this case, hurtful male acts. (For other, similar examples, see Gavey 1992.) If this woman's experience is not considered to be rape or some form of sexual assault very close to rape (by her *or* by the man involved *or* by police, judges, and juries *or* by researchers and social theorists), then what is it? Sex? If it can be accepted as just part of the realm of sex, then it redirects a critical spotlight onto heterosexuality itself.

It is worth noting that although Ann "resisted" seeing herself as a rape victim, this did not enable her to resist the assault physically. This illuminates how it would be misleading to assume that *not* being positioned in an overt discourse of rape or victimization somehow protects a woman from sexual assault. In a situation such as that Ann faced, the mark of gender difference imposed on what is a physical contest of sorts already incites certain responses, such as immobility and fear, that aid a rapist in his attack. To me, this suggests that in addition to directly challenging the overt discourse of rape, we need to create and promote discourses (both in language and in the normative practices of heterosexual interaction) that indirectly challenge the possibility of rape—for example, ways of understanding heterosex that don't leave room for ambiguity over a woman's entitlement to refuse unwanted sex.

A Feminist Response—The Methodology

With critical reflection on the research strategy of classifying some women as unacknowledged rape victims, what do we want to say in response to the critics but also as part of ongoing reflexive research practice? There is probably no straightforward answer, but I think it is important that we approach it as an open question rather than with formulaic answers. Why do so many women who have had experiences consistent with a legal definition of rape resist the label of "rape victim" (e.g., Koss 1985)? And how should feminist research respond to these women's rejection of the "rape" label? These questions raise complicated issues that are at the heart of feminist theory about research practice. If we see our role as giving women voice, then it may not be legitimate to "put words in their mouths," to describe experiences as rape that women themselves do not describe in that way. However, feminist research increasingly seeks to go beyond giving women voice and reporting on women's experiences, to offer analyses and critiques that help make sense of women's experiences as they are shaped and constrained by power relations in social contexts. When women's voices don't always tell "our story," it can be troubling to know how to proceed. (See also Fine 1992; Kitzinger and Wilkinson 1997.)

Evaluated in this light, the feminist empirical research on rape prevalence occupies an interesting position. In its use of traditional methods to produce conventional data dressed in the language of science rather than that of feminist politics, this research has been an important part of wider feminist action. This action has had some important successes—most notably, changes to rape laws, in many English-speaking countries and in portions of the United States, to recognize rape within marriage as a crime. Widespread publicity about date rape has also led to rape prevention programs on many university campuses. Despite the limited effectiveness of these changes so far (for instance, convictions for wife rape are extremely rare), this body of research has nevertheless had a subversive and transformative role in the changing representations of rape. It has generated a profound shift in the meaning of rape, to the extent that it is no longer impossible to think of a man raping his wife or a sporting hero raping a woman he dated (although this possibility is still more likely to be readily accepted if the man is black). Moreover, the research has subtly and covertly challenged normative heterosexuality. While this critique is often not explicit in the research, its message is obviously received by critics of the research, as evidenced in one of Neil Gilbert's (1994) criticisms of Koss's work on rape prevalence:

> Seeing rape not as an act of deviance, but as typical behavior of an average man, Koss notes that her findings support the view that sexual violence against women "rests squarely in the middle of what our culture defines as 'normal' interaction between men and women." (p. 23)

Gilbert offers no further critical analysis of this view, presumably in the belief that its flaw will be obvious to his imagined audience. In the context of his article, Gilbert's point can be read as an attempt to affirm the innocence of normal heterosexuality and cast as ridiculous any connection between it and rape.

Research and Complexity

The positivism of the empirical psychology research, however, has yielded the findings discussed above at a cost. It has forced closure on definitions of various forms of victimization and classified women's experiences into readymade categories of victims. This style of methodology necessitates disregard for nuanced and possibly contradictory meanings. Moreover, researchers seem to find it reasonably unproblematic that answers to such basic questions as whether or not a particular experience counts as "rape" are constructed through the research process. The resulting certainty that can be projected about the extent and nature of rape and sexual victimization may eventually undermine the authority of the findings, when it is found that the reductive and universalizing features of this style of research don't "speak to" the experience of all women whom it ostensibly represents. Not only are decisions about who is and who is not a rape victim not always straightforward, but the partiality of new truths about the effects of rape is sometimes overlooked.

In some instances, women's reactions may be contradictory and not consistent with either dominant traditional or dominant feminist constructions of rape. One woman participating in my research (Gavey 1990) described a situation with her boyfriend, whereby she said she wanted to say to him, "The very first time we had sex you raped me." However, she didn't always view the forced sex as rape, and she continued her relationship with this man for more than two years. She detailed a complex set of contradictory, ambivalent, and changing reactions to this and other coercive sexual experiences in the relationship. She also discussed how the usual feminist analyses of rape, such as those she later encountered at a rape crisis center, were not entirely helpful. Her reactions were not consistent with what she was hearing about how women respond to rape—because she loved the man who raped her, remembered some of their sex as "wonderful," and so on, she went through a stage of feeling that she must be a "sick" and "masochistic" person. Sharon Lamb (1996) has described the situation of a woman who eventually ended her relationship with her boyfriend not because he raped her but because he couldn't later acknowledge that what he'd done in forcefully holding her down and having sex with her was rape.

Feminist accounts of rape need to be able to take account of such women's experiences without, in effect, dismissing them as the result of false consciousness. Carefully listening to and theorizing such ambivalent and confusing experiences may illuminate the complex relationship between heterosexuality and rape. Moreover, it may produce feminist analyses of rape that are sympathetic to all women who are raped, no matter how they experience it.

Although there may be short-term political costs, embracing a more complex and less certain position on the ways in which rape can and does affect women may ultimately be an effective political strategy. By this I mean that psychologists, therapists, and activists should continue to work on understanding, helping, and speaking about the trauma of rape but at the same time be open to accepting, for example, that not all women are traumatized by rape. While many of us have accepted these complexities "in private," we have perhaps been reluctant to emphasize these possibilities in public because of the perceived political dangers of misrepresentation. Conventional empirical psychology research does suggest that while there are several common negative psychological reactions to rape, not all women who are raped experience them. Moreover, it has been claimed that "many differences [in psychological symptoms] between victimized and nonvictimized women disappear after three months, with the exception of continued reports of fear, anxiety, self-esteem problems, and sexual dysfunction. These effects may persist for up to 18 months or longer" (Koss 1993, p. 1063). However, the notion that it may be possible to experience rape and suffer no lasting devastating psychological effects is less often articulated than is the discourse of harm. But this "finding" about the effects of rape begs the question of whether such research, which once again must compress and order experience into finite categories, is adequate to perceive more subtle, idiosyncratic, and unpredictable psychological effects of rape. Moreover, even within medical model conceptualizations of psychological problems, a contrary suggestion about the effects of trauma holds that "it is not unusual for the symptoms to emerge after a latency period of months or years following the trauma" (APA 1980, quoted in Koss et al. 1987, p. 169).

Is Attempted Rape Sometimes Very Different from Completed Rape?

While some experiences of sexual coercion (and presumably most, if not all, experiences of sexual coercion that fit a narrow definition of rape) are surely victimizing, some possibly are not. Is it possible that our framework for conceptualizing *all* instances of sexual assault, and many instances of unwanted sex, as victimization actually helps constitute some of these experiences as victimizing, when they might otherwise have had effects that were less disabling? Although this question shares the anxiety typical of the backlash positions, it is an important question for feminists. In particular, are experiences of attempted rape and attempted sexual assault *sometimes* very different from actual experiences of rape and sexual assault?

I can think of a personal experience, when I was sixteen, that was probably attempted rape. This episode involved being tricked into stopping at an older male co-worker's place on the way to a party after we had finished work past midnight on New Year's Eve. I was thrown onto a bed that was just across from the front door of the flat, and he proceeded to jump on top of me and attempt to remove my pants. He was a relatively small man, and I was relatively physically strong from sports, and I remember having to struggle as hard as I could to prevent him removing my pants, with the intention (it seemed to me at the time) of having intercourse with me. (This point also reminds me how it is difficult to judge when a man's actions become "attempted rape" when a man and woman are acquainted and, at some stretch of the imagination, a mutual sexual encounter could be appropriate.) Despite the fact that both of us had been drinking alcohol with other workers at the restaurant where we worked before we left, I was never in any doubt as to my lack of sexual interest in this man—at all, let alone on this occasion. I was not ambivalent in my communication with him and told him clearly, verbally, that I did not want to have sex with him, and I resisted him physically as hard as I could. Yet he seemed to have one goal on his mind, which was unchanged by my refusal. I think it was my relative physical strength that enabled me to resist him vigorously and successfully, to the point that he possibly decided not to keep trying.

Ten years later, when I was working at a sexual abuse counseling agency, the subcultural milieu encouraged me to think back on and identify this experience as attempted rape and to wonder about its negative effects on me. While this was not a totally new way of interpreting this experience, it did sediment it with more certainty. And it did induce me to scrutinize my past to look for psychological effects of this experience. I recall that I was subsequently worried about this man's "interest" in me and arranged for my mother to pick me up from work on some of the following nights. I also recall that being able to successfully prevent a forceful attempt at unwanted sex left me feeling strong, determined, and invulnerable. Although I can't remember enough of the detail of what followed to be sure there were not also subtle negative effects on my identity and sexuality, it strikes me that such experiences of attempted rape that is successfully repelled are extremely different from experiences of completed rape, in terms of their effect on women. In my case, I did not feel like a victim. I despised his actions, but I did not feel I had been harmed. To the contrary, the effects of his attempt had probably been as empowering as they were disempowering. Was what happened "victimization"? Or is there a better way of describing it that recognizes and celebrates the power of this kind of physical resistance, of fighting back (what I flippantly like to think of as the "Xena factor"), rather than understanding the process in terms of the man's selfish and disrespectful intent?

Lois Pineau (1996) has also written about her personal experiences of attempted sexual assaults:

> By defeating the actual ends of an attack, I avoided feeling a submission which I by no means felt in the unwanted touches I endured while the battle was still going on. Insofar as the assault remained only an attempt, I was able to avoid the psychological implications of having lost the battle. I was thus able to screen out *the actual fact that the attempt itself was already a loss of integrity*. From the standpoint of my psychology it was just as well.
>
> (p. 104; my emphasis)

Later she wrote:

> While the sexual assaults I experienced served the purpose of general intimidation and forced me to the realization that I must maintain a higher state of alertness and caution, I was actually quite proud of myself for preventing the actual rapes. I developed a tough attitude, which I confess I still hold. . . . But this tough attitude masked an extreme vulnerability concerning my sexual integrity. I would have been totally devastated, unbearably humiliated, had any of the rapes succeeded. I am sure I would have needed serious psychiatric care. It is this very incapacity for enduring such humiliation that made it necessary for me to threaten my assailants with murderous intent.
>
> (p. 105)

The contradictory aspects of Pineau's experience resemble my own. However, while Pineau speaks of pride, toughness, and her lack of submission, she nevertheless accepts that these experiences were "already a loss of integrity." She implies that her nonexperience of this loss involved some sort of denial (she was able to "screen it out"), a defense mechanism to protect her from experiencing the harm she had received. Similarly, her "tough attitude" was the veneer that "masked" her real vulnerability. Through this way of writing, Pineau tacitly endorses a position that attempted rape (always) causes irrevocable psychological damage, even though she makes it clear that to have been raped would have been seriously worse.

I know that at the time I was imagining the possibility of identifying as an attempted rape victim, it seemed important to join together with women who had been sexually victimized by men, in part to make a political show of solidarity in the face of oppressive acts of male sexuality. However, I never really felt like I properly "belonged," in the sense that I didn't share the legacy of pain that some of the women around me had suffered. Moreover, it backed me into a speaking position that did not fully represent my recollected experience. That adopting an identity as an attempted rape victim would have silenced my different kind of story, which included traces of empowerment, seemed (and still seems) a relatively trivial concern in relation to the political and interpersonal importance of standing alongside women who *had* been harmed. However, perhaps there is more at stake here than some notion of making room for the "authenticity" of experiences like my own. Perhaps there is some political advantage in being able to tell lots of different stories about diverse experiences of sexual violence. In making room for a respectful plurality, we may be able to acknowledge the oppressiveness and potential pain of rape at the same time as igniting discourses that disrupt the possibilities of rape.

As a relevant aside, radical feminists have a long tradition of encouraging women to fight back against rape. Women's self-defense classes, for instance, have been an important part of feminist rape prevention action for many years. However, my impression is that we have been cautious and ambivalent about telling the stories of women who do fight back. Partly, I think, this has arisen out of ethical concerns about how such stories might be read in ways that contribute to self-blame by women who have been in circumstances where they were not able to fight back and were raped or sexually assaulted.

Clearly, not all attempted rapes are the same. Some experiences will involve violent and terrifying attacks, where a woman may literally fear for her life. However, the use of behavioral descriptions in surveys to measure the extent of sexual victimization does not distinguish these discrepant possibilities.

Emphasizing Women's Strength

In writing about therapy for women who have been sexually abused as children, Amanda Kamsler (1990) challenges what she sees as the traditional cultural story about childhood sexual abuse—that it leaves the child psychologically damaged for life. She argues that "there are many unhelpful, limiting and potentially oppressive ideas being applied in the service of therapy with women who were sexually abused as children" (p. 34). Instead, Kamsler proposes a narrative therapy approach that enables women to develop new, more empowering stories about their lives, which emphasize their resourcefulness and survival[6] rather than their pathology. Kamsler's approach to therapy recognizes the power of particular constructions of an event to determine how a person copes with its legacy. This analysis at least hints at the possibility that acts of child sexual abuse—and by implication, sexual abuse of adult women—do not have to coincide with a process of victimization. That the *potential* for harm and victimization exists strengthens the moral argument against sexual abuse, although arguably it should not be a requirement of this argument.

By extension of Kamsler's argument, we can consider how the normative practices of therapy for rape and sexual abuse victims may inadvertently help reinforce some of the effects of victimization through their concern with trauma, recovery, and healing. Again, a particular kind of psychological subject is assumed by such therapy approaches, and arguably, this "recovering" subject is always already constituted as lacking and in need of "betterment."

Whereas Kamsler draws attention to how particular constructions of sexual abuse can affect an individual's psychological well-being, Sharon Marcus (1992) considers how particular constructions of rape affect the very possibility of rape. In developing a postmodern feminist analysis of rape prevention, Marcus argues that in order to resist rape culture, we need to deny a necessary conflation between the act of rape and irrevocable harm. Marcus's feminist approach to rape is radically different from the approach of Susan Brownmiller's (1975) classic feminist analysis of rape. Marcus (1992) considers that "such a view takes violence as a self-explanatory first cause and endows it with an invulnerable and terrifying facticity which stymies our ability to challenge and demystify rape" (p. 387). She, in contrast, argues that

> in its efforts to convey the horror and iniquity of rape, such a view often concurs with masculinist culture in its designation of rape as a fate worse than, or tantamount to, death; the apocalyptic tone which it adopts and the metaphysical status which it assigns to rape implies that rape can only be feared or legally repaired, not fought. (p. 387)

Marcus instead argues for the need to "envision strategies which will enable women to sabotage men's power to rape, which will empower women to take the ability to rape completely out of men's hands" (p. 388). It is sometimes difficult to understand exactly how this sort of transformation could take place, but Marcus's dense argument is at least suggestive that it may be possible to conceptualize rape differently, in a way that somehow renders it less powerful without trivializing it.

I suggest that a small step in this sort of transformative direction would be the opening up of all sorts of narratives of resistance—by making room for stories about how potential rape was successfully fought, about how some women who are raped do not experience overwhelming psychological despair, and so on. As I suggested earlier, the potential cost of this strategy is that it may do violence to the experience of women who are victimized and traumatized by rape. Sensitivity to this possibility is necessary so that stories of particular kinds of resistance don't come to be privileged in ways that contribute once again to a silencing of women's experiences of victimization.

Apart from concern about the constitutive effects of the language of victimization, there are other questions that should be on the minds of feminists. As I signaled earlier, we may need to observe critically the effects of backlash discourse around "victimization." In the ensuing battle over the meaning of victimization, we may need to question which sorts of tactics are most likely to be effective in the political fight against rape. For instance, will the oppositional strategy of simply speaking a victim-advocacy position more loudly be sufficient, or will we need to engage in social deconstruction to contest the very terms of the debate? Aside from this direct pragmatic concern is another question about the political effects of a framework that construes the full range of sexually coercive acts, including very subtle ones, as victimization. I suggest that an unwanted kiss or touch doesn't always make a *victim*, and the effect of this rhetorical excess in the context of backlash activity may be to weaken the whole struggle against rape by acquaintances, dates, husbands, and so on. This point has been made by "post" feminist writers, but where they stop short of *feminist* analysis is in their willingness to forgo a critique of the conditions that foster ambiguity between rape and sex: that is, a culture of heterosexuality in which power is allowed to infuse sex in different ways for women and men—ways that consistently foreground men's rather than women's rights and desires. This is a cultural context in which even physical force can be ambiguously present—such as when a man's "heavy caress" is felt by a woman as "light choking" (Adams 1996). The concept of a continuum of sexual victimization can (but need not) work to obscure the critical work needed in changing heterosexuality, by implicitly posing it in its "mutually consenting" form as the good Other to sexual victimization. This implicit construal of an innocent heterosexuality renders it as something that can exist untarnished by the ever-present possibility of sex and violence being fused. In practice, this occurs when, for example, the claim is made that sexual harassment and rape are about "power, *not* sex" (as Pamela Jeffries, New Zealand's chief human rights commissioner, recently claimed on a national radio interview [Edwards 1998]).

Another problem with the way the framework of victimization is used is that it may implicitly require us to establish psychological harm in order to take a moral stand against sexual violence and against heterosexual practice that is offensive or disrespectful without necessarily being violent (in the usual sense). That is, the injustice of sexual coercion and sexual violence may become too closely tied with the "proof" of psychological damage. In New Zealand, for instance, state-funded lump-sum "accident compensation" for victims of rape and sexual abuse, which was available between the mid-1980s and the early 1990s, required a counselor's report and/or a specifically commissioned report by a psychologist or psychiatrist to establish that there had been mental pain and suffering and loss of enjoyment of life. I wonder if this restriction of financial compensation to those with expert "proof" of psychological damage is a reinstatement of the kind of "psychologization" of sexual violence that Burt and Estep (1981) hoped a victimization framework would avoid.

Supplementing the Language of Victimization

The new feminist research has come a long way, since Burt and Estep's article (1981), in describing the widespread problem of sexual victimization. But has it both gone too far and not gone far enough? Positivist methodologies have required us to iron out complexity, ambivalence, and contradiction. Public expectations of science have reinforced this drive for certainty in the form of concrete, definitive "findings." But when we peep behind the positivist mask, all sorts of discomforting questions arise: Are all instances of sexual coercion always victimizing? Do they always cause harm? For instance, in the arena of attempted sexual assaults, are women sometimes warriors, fighters, heroes? What are the effects of using these different kinds of language? Are the more subtle forms of sexual coercion, argued to be contiguous with rape by some feminists, best conceptualized on a continuum of sexual victimization? Or are there other ways of critiquing heterosexual practice, which routinely privileges men's sexual interests over women's? Or should both strategies be adopted simultaneously?

In case I've overstated my concerns about the language of victimization, I emphasize that I am not arguing for an abandonment of the victimization framework. Rather, I am suggesting that we need to question whether it is always appropriate or wise to talk about all the different forms and occasions of sexual coercion, sexual assault, sexual abuse, and sexual violence as *victimization*. Making connections between everyday sexual practices (such as sexual pressure in a marriage) and sexual violence has been important for highlighting the role of normative culture in sustaining problems such as rape. However, we have not always maintained a distinction between the theorization of, say, a continuum of sexual victimization and the implications for how we then understand men's and women's actions and experiences at the more normative end of the continuum. Using the language of victimization to discuss this territory of the continuum may be theoretically valid yet at the same time (wrongly?) give the impression that we believe every act that falls along the continuum is an act of "victimization," that it makes "victims." I don't think I want to insist that every time a woman experiences some unwanted sexual contact, it is an experience of victimization. But far from dismissing such experiences, it seems to me the challenge is to find different ways of critiquing the ways in which our culture(s) can tolerate all sorts of injustices, inequalities, and plain unfairness in the name of normative heterosexuality.

I close this chapter in a mood of uncertainty. I worry that my questions could lead to unnecessary and undermining problems for the feminist analyses of rape and sexual coercion that I value. Yet I raise these points in a desire to help strengthen and sharpen our critique of victimizing forms of sexual coercion, in ways that help prevent victimization and ameliorate the effects of potentially victimizing acts for individual women. If we don't ask these questions about the victimization framework, I sense we may risk leaving a fertile gap for backlash discourse to take hold. At the same time, this kind of move should create spaces for developing supplementary ways to critique both normative and violent forms of heterosexual practice— without losing sight of the possibility for both rape and more normative forms of sexual coercion to be victimizing. That is, it may enable us to issue new and more varied moral arguments against the cultural acceptance of a form of heterosexual practice in which it can be hard to tell the difference between "just sex" and rape.

1. This research, however, is often not explicitly identified as feminist.

2. In some of Koss's studies women were asked this direct question in addition to many more of the specific behavioral questions.

3. Although it is tempting to think that this is an out-of-date representation of heterosexual practice, the popularity of John Gray's books, such as *Mars and Venus in the Bedroom* (1995), which promote such a style of heterosexuality suggests that the representation still has widespread currency. (See Potts 1998, for a feminist deconstructive reading of Gray's work.) Researchers in the psychology of men have recently suggested that "nonrelational sex" is normative for men (Levant and Brooks 1997).

4. Of course, men are also raped and sexually abused, but not usually by women. As I am writing largely about the rape and sexual coercion of women in heterosexual relationships, I refer to those who rape as men and those who are raped as women.

5. Another common criticism of this work centers on the ambiguity of questions about unwanted sexual intercourse and unwanted attempts that occurred "because a man gave you alcohol or drugs." Due to the ambiguity of the question, the validity of scoring affirmative responses as "rape" has been questioned. Discussion of this problem with the research is beyond the scope of this chapter.

6. However, I note that the substitution of *survivor* for *victim* in many feminist accounts is a complicated act that does not necessarily imply much of a change in how we understand the process of victimization. It is arguably a more positive term in that it conveys a sense of resilience and of a woman's existence (through rape or abuse) being an active accomplishment that should be emphasized. However, at the same time, the common meaning of *survival* as existence through the threat of death conveys the sense that rape and sexual abuse are equivalent or nearly equivalent in severity to death. The possible downside of this is that it may be difficult for a woman to call herself a survivor without necessarily marking her self-image with the sense that severe damage has occurred (which is not to deny that rape *is* sometimes experienced as being as bad as or worse than death).

REFERENCES

Adams, D. M. 1996. Date rape and erotic discourse. In L. Francis (ed.), *Date rape: Feminism, philosophy, and the law* (pp. 27–39). University Park, PA: Pennsylvania State University Press.

Alcoff, L. M. Spring 1997. The politics of postmodern feminism, revisited. *Cultural Critique* 5–27.

Best, J. May/June 1997. Victimization and the victim industry. *Society,* 9–17.

Brownmiller, S. 1975. *Against our will: Men, women and rape.* Harmondsworth: Penguin.

Burt, M. R. 1980. Cultural myths and supports for rape. *Journal of Personality and Social Psychology* 38, 217–230.

Burt, M. R., and Estep, R. E. 1981. Who is a victim? Definitional problems in sexual victimization. *Victimology: An International Journal* 6, 15–28.

Deming, M. B., and Eppy, A. 1981. The sociology of rape. *Sociology and Social Research* 65, 357–380.

Denfeld, R. 1995. *The new Victorians: A young woman's challenge to the old feminist order.* New York: Warner Books.

Edwards, B. June 13, 1998. Interview with Pamela Jeffries, chief human rights commissioner. In C. Saunders (producer), *Top o' the Morning with Brian Edwards.* New Zealand: National Radio.

Estrich, S. 1987. *Real rape.* Cambridge, MA: Harvard University Press.

Feldstein, R. 1997. *Political correctness: A response from the cultural left.* Minneapolis: University of Minnesota Press.

Fine, M. 1992. *Disruptive voices: The possibilities of feminist research.* Ann Arbor: University of Michigan Press.

Gavey, N. 1990. Rape and sexual coercion within heterosexual relationships: An intersection of psychological, feminist, and postmodern inquiries. Unpublished doctoral thesis, University of Auckland.

———. 1991a. Sexual victimization prevalence among Auckland university students: How much and who does it? *New Zealand Journal of Psychology* 20, 63–70.

———. 1991b. Sexual victimization prevalence among New Zealand university students. *Journal of Consulting and Clinical Psychology* 59, 464–466.

———. 1992. Technologies and effects of heterosexual coercion. *Feminism and Psychology* 2, 325–351.

———. 1996. Women's desire and sexual violence discourse. In S. Wilkinson (ed.), *Feminist social psychologies: International perspectives* (pp. 51–65). London: Open University Press.

Gilbert, N. 1994. Miscounting social ills. *Society* 31 (3), 18–26.

Hollway, W. 1995. A second bite at the heterosexual cherry. *Feminism and Psychology* 5, 126–130.

Hwang, K. 1997. Excerpt from *The Humanist,* July/August 1997. Cited in Talking stick. *Utne Reader,* (84), 41.

Kamsler, A. 1990. Her-story in the making: Therapy with women who were sexually abused in childhood. In M. Durrant and C. White (eds.), *Ideas for therapy with sexual abuse.* Adelaide: Dulwich Centre Publications.

Kitzinger, C., and Wilkinson, S. 1997. Validating women's experience? Dilemmas in feminist research. *Feminism and Psychology* 7, 566–574.

Koss, M. P. 1985. The hidden rape victim: Personality, attitudinal, and situational characteristics. *Psychology of Women Quarterly* 9, 193–212.

———. 1988. Hidden rape: Sexual aggression and victimization in a national sample of students in higher education. In A. W. Burgess (ed.), *Rape and sexual assault*, Vol. 2 (pp. 3–25). New York and London: Garland.

———. 1992. Defending date rape. *Journal of Interpersonal Violence* 7, 122–126.

———. 1993. Rape: Scope, impact, interventions, and public policy responses. *American Psychologist* 48, 1062–1069.

Koss, M. P., and Oros, C. J. 1982. Sexual experiences survey: A research instrument investigating sexual aggression and victimization. *Journal of Consulting and Clinical Psychology* 50, 455–457.

Koss, M. P., Gidycz, C. A.; and Wisniewski, N. 1987. The scope of rape: Incidence and prevalence of sexual aggression and victimization in a national sample of higher education students. *Journal of Consulting and Clinical Psychology* 55, 162–170.

Lamb, S. 1996. *The trouble with blame: Victims, perpetrators, and responsibility.* Cambridge, MA, and London: Harvard University Press.

Levant, R., and Brooks, G. (eds.). 1997. *Men and sex: New psychological perspectives.* New York: John Wiley.

Marcus, S. 1992. Fighting bodies, fighting words: A theory and politics of rape prevention. In J. Butler and J. W. Scott (eds.), *Feminists theorize the political* (pp. 385–403). New York: Routledge.

Muehlenhard, C. L., Powch, I. G., Phelps, J. L., and Giusti, L. M. 1992. Definitions of rape: Scientific and political implications. *Journal of Social Issues* 48, 23–44.

Newbold, G. 1996. Commentary on Professor Mary Koss's keynote address: Redefining rape. In J. Broadmore, C. Shand, and T. Warburton (eds.), *The proceedings of 'Rape: Ten years' progress? An inter-disciplinary conference,' Wellington, New Zealand, 27–30 March 1996* (pp. 144–146). Doctors for Sexual Abuse Care.

Paglia, C. 1992. Sex, art, and American culture. New York: Vintage Books.

Pineau, L. 1989. Date rape: A feminist analysis. *Law and Philosophy* 8, 217–243.

———. 1996. A response to my critics. In L. Francis (ed.), *Date rape: Feminism, philosophy, and the law* (pp. 63–107). University Park, PA: Pennsylvania State University Press.

Potts, A. 1998. The science/fiction of sex: 'Mars and Venus in the bedroom.' *Sexualities* 1, 153–173.

Roiphe, K. 1993. *The morning after: Sex, fear, and feminism.* London: Hamish Hamilton.

Russell, D. E. H. 1982. *Rape in marriage.* New York: Macmillan.

———. 1984. *Sexual exploitation: Rape, child sexual abuse, and workplace harassment.* Beverly Hills: Sage.

Ryan, A., and Gavey, N. 1998. Women, sexual freedom, and the 'coital imperative.'

In R. du Plessis and L. Alice (eds.), *Feminist thought in Aotearoa/New Zealand: Connections and differences* (pp. 147–155). Auckland: Oxford University Press.

Shorter, E. 1977. On writing the history of rape. *Signs* 3, 471–482.

Sommers, C. H. 1994. *Who stole feminism? How women have betrayed women.* New York: Simon & Schuster.

Chapter 4

Recasting Consent

Agency and Victimization in Adult-Teen Relationships

Lynn M. Phillips

> Intercourse can be rape; it can also be profoundly plea-
> surable. Sexual experience with men or women can be
> abusive, objectifying, and degrading, but it can also be ec-
> static, inspiring, illuminating. It can also be—and here
> the inadequacy of a polarized discourse becomes clear—
> a particular mixture of all these things: objectifying and
> pleasurable, degrading and inspiriting. We must bring to-
> gether the complexities and contradictions: we must in-
> tegrate what we know with what we don't want to know.
>
> (Snitow, Stansell, and Thompson 1983, 42)

Since feminist activists and scholars began raising public awareness of gendered victimization in the early 1970s, attention has focused primarily on
adult women's experiences of rape and battering and on children's experiences of molestation and incest. In addition to fighting for new laws aimed
at protecting women and children and offering them forms of redress for
abuses they have endured, feminists have opened new conversations about
the nature of victimization itself (Donat and D'Emilio 1992; Kahn and
Mathie, forthcoming; see also chapter 3 by Nicola Gavey and chapter 5 by
Sharon Lamb in this volume). As a result of this work, previously nonexis-
tent concepts—such as marital rape, acquaintance rape, and sexual harassment—have entered the public discourse. For many, these developments
have represented a welcome (if painful) opportunity to name injustices

that were previously presumed to be simply inevitable aspects of hetero-sexual life. Yet they have also provided fertile ground for debate. As many in the feminist movement have struggled to open new avenues for women and children to name and heal from their own abuse, others have spoken out against these efforts, claiming that the category of "victimization" has be-come unreasonably broad and thus watered down beyond meaning (Paglia 1990; Roiphe 1993). While such backlash has frustrated many who have worked so hard to enable women and children to identify and seek justice for the wrongs that have been done to them, it has also served as a call for feminists and others to grapple anew with difficult questions about the complexities of power, consent, agency, and victimization.

Whereas earlier discussions of victimization tended to revolve around stranger rape, battering, child sexual abuse, and, later, date rape, the issue of statutory rape has entered the discussion much more recently. While it shares many themes in common with these other topics, the issue of rela-tionships between adults and teens adds new dimensions to the ongoing debate about the nature of victimization. As with more widely discussed forms of abuse, the controversies surrounding statutory rape revolve around questions about the nature and workings of power, consent, and agency. Unlike rape, battering, child molestation, and harassment, however, adult-teen relationships typically involve willing participation and some-times even initiation by the "victim," and often the teen involved reaps cer-tain benefits from the relationship in question. Although battered women, rape or molestation survivors, and those who have been subjected to ha-rassment have been called on to answer harsh questions about their partic-ipation in behaviors that led up to their victimization, few (other than those who subscribe to notions of female masochism) would claim that women and children enjoy or derive benefits from being beaten, raped, or harassed.[1] Yet in the case of statutory rape, adolescents often claim to be fully informed and willing agents in the very phenomenon that others may consider to be victimization (Phillips 1997). The experiences of young women in adult-teen relationships differ from those of "hidden" or "unac-knowledged" rape victims as well. Whereas unacknowledged rape victims acknowledge traumatic experiences that fit legal definitions of rape but do not regard themselves as rape victims/survivors (Kahn and Mathie forth-coming; Koss 1985; 1988), young women in adult-teen relationships often describe their experiences as both chosen and pleasurable (Phillips 1997). Because adult-teen relationships typically involve two willing partners, rather than one person imposing his (or her) will on another who does not wish to be subjected to the behavior, the notion of victimization becomes particularly murky.

The issue of statutory rape raises difficult questions about the relationship between willingness and consent. Legally, willingness and consent have been distinguished from one another (Sanday 1996). Indeed, the concept of statutory rape is based on the notion that the ability to consent to sexual relations is a function of age, rather than of willingness or desire. The argument is made that until a certain age, youth, however willing, are incapable of making informed sexual decisions for themselves. Thus, when an adult engages in a sexual relationship with a person who has not yet reached the legal age of consent, that adult is considered to have committed a form of rape.

Interestingly, although statutory rape laws have long been in existence in the United States (Donovan 1997; Sanday 1996),[2] their enforcement has been relatively rare, and few have highlighted this topic in discussions of victimization. As has been the case with other topics typically included in discussions of victimization, the definitions of and concern (or lack of concern) about statutory rape have varied across both history and cultures (Donat and D'Emilio 1992; Donovan 1997; Kahn and Mathie forthcoming; Sanday 1996). Even at the present time in the United States, the issue of adult-teen relationships may evoke varying cultural values regarding normative practices in hetero-relationships. But despite long histories of embracing relationships between adults and adolescents in certain cultures, current legal definitions and strategies fail to acknowledge such cultural variations (Phillips 1997).

It is also interesting to note that unlike the focus on rape, battering, harassment, and other issues that came to public consciousness through the feminist anti-violence movement, the renewed concern with statutory rape has evolved in large part from studies linking teen pregnancies to adult-teen relationships. Based primarily on analyses of birth records and questionnaires administered to adolescent mothers, such research has suggested that the majority of teen births are attributable to adolescent girls' sexual relationships with adult men, rather than with peers (Landry and Forrest 1995; Males and Chew 1996). Although subsequent analyses have called these findings into question (Lindberg, Sonenstein, Ku, and Martinez 1997), public response to the reported link between teen births and adult-teen relationships has nonetheless been swift and severe. Several states—including California, Idaho, Florida, Delaware, and Georgia—have moved recently to raise the age of consent, increase enforcement of statutory rape laws, and/or lengthen prison sentences for those who break such laws (Donovan 1997). Other states are currently considering similar modifications to their procedures for dealing with statutory rape. Presumably intended to protect teenagers and reduce teen birth rates by deterring adults from becoming involved with adolescents, the underlying and ensuing debates have tended to cast older men as "predators," thus relegating adolescent girls to the position of "prey."

While some have welcomed this crackdown on statutory rape, others have claimed that the prohibition against adult-teen relationships represents a form of sexual repression (Rubin 1984) and that numerical age is an arbitrary criterion by which to determine one's ability to give consent. Indeed, it is interesting to note that at the same time that some states are *raising* the legal age for sexual consent, many are also *lowering* the age at which adolescents can be tried as adults for crimes they have committed. This discrepancy—along with the varied ages at which one can drive, vote, perform military service, or marry—points to the ambiguities that linger in mainstream western thought about the ability of adolescents to assume responsibilities (or privileges) typically associated with adulthood. Why, then, it may be asked, should apparently willing participation in sexual encounters be illegal simply because of age? What makes a mature fifteen-year-old, for instance, any less capable of consent than a less mature eighteen-year-old? And what benefits are to be gained by prohibiting adult-teen relationships and severely punishing adults who violate the law?

As a feminist researcher and an advocate for both girls' sexual entitlement and girls' sexual safety, I find myself with very mixed responses to the issue of statutory rape and deeply conflicted about the heightened attention being paid to adult-teen relationships. On the one hand, I am hopeful that a focus on adolescent women's participation in relationships with adult men can provide feminists with a rich opportunity to probe further the nuanced meanings of such presumed dichotomies as consent and coercion, victimization and agency, danger and desire. Since my own research points to some troubling power imbalances in adult-teen relationships (which I discuss later in this chapter), I am also hopeful that the current attention being paid to this issue will lead to further feminist research and analyses that can inform educational strategies to prevent young women's exploitation in these (and other) relationships.[3] And most important, I am hopeful that careful attention to girls' perspectives on adult-teen relationships can illuminate otherwise unmet needs they believe these relationships can fill. As I discuss further in this chapter, many girls find that relationships with adult men offer them a sense of emotional fulfillment, maturity, and economic stability that relationships with peers or families may not provide. The reasons girls give for their attraction to adult-teen relationships may point to social, emotional, and material needs that are currently unsatisfied on both societal and interpersonal levels. And with an understanding of those needs, concerned adults may better be able to address them in proactive ways, rather than relying solely on individualistic and punitive approaches after the fact.

Yet, despite these hopes, I have serious misgivings about the ways in which popular discourse and public policy appear to be unfolding. I am deeply wary of the reactionary and exclusively punitive approaches that have emerged in an effort to "solve" statutory rape. Such responses attempt to locate "the problem" in an individual "perpetrator" and to eradicate the problem through simplistic legal strategies—by increasing the number of relationships that fall within the realm of illegal activity (i.e., through raising the legal age of consent) and by subjecting adult violators to increasingly severe penalties. Largely absent from current policy debates are considerations of girls' agency, attention to cultural variations, discussions of educational strategies, and examination of the underlying needs that may attract adolescent girls to adult men in the first place. This absence is reflective not only of a paternalistic stance toward adolescent girls but also of a lack of research on the ways in which girls actually conceptualize their relationships with older men. That research which is available tends to focus narrowly on the incidence of adult-teen relationships, on demographic characteristics of the participants (East and Felice 1996; Nakashima and Camp 1984), or on the percentage of pregnancies or sexually transmitted infections that are attributable to sexual relationships between adolescent girls and adult men (Landry and Forrest 1995; Lindberg et al. 1997; Males 1992; Males and Chew 1996). While such research can certainly be useful to ascertain the scope of the phenomenon, these studies tell us little about girls' experiences in those relationships or the implications of their involvement after those relationships end. Thus, I worry that while girls' involvement with older men may, indeed, be cause for some alarm, that alarm—like the strategies that have accompanied it—is based on reactionary and paternalistic presumptions, rather than on an understanding of the complex and varied meanings young women construct regarding their own sexualities and relationships. As I have grappled with both my hopes and my misgivings, I have come to believe that if feminists are to lend constructive voices to the debates about adult-teen relationships, we must suspend preconceived notions and resist the dichotomous thinking that has often permeated discussions of victimization. (See chapter 3 by Nicola Gavey, chapter 1 by Janice Haaken, and chapter 5 by Sharon Lamb, this volume.) Rather than presuming either that adult-teen relationships are *really* a form of victimization or that they *really* represent unproblematic, consensual partnerships—rather than maintaining either that willingness means consent or that an age difference means an inherent inability to consent—we need to step back and probe the nuances of adult-teen relationships from the perspectives of young women who participate in them. Further, if we are to develop educational strategies aimed at discouraging teen women from becoming involved in potentially exploitative relationships, those strategies must speak to young women's lived realities and the cultural and personal values that they, their families, and their communities hold regarding this issue. Again, this requires an understanding of *their* understandings and a respect for the priorities they bring to their own decision-making.

At the same time, it is important to keep in mind that young women's renderings of their experiences do not necessarily represent the final truth about adult-teen relationships. This is not to suggest that girls' voices do not have merit in their own right. Rather, it is to say that their positions, like any, are partial and constructed (Gergen 1985; Marecek and Hare-Mustin 1990; Shweder 1990) and that there may be important dimensions and implications of adult-teen relationships that those who are currently in them are unable to see. Thus, while we need to learn more about girls' experiences and understandings, we can also benefit from listening to the insights of older women who have had experiences in adult-teen relationships as adolescents. And we need to examine young women's perspectives critically through a consideration of power dynamics and potential outcomes of adult-teen relationships.

In the following sections I begin such an examination, with the hope of shedding some light on the complex interplay of power and agency in adult-teen relationships. I draw here on data collected through a qualitative study that I conducted in collaboration with Planned Parenthood of Greater Northern New Jersey in 1997.[4] In an effort to understand better the meanings of adult-teen relationships to those involved, as well as to their families, peers, and community members, I spent a year conducting focus groups and individual interviews with a racially and socially diverse group of 127 adolescents and adults in urban, suburban, and rural areas across northern and central New Jersey. The participants ranged in age from four-teen to forty-six years old. They included adolescent women and adult men who were involved in adult-teen relationships at the time of the interviews; adult women who had been in such relationships as teenagers; and adoles-cent and adult men and women who had friends or family members in such relationships. In each of the interviews and focus groups, participants discussed their views on adult-teen relationships in general, as well as their personal experiences and observations of the costs, benefits, and power dy-namics of these relationships. Because the research was part of a teen preg-nancy prevention study, the adult-teen relationships addressed here refer specifically to relationships between teen females and adult males. The study did not include relationships between teen males and adult females or between same-sex adults and teens, since these types of relationships do not result in teen pregnancies.[5]

Perhaps to some readers' relief and others' frustration, I do not attempt to determine here whether adult-teen relationships should be legal or ille-gal or whether they should be considered *inherently* abusive. Indeed, after a year of research and a great deal of reflection, I admit that I remain con-flicted about such questions. Instead, I wish to present the perspectives of several adolescent women involved with adult men, to juxtapose these with the reflections of adult women formerly involved in adult-teen relation-ships, and to tease apart issues in need of further feminist consideration.

Exploring Adult-Teen Relationships: What Do Adolescent Women Say?

How do teen women view their relationships with older men? And what do they think about the renewed concern with issues of statutory rape? My dis-cussions with adolescents involved in such relationships point to marked distinctions between their perspectives and those of legislators and others hoping to toughen enforcement of statutory rape laws. Indeed, in sharp contrast to many adults' fears about adolescents' exploitation and inability to make sexual decisions for themselves, across the interviews, young women in adult-teen relationships focused on their maturity, their entitle-ment, and the material and psychological benefits they reaped from their involvements with adult men. For many,[6] adult partners represented a chance to confirm their own feelings of maturity and an opportunity to step into the much-anticipated realm of adulthood. Indeed, rather than appearing as naive and exploitable children, these young women portrayed themselves as active agents making constructive decisions to affirm their identities and bring them the benefits they sought from their relationships.

At fifteen, for instance, Donelle[7] is frustrated with her male peers and their interest in activities she sees as childish and trivial. Like other adolescents involved in adult-teen relationships, she describes herself as particularly mature for her age. Thus, she finds that she has more in common with adult men. She also finds that older partners allow her to access "adult" activities, such as movies and clubs, which adolescent boyfriends do not:

> I like to go out with older guys because they are more mature. They understand me better, because I just got out of a relationship with a little boy. He was my age, and all he wanted to do was like go bike riding, hang out with his friends, and I wasn't used to that, because he was the first guy I've ever dated that was young. All the other guys were older. The older guys were like, "Do you want to go to the movies, do you want to go to a club?" Things like that . . . It's like, little boys just want to like, I don't know, hang out with their friends, bike ride, do little things. At least with older guys, like, I don't know, they are more mature about things.   (Donelle, 15, Latina)

While it might be argued that fifteen-year-olds should not be attending nightclubs at all, Donelle nonetheless explains that she sees her adult partners' invitations to such places as a sign of respect. They are also consistent with her own construction of a "real date." In her view, despite the age difference inherent in adult-teen relationships, older men are her psychological peers, whereas her chronological peers are "little boys." Thus, she finds the increasing public concern about adult-teen relationships misplaced. Far from feeling exploited, she feels that adult partners show her greater respect and fulfill her sense of entitlement to be treated as an equal, not as a "little girl."

For many teens, relationships with adults also represent access to material benefits that are otherwise unobtainable for them. Although adolescent women involved with adult men tended to focus on the emotional intimacy and sense of respect they found with older partners, most also acknowledged several luxuries and conveniences that came to them as a result of dating an older man. Males and females across age groups noted that adult men are much more likely than adolescents to have a car, an apartment, and a job that would allow them to buy gifts and take young women to expensive places. As seventeen-year-old Samera put it:

> Don't nobody want to walk no more. You have to have a car, your own apartment, or a job. Mainly a car. Everybody wants somebody with a car and

somebody, most likely, seventeen is not going to have their own car. So they figure they'll find somebody older, they got a car, a job, and apartment.

(Samera, 17, African American)

Although many in the study speculated that adolescent women's attraction to adult men reflected primarily materialistic interests, young women in adult-teen relationships noted that their interest in material benefits also reflected a social need. While they enjoyed the comforts of rides, money, and dining out, and they welcomed the privacy of adult men's apartments, many focused on the social status that came from being seen in nice cars and being able to show off expensive gifts to their friends. Indeed, in a society that continues to promote traditional, gendered scripts teaching women to expect confirmation of a man's commitment (and perhaps their own worth) through the gifts he gives, the money he spends, and the comforts he provides, many of these young women and their peers have learned to translate men's financial capital into their own social capital. While young women can certainly critique this traditional script, and some may find it distasteful, they nonetheless have been inundated with such images through movies, women's and teen magazines, television shows, and their experiences with their own friends. As Samera explains, cars and money connote both the freedom and independence of adulthood and the satisfaction of being seen as a valuable partner. For her, being associated with an adult man increases her social standing and sense of belonging among her peers:

It's mainly because, I don't know, part of belonging. Everybody else's boyfriend got a car, and I want a boyfriend with a car, and they look like they're having fun together, and so it's like that.   (Samera, 17, African American)

While young women often found that adult-teen relationships facilitated social acceptance by their peers, most reported that their families and other adult community members disapproved of their association with older men. It is interesting to note that several Latino men in the study referred to cultural values that promoted adult-teen relationships, noting that adult men in their communities were often encouraged to pursue adolescent women (particularly virgins) as sexual and/or romantic partners.[8] Yet few adolescent women actually involved with older men referred to such cultural or community support of their relationships, and none discussed cultural issues as a factor in her decision-making. Seventeen-year-old Tamiqua, however, notes a conflict between what is acceptable in her home culture and what most (including her parents) consider acceptable in the United States:

In Spanish countries it's, there's no problem with that. It's like that over there. I mean when my mom got married at fifteen and my father was twenty-two, you know? Like that, it's like nothing big over there. Like over here they make it a big deal. Over there, it's like a common thing, you know, unless it's like somebody forty or something like that, you know?   (Tamiqua, 17, Latina)

Many girls noted that they felt a sense of personal satisfaction from simply knowing (and having others know) that an adult man found them attractive. Seeing older men as more sophisticated than their peers, and assuming that adult men could date older women if they so chose, adolescent women tended to find older men's interest in them particularly flattering. For Lois, receiving sexual attention from an older man serves as a confirmation of her desirability and self-worth:

I feel it's kind of flattering when an older guy likes the younger girl, like . . . I'd be flattered to know that the guy who was older than me by, you know, like a pretty decent margin, is interested in someone [like me]. And it kind of makes you feel like, I don't know, a little bit better about yourself knowing that, like, you always want to be better than everyone around you . . . and it's like, by having an older guy, you know, interested in me, I think that, I don't know, it's kind of inspiring.   (Lois, 15, Caucasian)

In addition to being desired and treated with respect in social situations, young women in the study emphasized their desire to be treated respectfully in the sexual aspects of their relationships. Ironically, in contrast to many adults' worries that older men "prey" on young, unsuspecting girls for sex, several teen women suggested that older men are *less* likely than teenage men to push for a sexual relationship before girls are ready. The young women I interviewed frequently saw adolescent men as "players," "manipulators," or "only interested in one thing." Thus, their involvements with adult men were part of a conscious strategy to reduce their chances of victimization by their male peers, whom they saw as sexually irresponsible. According to Tamiqua, who has had relationships with adult men since she was twelve, teenage boys are "too immature" and too preoccupied with sex to make serious partners. For her, having a relationship with an older man means being treated with respect, rather than being seen as a sexual conquest:

Well, I always go out with an older guy because I consider most of them to be a little mature, you know, on my level. I mean, when you go with a younger person, they're too immature. . . . They look at sex, like, in a different kind of way. I don't know, I just can't, I can't deal with a person, a guy of my age. . . . They look at it like, "Oh, she gave it up to me in one day, you know, like well, she gave it up to me in a week." You know, that's like real stupid. An older person will, like it doesn't matter when you, to me, it doesn't matter how long it took you to, you know. It's when you're ready, you know?

(Tamiqua, 17, Latina)

Fourteen-year-old Adriana agrees. Like many of her female peers, she is looking for romance, which she equates with tenderness, understanding, and mutuality. Adriana sees sexual expression as an important aspect of romantic involvement. But she is drawn to partners who demonstrate a desire for intimacy, rather than simply a desire for sex. Having dated both peers and adults, she finds that older men are more patient and less likely to pressure girls into having sex. She also finds that older men are more sensitive lovers, who understand that younger girls might be nervous about beginning a sexual relationship:

I think that guys our age, they are more into pressuring you than an older guy because the older guy, they are like, willing to wait for it. Or like, if it's a thirty-one-year-old guy and a fourteen-year-old girl, they know that, you know, they are young and, you know, they are kind of scared. But the same kind of age, they are like, "What, you don't want to give it to me or something? You know, I'm with you right now." So I think that a guy your age would pressure you more than an older guy.   (Adriana, 14, Latina)

Interestingly, some young women felt that older men were more likely to be monogamous, because they presumably had already "played the field." Frustrated by adolescent men who cheated on them, they reasoned that adult men, with "less to prove," would be more willing to settle into a serious, monogamous relationship. Although Mirabelle is generally rather cynical about all men's fidelity, she believes that adult men are more apt to remain faithful than teenage partners:

I didn't like dating a young guy, because younger guys, they were immature, they want to play the field, you know? Play with you . . . I mean older guys cheat on you, but not as much as the younger guy, because [older guys] behave, they had their cake and ate it too, you know what I'm saying?

(Mirabelle, 17, African American)

This faith in adult men as more trustworthy was echoed by teen women who felt that older men, with their presumed maturity and greater access to material resources, would be more likely to assume responsibility for their children, should a pregnancy result from their relationship. As seventeen-year-old Carla reasons, adult men are more *likely* to be responsible because they are more materially *able* to be responsible:

> An older guy probably will be responsible because he has that mentality of an older guy. He can be like, "Oh, you know, I got this girl pregnant, I got to stand by her. Even though I'm not with her, I have to support the kid." But with a younger guy, they don't have a job there. What, they are going to try to support a family working at McDonald's? Minimum wage? You know, it's not going to, it don't work like that. (Carla, 17, Latina)

For some young women, an adult male partner meant access to wisdom and guidance they felt were lacking in their own homes. Sixteen-year-old Jill, for instance, feels that her thirty-three-year-old partner, Carlos, has saved her from a life of abuse, drug use, and academic failure that were condoned by her mother and her grandmother. She is frustrated with Carlos for being jealous and overbearing at times. Yet she values the stability he has brought to her life, and she feels deeply indebted to him for his support. Since both partners agree that he is wiser and more experienced than she, Carlos typically makes decisions for the couple and tells her what to do "for her own good."[9] Although she sometimes "rebels" by not following his advice, both partners say that she ultimately apologizes and follows his lead. As Jill explains it, "He treats me good. He knows what he's doing. . . . You know, he's overprotective of me because I'm young." For her, an overprotective partner is preferable to the lack of care and support she experienced when living in her mother's home.

Looking across these young women's narratives, it appears that their decisions to participate in adult-teen relationships stem from conscious efforts on their part to find pleasure, to reap certain benefits, and to increase the odds of finding a sensitive, respectful, and responsible partner. In contrast to a traditional victim/villain script, these adolescents do not present themselves as helpless objects of a victimizer's abuse. Indeed, taken at face value, their renderings of their own relationships and decision-making processes seem to have little to do with victimization. Far from being unwilling victims or "prey," these young women see themselves as active agents making proactive decisions that increase their likelihood of finding meaningful and pleasurable relationships. Does this, then, mean that adult-teen relationships are unproblematic? Do girls' willingness and even desire to participate such relationships mean that they are consensual and that we therefore have no cause for concern?

A Different Vantage Point: Perspectives of Older Women

Some light can be shed on these questions by turning to the perspectives of somewhat older women who were in adult-teen relationships themselves as adolescents. While their insights do not negate the validity of adolescent women's experiences, they offer us a different vantage point from which to view the power dynamics and implications of relationships between adults and teens. In particular, adult women are able to speak to outcomes that girls currently in adult-teen relationships may not yet have experienced and may not anticipate.[10] Thus, we may develop a fuller picture of adult-teen relationships by considering each group's perspective against the backdrop of the other.

Like current teens, older women with experience in adult-teen relationships note that as adolescents, they felt more mature than their peers. And like current teens, they sought relationships that would allow them to experience more fully that sense of maturity. But whereas adolescent women speak with great conviction about their unusually high maturity levels, adult participants, reflecting back on their teenage years, note that they were not nearly as mature as they believed at the time. In retrospect, many now say that their desire to separate themselves from adolescent activities and peers was not so much a reflection of their greater psychological maturity as it was a reflection of their impatience to leave behind an adolescence filled with emotional, social, and material insecurity. In a society that associates adulthood with independence and privilege and childhood with powerlessness and dependence, they now feel their attraction to older men (and the comforts they promised) represented an eagerness to escape adolescence, rather than a readiness to assume the responsibilities of adulthood. Sherraine, now thirty-six, recalls her own relationships with older men when she was a teen. Although she insisted at the time that she could handle such relationships, and she remembers finding them fun and exciting as a teen, she now says that she was overwhelmed and exploited. She looks back at her adult partners with disdain and expresses deep skepticism about any man who is involved with a teen:

> As we all know, when you're thirteen, fourteen, fifteen years old, you don't know your ass from a hole in the ground, okay? You just don't know. All you know is that you can't stand being thirteen, fourteen, fifteen years old. You want to appear to be older to everyone else around you. So here is this pervert who is willing to give you this maturity, and he knows you don't know

what you're talking about, for crying out loud. You barely know your multi-
plication, you know? (Sherraine, 36, African American)

Whether or not older men consciously seek to exploit their adolescent
partners, women who had been in adult-teen relationships tend to feel, to
varying degrees, manipulated, dominated, or cheated out of their youth as
a result of their involvement with adults. Many note that their older partners tended to be jealous and possessive, restricting their activities and encouraging them to break off ties with their peers. Although, like Jill, these
women often interpreted their partners' jealousy as a sign of love and de-
votion at the time, they look back now and see opportunities and relationships that they forfeited to please the men with whom they were involved.
Ironically, whereas teen women in the study frequently cite an eagerness to
reach adulthood and often associate adult-teen relationships with freedom
and independence, many adult women attribute their current economic
and social burdens to their adolescent involvements with adult men and
lament the loss of their childhoods.

As Rosa says, with tears in her eyes, "It's hard, you know, it makes me cry,
knowing that my whole childhood just went in a snap, and I didn't even get
to say goodbye." Shortly after her mother kicked her out of her home when
she was sixteen, Rosa became involved with Antonio, who was then twenty-
eight. At first, she saw his age as an asset and enjoyed the access he gave her
to clubs and other adult activities. Although he was controlling and forbade
her to go out alone, her desire to please him was sufficiently strong that, she
says, "I wanted to even kind of change just to be with him." She later learned
that he was married, and he left as soon as Rosa told him she was pregnant.
While she acknowledges that a peer might also have left her when she became pregnant, she does not believe that she would have made the same
sacrifices—such as dropping out of school or cutting ties with family and
friends—for an adolescent partner. Thus, she says, she would have been less
vulnerable when her relationship ended. Now, she is left on her own with a
young daughter, severe financial difficulties, no high school diploma, and
little social support:

This guy that I was with was twenty-eight, and I have a daughter from him.
I started going out with him when I was sixteen, and I got pregnant when I
was seventeen. Right now we're not really together . . . but my childhood, like,
I've grown up too fast because he was mature, and that's what I liked, but
who can expect my life was going to have to change into being suitable for

his life? And this started with all the childhood games and everything, fun, and I wind up having a kid, and now I'm never going to have that childhood again.   (Rosa 19, Latina)

In several cases, women note that older partners persuaded them to go against their own better judgment when making important life decisions. Trusting that adult partners would be more responsible than adolescent men and believing the promises older men made, some, like Sheryl, agreed to carry unwanted pregnancies to term. Sheryl moved in with twenty-three-year-old Robert when she was sixteen. Although she soon decided that this was "a big mistake" and tried to end the relationship, Robert convinced her to stay by making her feel sorry for him, telling her that he loved her and had nowhere else to go. When she became pregnant six months into their relationship, Robert began drinking heavily and started hitting her, throwing her to the ground, and jumping on her stomach on a regular basis. Sheryl decided to get an abortion, but Robert pressured her into carrying the pregnancy to term, promising that he would stand by her and the baby. Although she still did not want to have a child, she believed his promises and reversed her decision. Shortly after she gave birth, he left her, and he has seen their eighteen-month-old son only once since the child was two months old:

> I didn't want to be [pregnant]. I wanted to get an abortion, but he was like, "No, don't get an abortion." So I said, "All right, I won't." But then I ended up having the baby and he ended up leaving, so okay. . . . I figured since he was there when I had the baby and everything and a little while after, I would say, "Well, he's going to be there for my son." But then like, the visits got shorter and like, spread around. Like he would come, he used to come every week, then it was like every two weeks, every three weeks, and then he didn't come at all until now.   (Sheryl, 20, biracial: African American/Caucasian)

Even those few women whose adult partners stayed after children were born note that the age difference that first attracted them became an ongoing problem in their relationships. Cindy, for instance, became involved with a twenty-six-year-old man when she was sixteen. She attributes her initial attraction to her partner to her need for a "father role model."[11] Looking up to her partner and feeling indebted to him for "saving" her from a troubled adolescence and severe family problems, she was willing to sacrifice her own needs for his desires. She had their first child when she was seventeen, dropped out of high school, and married him. Although she considers herself lucky compared to adolescents whose partners left them, she notes that the combination of young motherhood and an older partner has left her feeling "stuck" and unable to pursue opportunities she would like. At twenty-four years old, she says, "Right now, I have to put [my needs] on hold all these years. I'm not myself that I would have been."

Cindy acknowledges that if she had known at sixteen what she knows now, she would never have become involved with an older man. Indeed, she finds adult-teen relationships problematic in general, and she recommends that girls avoid them:

> I think it is like having the years, a lot of years in between each other, it is really, you know, it shouldn't be like that. . . . But I have a niece that's fifteen now, and I try to give her advice on staying with the men that are in her age group, you know, nobody that is over eighteen or nobody that is over her age herself, because of some of the problems that I experienced and go through. . . . I really think it's the age and I, you know, when I was sixteen, if I would have known this would have been a problem, you know? But the thing is, we never do.   (Cindy, 24, Caucasian)

Looking up to adult men, valuing their maturity and experience, and often feeling indebted to them, women acknowledged that they often were quite willing to defer to older men and to sacrifice their own wants and needs in order to please their partners. Yet, in retrospect, many came to believe that their partners were not so mature after all, and they regretted allowing them to determine the dynamics of their relationships. While they typically did not refer to themselves as passive "victims," they explained that their young age rendered them vulnerable to older men's greater experience and persuasiveness, making the girls easily manipulated and exploited. As Nora says:

> When I was fifteen, I went out with someone who was ten years older than me, so he was twenty-five. And I didn't, at the time, he was a lot deep into, I just didn't even know how to deal with some of the things he was doing, and I just agreed with him and did everything.   (Nora, 21, Caucasian)

Particularly troubling were stories in which adolescents gave in to adult men's pressure to have intercourse without using condoms. Although teens are not particularly likely to practice safe sex in general (Abma, Chandra, Mosher, Peterson, and Piccino 1997),[12] some participants said they would have refused to have intercourse with a peer who would not wear a condom; yet they agreed to have unprotected intercourse with an adult partner, because their desire to please him outweighed their commitment to protecting themselves.[13] Many cited fears (fueled by men's threats) that if they did not give their partner the sexual pleasure he expected, they would be left for an older, more "sophisticated" woman. Some women noted that they felt less of a need to insist on contraception use because they believed adult men's claims that they would stand by them if they did become pregnant. Persuaded, like Carla, that older men possessed both the maturity and the resources to support them and their potential children, they said they were more likely to "let my guard down" with adults than with adolescent partners. Unfortunately, those adult partners typically left as soon as a teen announced that she was pregnant or soon after she gave birth.

It is important to note that misgivings about adult-teen relationships were not limited to those who became pregnant as adolescents. In contrast to the enhanced sense of self-worth many teens anticipated from their involvements with adult men, several adult women felt ultimately that their sense of self-respect, trust, and independence was diminished as a result of their earlier relationships. For instance, whereas some women shared Mirabelle's belief that older men were less likely to cheat on them with another woman, many later learned that their partners were actually married or in serious relationships at the time of their involvement. Thus, they experienced considerable confusion and disillusionment when they came to realize that *they*, in fact, had been "the other woman." Some women, like Lydia, found that the initial thrill of being able to attract older men soon gave way to feelings of worthlessness, as she realized that men valued her for her body and her youth but not for her character or her mind. In time, she began to internalize their views, seeing herself as only "a body" or a "trophy broad":

> It's not a love thing, it's not whatever these kids think is going on, or whatever these immature men think is going on. It's a power trip for them on some level. I dated a lot of guys that were a lot older than me when I was younger. I was the little trophy broad, getting into bars when I was fifteen, and they loved it . . . It was not all fun. . . . Of course, they had nice cars and they took me places, they got me loaded, they did all kinds of nice jewelry and stuff. I loved it, you know, but it's still statutory rape, because it was a power trip for them. I wasn't on an equal basis with them . . . but it always backfires, because a power trip like that, you're going to feel like garbage in the end. . . . I was only looking on myself as a body, and the more I perpetuated that, the worse it got. I was nothing, except for my physical appearance. (Lydia, 46, Caucasian)

In stark contrast to the teen women currently involved in adult-teen relationships, these adult women offer stories of control, irresponsibility, and opportunities lost. We cannot know, of course, the extent to which their current difficulties are a direct result of their earlier participation in adult-teen relationships; indeed, some of these women may have made similar decisions if their partners had been peers. However, across race, culture, and socioeconomic status, women with prior experience in adult-teen relationships note that the power differences between them and their adult partners—differences they could not see clearly at the time—led them to enter situations and make decisions for which they were not yet prepared. These women remember perceiving the same benefits to which current teens refer. But while adolescent women tend to see their partners' gifts, cars, money, and other resources as symbols of fun, freedom, and a committed relationship, older women look back and see those resources as promoting an imbalance of power within their relationships. Further, adult women's stories suggest that when adult-teen relationships end, teens are often left with children to raise, little money, diminished social and familial ties, and a sense of having been exploited. Yet adult men are likely to retain the same resources with which they entered the relationships. In short, while both partners seem to receive certain benefits from their association with one another, these benefits are often fleeting. And while adult men's costs are typically minimal, young women's costs—both material and psychological—may be both severe and enduring.

Re-examining Agency and Victimization in Adult-Teen Relationships

As I noted at the beginning of this chapter, the issue of adult-teen relationships raises particularly difficult questions about the dynamics of consent and coercion—questions with which I continue to grapple. On the one hand, the young women's narratives suggest that they are quite willing to enter these relationships, that they perceive clear benefits from them, and that they see themselves as active and consenting agents in their own decision-making. On the other hand, older women with experience in adult-teen relationships point to power asymmetries that may result in considerable pressure for girls to comply with older partners' wishes—wishes that may go against teen women's present or future best interests. If we were to listen only to young women's stories, we might conclude that adult-teen relationships are freely chosen, mutually beneficial, and therefore unproblematic. If we were to listen only to the voices of adult women with experience in adult-teen relationships, we might conclude that teen women are, in fact, overwhelmed victims who are preyed on by older men. Yet, by taking both perspectives together, we begin to see a fuller picture than either perspective can provide on its own.

The strength and conviction of girls' voices certainly call into question the portrayal of teens as passive "prey." The young women in this study are by no means naive to potential sexual dangers, and they are quite cognizant of the societal tolerance for men's sexual misbehaviors. Indeed, they have learned well what Wendy Hollway (1984) has called the "male sexual drive discourse"—a set of pervasive cultural messages claiming that men possess an uncontrollable and aggressive sexual drive that, once aroused, must be satisfied. Having learned from this discourse, as well as from their personal experiences, that "boys will be boys," these young women have come to expect sexual pressure and a lack of responsibility from their male peers. Interestingly, however, they appear to make exceptions for older men, reasoning that they are more likely than adolescent men to have already "sown their wild oats" and that they are therefore more likely to be responsible and sensitive in their sexual relationships. Thus, we see young women making active and, from their perspective, informed decisions to seek out partners they believe will be *less* likely to exploit or abuse them. Unfortunately, social policies based on reactionary and paternalistic assumptions tend to overlook girls' capacity for agency in their sexual decisions. As these teens' stories demonstrate, the presumption that girls leap into adult-teen relationships without thinking reflects a misunderstanding of young women's decision-making process.

Young women's narratives suggest several otherwise unmet needs that relationships with adults appear, at least temporarily, to fill. For young women who are struggling with social and emotional difficulties, adult-teen relationships appear to be a bridge into what they perceive as the relative freedom and security of adulthood. For those who are wary of the often insensitive sexual behavior of their male peers, adult partners appear to be a welcome source of affection, respect, romance, and sexual pleasure. For those who lack warmth and stability in their home lives, older men appear to provide the wisdom and experience of what many women termed a "father figure," as well as the benefits of a more experienced lover. And for those who equate men's commitment or their own self-worth with gifts and other material benefits, adult men's greater access to money, cars, and apartments appears to offer girls a sense that they are special and respected.

Yet, despite girls' rather laudable efforts to think strategically about their own needs and relationships, older women's experiences suggest there may be important dimensions to adult-teen relationships that adolescent women are less likely to perceive or foresee. While it may be argued that adults look back on many adolescent decisions with regret, by these women's accounts, the stakes in adult-teen relationships are particularly high. If, as the older women in this study indicated, adolescent women are more likely to be persuaded by adult partners than by peers to cut ties with families and friends, to forgo safer sex practices, to carry unwanted pregnancies to term, and to forfeit educational opportunities, then we need to consider the likelihood that adult-teen relationships involve particular power imbalances that are skewed against adolescents' best interests. Since teens, by virtue of their age, typically are unable to have independent access to well-paying jobs, housing, and the educational attainment that may be enjoyed by their adult partners, they may feel less able to leave unsatisfying relationships. And since the benefits they receive from adult partners are dependent on their continued involvement, they may suffer more severe consequences than adults—such as financial hardship, homelessness, single teen parenthood, an incomplete education—when their relationships end. Indeed, although young women like Carla may reason that well-resourced men are more likely to stay, those men are also better able to leave without incurring the costs that would befall a less-resourced (and therefore more dependent) teen. Thus, while girls may *enter* these relationships of their own accord, it may be argued that many are less able *to negotiate within* or *to leave* such relationships without considerable social, emotional, and material repercussions. And if girls find that they cannot say no without repercussions within the relationship, what sense are we to make of their ability to say an informed yes?

As feminists have demonstrated in cases of battering, acquaintance rape, and harassment (Riger 1992; Sanday 1996), the question of context is central to an understanding of victimization. If one's willingness to participate in a relationship occurs in a coercive context, the notion of consent must be problematized. While the young women in this study did not describe themselves as "coerced" into becoming involved with their adult partners, they often alluded to age-based power asymmetries. And older women pointed consistently to strong pressure and inequitable power dynamics they experienced in adult-teen relationships. If adult women were the only participants to refer to such dynamics, one might conclude that they had simply rewritten their memories in a way that helped them explain their current difficulties. But even current teens involved with older men acknowledged throughout the study that while they enjoy benefits from their relationships, they feel more compelled to please adult partners than adolescent partners. Even as young women spoke with affection and appreciation toward their partners, they often lamented, "If only he weren't so jealous" or "If only he were less controlling." As seventeen-year-old Brenda put it:

> If you go out with an older guy, like, let's say it's not a good relationship and you know, you feel that you have to like, put on an act for, not an act, but you have to make them happy. Like you forget the fact that you are in a relationship, a two-way relationship which means they have to make you happy also. And all you think about is well, I have to make sure he's happy. I have to make sure I talk to him the right way. I have to make sure I'm living up to his standards. And then you start to lose sight of what a relationship is.
>
> (Brenda, 17, Caucasian)

It seems that while girls' choice of older partners represents an act of agency, that agency often becomes compromised within their adult-teen relationships. Of course, given the cultural privileging of male desire (Fine, Genevese, Ingersoll, McPherson, and Roberts 1994; Hollway 1984; Phillips, forthcoming; Tolman and Higgins 1996), both adolescent and adult women may defer to same-age male partners as well. But in cases where girls perceive their partners as wiser, more mature, and better resourced by virtue of their age, they may see them as more important to please; thus, they may be considerably more apt to put their own needs on hold. And since teens are at a critical point in their development in terms of education, sexuality, peer social relationships, and the laying of the groundwork for future economic stability, compromises to their well-being in adolescence may have negative consequences that endure well into adulthood. Thus, we can see a compelling irony in these teens' sexual decision-making processes. While young women appear to be strategizing actively to cope with difficulties or to fill otherwise unmet needs in their lives by becoming involved with older men, their strategy may lead them to make decisions that actually exacerbate the very problems they are trying to solve.

As I stated at the beginning of this chapter, I remain conflicted about the current legal focus on adult-teen relationships. The data collected in this study suggest potential problematic implications for adolescent girls, and I in no way wish to excuse men from their responsibility for these outcomes. Indeed, if adult men exploit young women's typically greater vulnerability, it makes sense that they should be held accountable for their actions. As Lydia asks:

Are we gonna let these guys who are older, and are supposed to be held to a certain standard of behavior because they're adults, are we gonna let them take advantage of the situation, of the fact that this kid's parents didn't do, you know, the job that she should have done or he should have done in raising this child? And isn't that [what] these girls are seeking? They're seeking some kind of love or approval from these older guys. So are we gonna say to the guys, "You can just have carte blanche, go ahead and take advantage of the situation," when these kids didn't get the upbringing maybe, you know, we would have liked them to get?   (Lydia, 46, Caucasian)

At the same time, I wish to suggest that the responsibility for adult-teen relationships goes much further. Many of girls' vulnerabilities appear to predate their involvement with older men. Indeed, many of the needs girls wish to fill though adult-teen relationships point to a failure of social support systems, a lack of material resources, and a culture that both tolerates adolescent male sexual irresponsibility and encourages young women to gain status and security through their attachments to men. Since adolescent women voice very real concerns about sexual exploitation in their *peer* relationships, it is shortsighted to focus on age differences as the sum of girls' problems. If we wish to fortify young women to avoid exploitative relationships and craft futures of their own making, we must continue feminist efforts to investigate and problematize underlying gendered power imbalances, as well as those related to age. We must listen closely to teen women's stories of alienation as well as their stories of agency and resistance and help them on a societal level to meet their needs, rather than leaving them to attach to adult men as their most viable (however tenuous) route out of a difficult adolescence. We must ensure that young women and their families have access to adequate resources so that teens might feel less of a need to rely on older men for the material benefits they can provide. And we must work with both adolescent men and women (as well as adults) to help them envision relationships based on mutual pleasure and mutual respect.

The renewed public focus on statutory rape affords feminists an opportunity to raise consciousness about adolescent girls' needs, as well as the complexities of consent and coercion. Current reactionary legal strategies and oversimplified portrayals of young women as "prey" suggest the need for continued feminist efforts to illuminate the perspectives of teen women while redirecting attention to the often problematic contexts from which they make their sexual decisions. Rather than reifying the dichotomization of agency and victimization, we may further understandings of power in hetero-relationships in general, and adult-teen relationships in particular, by exploring the nuanced and dialectical nature of consent and coercion in young women's experiences. While individualistic, punitive, after-the-fact approaches to adult-teen relationships may temporarily ease the anxieties of adults who wish to advocate for girls, true advocacy must involve broader efforts to provide them the resources they need and the justice they deserve, both within and outside their relationships.

NOTES

1. It may be argued that battered women who lack the resources to leave may benefit materially from staying in abusive relationships, that incest or molestation survivors may be offered "rewards" for their compliance with adults' sexual demands, or that those who experience workplace harassment may benefit from job security if they tolerate the behavior. But in these cases, the benefits stem from enduring unwanted behavior. Any "advantages" gained come *in spite of* their victimization, not as a result of the victimizing behaviors.

2. The legal age of consent varies from state to state, ranging from fourteen in Hawaii to eighteen in several other states. The majority of states set the age of consent at sixteen, although most states have various degrees of offenses, depending on the minor's age and the age gap between the minor and the adult (Donovan 1997).

3. For an encouraging example of such an educational approach, see Planned Parenthood of Greater Northern New Jersey's forthcoming curriculum *Unequal Partners*.

4. This study was part of *New Findings, New Approaches: Preventing Adolescent Pregnancy*, a research project of Planned Parenthood of Greater Northern New Jersey. The research was made possible by a generous grant from the Geraldine R. Dodge Foundation.

5. For a fuller description of the sample selection, methodology, and analysis used in the study, see Phillips 1997. The aim of the study was to learn more about the nuanced understandings and experiences of a diverse group of participants, rather than to document the prevalence of particular characteristics or responses across a random sample. Therefore, readers should note that I am not attempting to generalize these findings to other groups.

6. Because data were collected primarily through focus groups, precise numbers of participants sharing particular views or experiences cannot be known. This is because some participants may not have voiced all of their experiences or opinions during the focus group.

7. To protect the anonymity of the participants, all names used in this study are pseudonyms.

8. Although several men across race and cultural groups recalled receiving messages that encouraged them to seek younger women or girls as sexual partners, only Latino participants attributed these messages specifically to their own culture. Since this chapter is based on the voiced understandings of women currently or formerly in adult-teen relationships, men's narratives are not included here. For a fuller discussion of men's views, readers are referred to Phillips 1997.

9. This quote is taken from an interview with Carlos for the same study (Phillips 1997).

10. The point here is not that adult women have a necessarily more accurate understanding of the merits and limitations of adult-teen relationships, since their perspectives are also constructed and their memories may highlight certain elements of their past relationships while diminishing other aspects. However, they do offer us an opportunity to explore the longer-term implications of such relationships and to witness the understandings of women with broader relationship experiences.

11. It is interesting to note that while adolescent women often referred to adult men as wise, supportive, stable, and responsible, they typically did not use expressions such as "father figure" to describe their adult partners. Yet older women reflecting back on adult-teen relationships used this expression quite frequently.

12. According to the National Center for Health Statistics' 1995 National Survey of Family Growth (Abma et al. 1997), 54 percent of adolescents reported using condoms at first intercourse in the 1990s. Although this represents a tripling of adolescent condom use at first intercourse since the 1970s, it also means that nearly half of those who had first intercourse as adolescents were unprotected.

13. These women's experiences are consistent with the findings of Miller, Clark, and Moore (1997). In their study of 150 black and Latina girls, ages fourteen to seventeen, these researchers found that compared to girls with same-age first partners, girls with first partners at least three years older reported significantly less condom use at first intercourse (82 percent versus 63 percent), at last intercourse (44 percent versus 29 percent), or in the six months prior to the study (66 percent versus 44 percent). They also found that girls with older first partners were more than three times as likely as girls with same-age first partners ever to have been pregnant (38 percent versus 12 percent).

REFERENCES

Abma, J. C.; Chandra, A.; Mosher, W. D.; Peterson, L. S.; and Piccino, L. 1997. Fertility, family planning, and women's health: New data from the 1995 National Survey of Family Growth. National Center for Health Statistics. *Vital and Health Statistics* 23(19).

Donat, P. L., and D'Emilio, J. 1992. A feminist redefinition of rape and sexual assault: Historical foundations and change. *Journal of Social Issues* 48, 9–22.

Donovan, P. 1997. Can statutory rape laws be effective in preventing adolescent pregnancy? *Family Planning Perspectives* 29(1), 30–40.

East, P. L., and Felice, M. E. 1996. *Adolescent pregnancy and parenting: Findings from a racially diverse sample.* Mahwah, NJ: Lawrence Erlbaum Associates.

Fine, M.; Genevese, T.; Ingersoll, S.; McPherson, P.; and Roberts, R. 1994. White li(v)es: Looking for a discourse of male accountability. In M. Lykes, A. Banuazizi, and R. Liem, (eds.), *Unmasking social inequalities: Victims and resistance.* Philadelphia: Temple University Press.

Gergen, K. 1985. The social constructionist movement in modern psychology. *American Psychologist* 40, 266–275.

Hollway, W. 1984. Gender differences and the production of subjectivity. In J. Henriques, W. Hollway, C. Unwin, C. Venn, and V. Walkerdine (eds.), *Changing the subject: Psychology, social regulation, and subjectivity.* New York: Methuen.

Kahn, A., and Mathie, V. A. Forthcoming. Understanding the unacknowledged rape victim. In C. B. Travis and J. W. White (eds.), *Sexuality, society, and feminism: Psychological perspectives on women.* APA Press.

Koss, M. 1988. Hidden rape: Sexual aggression and victimization in a national sample in higher education. In A. W. Burgess (ed.), *Rape and sexual assault, vol. 2.* New York: Garland Press.

———. 1985. The hidden rape victim: Personality, attitudinal, and situational characteristics. *Psychology of Women Quarterly* 9, 193–213.

Landry, D. J., and Forrest, J. D. 1995. How old are U.S. fathers? *Family Planning Perspectives* 29(2), 61–66.

Lindberg, L. D.; Sonenstein, F. L.; Ku, L.; and Martinez, G. 1997. Age differences between minors who give birth and their adult partners. *Family Planning Perspectives* 27(4), 159–161 and 165.

Lorber, J. 1994. *Paradoxes of gender.* New Haven: Yale University Press.

Males, M. 1992. Adult liaison and the "epidemic" of "teenage" birth, pregnancy, and venereal disease. *Journal of Sex Research* 29(4), 525–545.

Males, M., and Chew, K. S. Y. 1996. The ages of fathers in California adolescent births, 1993. *American Journal of Public Health* 86(4), 565–568.

Marecek, J., and Hare-Mustin, R. T. 1990. Toward a feminist poststructural psychology: The modern self and the postmodern subject. Paper presented at the meetings of the American Psychological Association, Boston, MA.

Miller, K. S.; Clark, L. F.; and Moore, J. S. 1997. Sexual initiation with older male partners and subsequent HIV risk behavior among female adolescents. *Family Planning Perspectives* 29(5), 212–214.

Nakashima, I. I., and Camp, B. W. 1984. Fathers of infants born to adolescent mothers. *American Journal of Diseases of Children* 138, 452–454.

Paglia, C. 1990. *Sexual personae: Art and decadence from Nefertiti to Emily Dickinson.* New Haven: Yale University Press.

Phillips, L. Forthcoming. *Flirting with danger: Young women's reflections on sexuality and domination*. New York: New York University Press.

————. 1997. *Unequal partners: Exploring power and consent in adult-teen relationships*. Hackensack, NJ: Planned Parenthood of Greater Northern New Jersey.

Riger, S. 1992. Gender dilemmas in sexual harassment policies and procedures. In E. Wall (ed.), *Sexual harassment: Confrontations and decisions*. Buffalo: Prometheus Books.

Roiphe, K. 1993. *The morning after: Sex, fear, and feminism on campus*. Boston: Little, Brown and Company.

Rubin, G. 1984. Thinking sex: Notes for a radical theory of the politics of sexuality. In C. Vance (ed.), *Pleasure and danger: Exploring female sexuality*. Boston: Routledge and Kegan Paul.

Sanday, P. R. 1996. *A woman scorned: Acquaintance rape on trial*. New York: Doubleday.

Shweder, R. 1990. Culture: What is it? In J. W. Stigler, R. A. Shweder, and G. Herdt (eds.), *Cultural psychology: Essays on comparative human development*. Cambridge: Cambridge University Press.

Snitow, A.; Stansell, C.; and Thompson, S. 1983. Introduction. In A. Snitow, C. Stansell, and S. Thompson (eds.). *Powers of desire: The politics of sexuality*. New York: Monthly Review Press.

Tolman, D., and Higgins, T. 1996. How being a good girl can be bad for girls. In N. Bauer Maglin and D. Perry (eds.), *Bad girls/good girls: Women, sex, and power in the nineties*. New Brunswick, NJ: Rutgers University Press.

Chapter Five

Constructing the Victim
Popular Images and Lasting Labels

Sharon Lamb

There has been quite a change in thinking since the victim-blaming atmosphere of past decades, where victims of abuse—such as rape, battering, sexual harassment—used to be afraid to come forward lest they not be believed or they be blamed for the abuse they suffered. Not so long ago, small girls were seen as "seductresses" (Bender and Blau 1937), and rape victims were viewed as being provocative. But this kind of treatment of a child who has been abused or a woman who has been raped is no longer as common as it was earlier in the twentieth century.

In place of the victim-blaming that occurred decades ago, we—and by "we" I mean psychologists, researchers, therapists, feminists, victims' rights organizations, the media, activists, and survivor groups—have offered up for public discourse a different version of the victim that has its own problems. Here, the image of the victim is one who is pure, innocent, blameless, and free of problems (before the abuse). This version is often presented in juxtaposition with the perpetrator as evil monster.

Clearly, there are counterdiscourses within these groups; psychologists, researchers, and therapists are rarely so naive as to see only one side of any issue. But in this chapter, I focus on a dominant theme that pervades their discourse on victimization, a motif that recurs and overwhelms the ambiguities that might otherwise surface.

This chapter looks at our current definition of *victim*; what is required from victims and what the implications of these conceptualizations are. I first examine in detail the kinds of pathology that victims are required to develop and how being victimized has become equivalent to having a chronic mental illness. I also attempt to show how this pathologizing begins with a reading of the victim's body that requires long-standing suffering, thereby setting up a version of a victim that is damaging and exclusionary. Both pathology and long-standing suffering rob victims of agency, and victims become reactors rather than actors. I then look at the irony as well as the difficulty of becoming a "convincing victim."

The second section of the chapter raises questions about the labels "victim" and "survivor." I question the meaning and function of these terms for victims and their implications for feminist thinking. I pursue this analysis through two victims' stories. These stories are meant to show how our expectations of victims enter into and shape the victims' own conceptualizations of their experience, and how victims are starting to avoid the label "victim" because of the negative associations of this label. I examine the struggle of these victims to remain "agents" of their acts, that is, to see themselves as planful actors, as they describe their victimization.

In the final section I offer a critique of two concepts, the label of "victim" and the metaphor of "voice." My alternative to the version of victim in dominant discourse is one that recognizes agency as well as passivity, strength as well as vulnerability, resistance as well as dissociation. In like manner, the metaphor of "voice," while particularly useful in describing agency and resilience, is an overused one that can work against victims as well as for them.

This examination of resiliency, resistance, and voice calls for a discussion of the politics—and sometimes lack of politics—of abuse and victimization. It is ironic that seeing abuse as widespread and common, not as a "special" event, will help feminism and psychology reclaim the activism once associated with the area of abuse.

I agree with many a reader that victimization of women by men is a frequent occurrence in our culture. But my purpose beyond that stance is to point out that the way we have thought about and labeled victims has hindered the possibility of acknowledging the pervasiveness of abuse[1] on a political level and has made us focus on extreme and pathological versions. While I see abuse as pervasive, I do not see all abuse as severe or traumatic. It exists on a continuum of severity and harmfulness. There are smaller, everyday exploitations that don't count as abuse in dominant definitions, which focus heavily on extreme cases. To the extent that abuse is a "normal" (meaning typical) occurrence in the lives of women, a narrow and extreme prototype of victimization serves only to divide women from one another and work against a large-scale reshaping of gender relations in society, which the problem ultimately requires.

I. The Public Construction and Consumption of the "Victim"

Pathologizing the Victim

Feminism lost its power to suggest interpretations of abuse to the American public almost as soon as the media seized on victimization of women and girls as a popular subject. This loss of a political movement that saw abuse as primarily a gender issue became a gain for the public health and mental health professionals. Discussions of power and dominance yielded to discussions of symptomatology and long-term effects. It was as if the most effective way to stop abuse or to make the public recognize the problem was to prove that abuse inevitably and overwhelmingly leads to psychological distress. There seemed to be no other reasons to bring a stop to the abuse of women and children—-moral reasons were not discussed, except perhaps a washed-out kind of secular liberalism that based moral "badness" on feeling bad or psychological harm. The wrongness of abuse could have been founded on some kind of universal or shared belief about how people ought to treat one another, instead of on the concept of psychological damage; and if it had, a movement directed at social and political change might have survived. As Louise Armstrong rightly complains about the current state of affairs in the United States, "It is the degree of . . . suffering (not the grotesqueness of the injustice) that speaks of the wrongness of the assault" (1996, p. 300).

Child sexual abuse, more than rape or battering, for example, seems to have become a mental health issue instead of a social one. Workers in battered women's shelters have dealt with this issue head-on for some time, debating whether offering counseling to battered women is problematic. Some shelter directors have vehemently maintained a no-counseling philosophy, so that women would know that the problem of being beaten lies with the man who beats, not with the woman who is beaten, thus taking a more political response to the problem.

Treatment of victims of sexual abuse, however, focuses on the woman's reactions and the mental illness or trauma the experience is assumed to have caused. The "altered state" of mental illness makes people believe in the horror of abuse, because it emphasizes victim powerlessness. It also fits into a prevailing model of women as more vulnerable to mental illness and disease. The demonstration of long-lasting harmfulness of abuse even helps, some would say, to hold men responsible for their crimes, by making the crimes seem more serious.[2]

The list of symptoms experienced by victims of sexual abuse is enormous: depression, suicidal tendencies, anxiety, phobias, addictions, dissociative identity disorder, eating disorders, sexual dysfunction, and so on. The advancing of these lists was politically important at one point in the history of exposing abuse, to force the public to take it seriously. Lindsey O'Dell (1997) writes of the "highly emotive" language used to describe the symptomatology.

These symptoms are not invented or pulled out of thin air. There are victims of severe sexual abuse who suffer from these and concomitant disorders, some briefly and some long-term. But reactions to abuse vary. Often, the mental illness–like qualities of women who have been beaten disappear in the years shortly after leaving the abusive man. And sexual abuse researchers have documented recently that the majority of sexual abuse victims do not show severe symptomatology (Finkelhor 1990). Many victims cope; many recover. In an analysis of the research that supports the idea of long-term suffering, O'Dell (1997) found questionable methodologies and articles in which authors tended to take small points and elevate them to findings, as well as taking single cases and generalizing to all victims.

Although some authors address victim resistance and recovery, there has been little written about the many victims who have truly "survived"—that is, moved beyond these all-too-common abusive experiences. Positive messages are absent (Lamb 1996; O'Dell 1997). When a victim does "move on," she herself becomes wary of continuing to call herself a "victim," because the label has become associated with the multiproblem, dysfunctional image.

One of the worst thieves of victim agency/victim resiliency is the diagnosis of post-traumatic stress disorder (PTSD), a syndrome that describes a pattern of symptoms sometimes found in a person who has been traumatized. Research shows that while 95 percent of rape victims show PTSD symptoms a few weeks after the rape, fewer than 25 percent remain this distressed two years later (Rothbaum, Foa, Riggs, Murdock, and Walsh 1992). PTSD makes sexual abuse "treatable," in the sense that insurance companies reimburse for diagnosed disorders more readily than they do for reactions to stress. An "adjustment disorder," which is a diagnosis that describes a person coping with a major change such as the death of a loved one or loss of a job or divorce (APA 1994), is usually reimbursable only for six months. Thus, the medicalizing of victims' reactions, through diagnosing PTSD, has served the purpose of making extensive treatment more likely to be covered by mental health insurance.

But financial considerations aside, why are these reactions to a stressor considered a mental illness? There are other kinds of reactions to environmental stressors that are not called "syndromes." Take, for example, an inner-city youth who doesn't show an interest in education: his eyes glaze over; he is listless; he engages in some delinquent behavior outside of school. His stressors may be poverty, lack of opportunity, an uncaring parental or school system. These stressors cause his disinterest about as often, if not more often, than violence and trauma cause PTSD (Lamb 1996). Could the label of his syndrome be "school dissociation disorder"? Of course it could; but the culture doesn't acknowledge this as a mental illness.

PTSD is seen as involuntary and thus arising from a deep biology of sorts. And recently in our culture, we have begun to invoke biology to avoid tricky questions of social or personal responsibility. But there is a sad consequence for women if the culture adopts this perspective on their reactions to abuse. If we see symptomatology as produced by external sources (e.g., the trauma), if we see it as involuntary, outside a person's control, then we are very close to a notion of a woman as damaged—or "damaged goods" as the older, viler saying used to go. Our new medical conceptions of the ravages of trauma start sounding very much like older hushed-voice opinions that a girl who is raped or sexually abused is now "damaged" and consequently worthless (Haaken 1998). While modern-day thinkers may be more sympathetic to a victim, it is clear that her body is no longer a "good" body, one that behaves and follows her wishes. Female passivity is thus re-created and reinforced.[3]

In addition to PTSD, abuse has become associated with severe pathologies such as "borderline personality disorder" (Becker 1997) and "multiple personality disorder" (Putnam, Guroff, Silberman, et al. 1986; Ross, Miller, Reagor, Bjornson, et al. 1990; Coons 1994; Keaney and Farley 1996), as well as more commonplace problems such as eating disorders and disorders of sexuality. Multiple personality disorder (MPD) and borderline personality disorder (BPD) are rare diagnoses. And with regard to the more commonplace problems, many women who have not been abused also show difficulties in eating and sexuality. Rather than narrowly viewing abuse as a cause of so many female maladies, severe and commonplace women's disorders might be seen as stemming from institutionalized practices (male violence, privilege, and objectification of women) that contribute to the dissociation of body from spirit in women.

All of the difficulties associated with abuse, whether unusual such as MPD or more typical such as sexual arousal problems, fetishize the body; that is, they focus on the body over the rest of the person in an exaggerated fashion (see Chapter 7 by Jeanne Marecek for specific examples of therapists doing such). Each of these disorders creates the appearance of a victim being victimized by her own body, a body that, like her perpetrator, has somehow turned against her. It has been argued that this is precisely what traumatization does to a person (Herman 1992). Trauma invades the victim in such a way as to internalize the perpetrator, and this internalized perpetrator continues to abuse the victim endlessly. There are psychoanalytic notions that explain this (the internalized aggressor), as well as biological explanations (reconfigured endorphin systems); but no matter what discipline the explanation comes from, the effect on the public mind is the same. These notions are pleasing to U.S. culture because they reproduce a notion of girlhood or womanhood that we would like to preserve: the helpless female—slight, airy, voiceless—who needs reviving (as with Ophelia) or rescuing. The idea of "voice" (which I will discuss later) is about a disembodied voice—one that conveys the betrayal of the body. This betrayal of the body is an image acceptable to the mental health field. It also provides a substitute for recognizing the large-scale betrayal of women by men (a view that would be a more political stance). The category of "victim," then, serves to re-objectify the female body; she is not a person but an object.

The Eternal Suffering of the Victim

The expectation that an abuse victim will develop symptoms is clear. It is also clear that victims' suffering must be long and severe, or else their victimization is trivial and does not "count." This expectation is endorsed, ironically, both by victim advocates who cannot believe that someone's abuse is not the central meaning-making incident in their lives and by backlash authors who do not count minor abusive experiences as "real" abuse, calling victims "whiners" for so labeling these experiences. For abuse to *count*, the suffering can never go away.

Why have well-meaning therapists and victim advocates focused so overwhelmingly on extreme symptomatology, and why have they seen the suffering of victims as so long-lasting? As I have said earlier, in the beginning of this movement about abuse and victimization in the 1970s, the point needed to be made that abuse does cause harm. Therapists and other victim advocates wanted very much to differentiate themselves from perpetrators who denied harm and to take sides with the victim, so that any yielding on these points may have seemed like minimization of the abuse. Minimization of abuse is something that perpetrators actually did, saying, "It was just sex education" or "There was no harm to it; I think she liked it." Minimization of the abuse is something that families, particularly mothers, were said to have committed: "Let's not think about it and it will go away"; "Uncle Don is just a little sick in the head." Thus, victim advocates in general were being careful not to minimize any symptom, any harm done.

There is also an aspect of long-suffering that conveys a sense that a victim is "morally superior" to the rest of the population who have not been victimized (Fillion 1996). In a false duality, suffering or the bearing of oppression becomes equated with moral superiority because it is so clear that oppressors are morally inferior people. Thus, the version of the victim as long-suffering simplifies the moral picture of good and evil regarding abuse.

The rise of professionalism in the United States may also have contributed to the need to see victims as eternally suffering. A focus on abuse and victimization created an opportunity (in the fields of psychiatry and mental health) for women to obtain prominence as experts in a field that was gaining a great deal of exposure. It is important to remember how male dominated the psychiatric profession was several decades ago in the United States. There is still an obvious hierarchy in hospitals across the United States; psychiatrists are seen as superior to psychologists, who are superior to social workers, who are superior to mental health workers, and so on. Psychiatrists are still predominantly white men, who make more money and have more decision-making power in hospital and clinic settings than the social workers, who are predominantly women. (Psychologists lie somewhere in between.) With the new specialty in abuse and victimization, satellite clinics and units within hospitals were formed, and many of these were led by women. Did male doctors think this particular female complaint was better left to women because the perpetrators were men? Did sympathetic mental health professionals think that women would be more comfortable speaking to other women about their abuse? Or did the beginning of this new specialization simply coincide with the rise of women in fields such as psychology and psychiatry? Linda Gordon (1988) has written about the professionalization of social work at the beginning of the twentieth century and how the profession edged out the influence of feminists and social reformers. Perhaps the professionalization of the field of sexual abuse edged out an activist kind of feminist. Professionalization required women to work within a system, in this case, the system of diagnoses and disorders.

The media, in addition to mental health workers, have also required long-term suffering from victims for their victimization to be compelling. Suffering creates drama. And not only long-term suffering but heroic recoveries from abuse became important, as the word *survivor* came to replace *victim* in the public vocabulary. As talk-show TV has expanded, the mildly distressed has become commonplace and less interesting than the awfully distressed.

This emphasis on the pain and suffering of victims ignores several alternative realities. Most important, therapists and a sympathetic public have had to ignore victims who have moved on. When a victim says she is "over it" or that it was "a long time ago," she becomes suspect. It is assumed that she must be retaining a lot of anger and harboring resentment or hatred toward men. It is expected that her suffering will need to emerge in a matter of time. Will she just explode? Will she kill herself? Or will her symptoms appear in the bedroom?

A subtle but different perspective about the long-term suffering required of victims is that victims are seen as continually reacting to their abuse, as if no other life circumstances could compare with this trauma for influencing the course of events in their lives as they continue. In *The Trouble with Blame: Victims, Perpetrators, and Responsibility* (1996), I wrote a two-sentence statement about my own experience with abuse because I wanted to show other victims that I wasn't writing from the position of an outsider. I wrote that when I was small, a teenage boy tickled me in order to carry me into a cellar and there molest me: "Though terrifying at the time, in the grand scheme of abuse experiences, this experience was minimal and not difficult to overcome" (Lamb 1996, p. x). However, a reviewer of my book transformed my personal history to be years of horrible abuse and stated that it was the motivation for my writing a book on abuse—as if I could not possibly have been telling the truth when I said I was "over it," even though it happened thirty-six years ago (Anisfeld 1997).

Thus, it is the long-suffering victim who has become a mainstay client of therapists in private practice and clinics. Forever a victim, her therapy focuses on making meaning of the abuse (Silver, Boon, and Stone 1983), surviving the event, finding her voice, getting in touch with her anger, seeking out other victims for support, sometimes confronting the perpetrator, but rarely moving on.

Not only are victims seen as ever suffering, continually reacting to their abuse, as if no other life circumstance compares with the trauma; they are also seen as not responsible for their reactions to the abuse. This is perhaps an even more important point. It is tricky to argue that someone is responsible for how she or he reacts to a trauma; but I would argue that the person is, at least in part, by using two examples. The first case involves a man who was sexually abused throughout his boyhood and who raped a woman when he grew up. Do we excuse his raping her because it was a reaction to his own sexual abuse? Do we see him as unable to stop his raping (his reacting to his abuse in this harmful way)? Do we see him as able to make a choice not to rape?

The second example is more complex. I once interviewed a woman who, as a child, experienced horrible, numerous incidents of abuse and rape from multiple perpetrators. As a mother, she allowed a known sex offender to baby-sit her daughter. How did she know he was a sex offender? He had already served time for molesting both of her sons years before. Would we hold her responsible, to some extent, for her daughter's abuse? Yes, of course. But would we hold her responsible if she had put herself in a dangerous situation and allowed herself to be raped again? I suggest that, customarily, we would assess the latter situation differently, and we might not blame her. We might excuse her as incapable of doing otherwise because she was *reacting to her abuse*. Is this not illogical? Is she less responsible for herself than she is for her daughter?

The Convincing Victim

Therapists are not the only ones who prefer to see victims as helpless; the general consuming public does as well. The public sees victims as long-suffering and believes it is very hard to get over abuse, because it "jibes" with what we have learned and continue to learn through experts who appear on the news and through other media sources. But when resilience is ignored, a traditional view of women as the weaker sex, in need of protection and special services, is reinforced.

I saw two girls in therapy a few years ago who were preparing to go to court (in separate cases) to confront their abusers. In both cases, the lawyers (a district attorney for one and a private attorney for the other) were concerned that they would not be convincing "victims" because they were doing so well. Both were straight-A students. Both had good friends and got along with their parents. Neither met the criteria for a DSM-IV (or standard) diagnosis. While they got sad and were upset when thinking about their abuse, both seemed able to talk about it, as well as put it aside when it got too upsetting to remember. They contradicted our accepted notion of what it means to be a victim.

Another client, a woman who was date-raped, was doing exceptionally well one year after the rape. This was of concern to her lawyer, who kept asking me to describe the ways in which I thought she would have long-term suffering and damages because of the rape. It seemed to me at the time that she was very much recovered, even though she had suffered a great deal immediately after the rape—thinking constantly of the injustice, fearfully putting off plans to travel, showing some phobic reactions, distrusting men, and so on. As her therapist, I found myself forced to decide whether I wanted to give her the impression that she would suffer from this experience her whole life, or offer an opinion that would likely result in a smaller settlement for her in court.

In a similar situation, when another child I was seeing in therapy went to court, the lawyer complained during a recess from the proceedings that the child's testimony was sounding too "rote," and because of this, the jury might think she was making the abuse up. Later in the proceedings, when the girl began to cry and was so upset that she could not finish, the lawyer was satisfied that she looked "good" for the jury.

If the public looks to the media or the courtroom for public displays of the culturally approved victim, it is these sorts of images that are reinforced: innocent, young, thin, attractive, and from the middle class. She will cry and show humiliation in having to describe sexual acts. She will never be angry or bitter (Benedict 1992; Madriz 1997).

Amanda Konradi (1996) spoke to victims who had an even greater investment in understanding the culture's definition of victim than we theorists and practitioners do. If these victims didn't "pass the test," their perpetrators would be set free. Konradi interviewed thirty-two women and made twelve courtroom observations. She found that the women researched and played the role of victim to get what they wanted—a guilty verdict for their perpetrator.

What the women first did was what Konradi called "appearance" work. This occurred across class lines; all went shopping to buy clothes appropriate for a victim going to trial. One woman was particularly concerned that the jury not know that she was an avid backpacker because they might see her as too "self-reliant."

A second kind of work Konradi called "emotion" work, based on the theory of Arlie Hochschild (1988). The ideal victim, in the eyes of these women awaiting trial, was someone who was polite, composed, deferential, and overcome by tears only when recalling her rape. In one case a woman had to go through a second trial because the first jury was unable to reach a decision. Angry that she was forced to go through the whole trial again, she became, then, a "real" victim. She told the interviewer, "I was just going to have to lose it. . . . The jury wanted someone hysterical on the stand; they were gonna get one."

A side issue that Konradi writes about is that much has appeared in the literature about the passive victim who is "raped again" by the legal system. This, of course, happens, and with some frequency, when one considers how difficult it is to prosecute rape and abuse cases successfully. But Konradi's interviews speak of something else. They speak of victim agency in the process, a previously unacknowledged aspect of courtroom victims.

Why hasn't this aspect of trial work for victims come to light? It is true both that women are often victimized again by the judicial system and that women work hard to present their cases in the best light possible. Rather than embodying a version of a victim who is defeated and condemned to a multitude of disorders, they actively prepare their cases with lawyers and make plans to influence juries, determining how best to fit into our common understanding of what a victim should be like. The backpacker knew well that the American public does not want its victims to be too self-reliant!

Victim versus Survivor

A Rose by Any Other Name?

Sexual victimization is in some ways an exciting topic, captivating the public's imagination and interest for longer periods than homelessness or child neglect. Why does it "turn us on"? It is because of the almost archetypal images evoked of victim and perpetrator. The victim is pure, innocent, helpless, and sometimes heroic. The perpetrator is monstrous and all powerful. These images are dichotomized; they never are integrated.

The push-and-pull that shapes a victim into a caricature has its problems even among victims. Ironically, while the media and psychology books have increasingly pointed out that everyone wants to be a victim, victims have vehemently argued that they are not victims.

When abuses such as child sexual abuse, battering, and rape were widely acknowledged in the 1970s and 1980s, massive numbers of women stepped forward and disclosed such experiences from their past. This recognition of victimization produced a sort of solidarity among women around issues of abuse. But very soon after, disrupting the process of recognition of victimization, sexual abuse victims demanded to be called "survivors."

The word *survivor* was meant to convey an aspect of a traumatic event that actually occurs infrequently in relation to abuse—that the victim's life was at stake and that the victim survived an event on a par with a genocide. To the extent that this is what was meant by the term *survivor*, it was a grand term to use in this context. Particularly for victims of sexual abuse, rarely was a life at stake. It is possible that the use of such a grand term caused some victims to feel as if they were faking it, compounding the self-blame that normally accompanies abuse.

The second aspect of the word *survivor* was that it evoked the "worst of it" in terms of situations of abuse. Even though it was infrequent that girls' and women's lives were actually at stake, it was still true that women and girls were occasionally being killed or experiencing horrendous tortures *simply because they were women and girls.* The use of *survivor* was meant to help draw attention to the abuse of women and girls as an institutionalized practice in our culture, something common, unquestioned, and almost expected. The accentuation of the worst—that women and girls were dying—was to show the public how far the "typical" could go, to show how horrible it could get for women along this continuum of hardship.

The third quality that the term *survivor* evokes is one of heroic adaptation. The new label was the first suggestion that the victim was an active resister in her abuse, and that whatever she did, whether it was to dissociate, kill her oppressor, dress up for him, or not tell her mother, she did this to "survive." In contrast, Angela Ginorio (1998) writes that her students in a course on violence prefer the word *victim* to *survivor* because some victims don't actually "survive."

Why did victims resist being called "victims"? It is shameful to be a victim in our culture. No matter how much victims' rights advocates and therapists have told victims that they are not to blame for their abuse, that they did not provoke it, and that it had nothing to do with them, it is still shameful to be a victim. Where does this shame come from? Why is there such a deep feeling of humiliation associated with being overpowered or vulnerable or hurt or unable to come to one's own defense? It is because no matter what therapists tell victims, they feel that they have been weak, and weakness is shameful in our culture.

But they are victims—though some are survivors as well. And while victims often do cope with, struggle against, and resist their abuse, they also yield, look the other way, and "take it." Their ambivalence about passivity and weakness, their unrealistic expectations of themselves that they could have prevented or stopped the abuse, gets translated into grandiose versions of their struggle within the abusive experience. They believe they were survivors, not victims. Of course, they were both victims and strugglers.

Though labeling herself a survivor may help a victim to repudiate her passivity, it may also help her avoid an examination of her feelings of humiliation about having been vulnerable. In this, she falls into collusion with backlash forces that view the acknowledgment of victimization as mere whining and that associate this acknowledgment with hysterical females making much ado about nothing. While feminist authors have pointed out the empowering aspects of naming and thus reclaiming one's own experience as "bearing witness to oppression" (Ginorio 1998, p. 79), they sometimes forget that this renaming can derive from and support oppressive forces themselves. It used to be that women were afraid of not being believed or of being accused of provoking the abuse (which assumes, if you think about it, a significant amount of power on the woman's part). But now, calling oneself a victim can mark the victim socially as self-involved, lacking responsibility, and whining.

What I see in this trend is an across-the-board lack of empathy for those who have suffered, an attitude of stinginess. But perhaps this ungenerous attitude grew out of what the public saw as exaggerated claims of the victim. Perhaps it grew out of the huge victim industry that developed around treatment and service for people who had suffered from these experiences (Kaminer 1996).

The other problem with victims no longer willing to call themselves victims is that this trend has undone a sense of unity among women. The category of "victim," when it meant something simple rather than something so grand as survival of the most horrendous abuses imaginable, could include many more women. A majority of women have experienced sexual abuse, or rape, or unexpected gropes from strangers, or "flashes" from men in parks, or lewd gestures, and these experiences unite women. They create solidarity because they come from one source that can be fought: male hostility, objectification, and exploitation of women. But the fear of being called a victim, of being seen as "exaggerating one's claims," looms so large that women will separate themselves from other women in order not to be labeled in this way.

Nobody wants to be labeled. In our Western democratic individualism, our belief that we are our own, unique creations is powerful. And so it is understandable that solidarity or even "identity politics," as it is applied to victims, is a vulnerable concept. Jodi Dean (1996) writes of a stage in feminist politics where differences among feminists challenged the identity of the group. She writes that the challenge of "reflective solidarity" is to find a way in which differences are not melded into a unitary vision but are acknowledged and appreciated within an overarching purpose. Even though victimization was so widespread, it varied tremendously, and because these variations were not acknowledged, there was no longer a basis for solidarity among women and no longer a clear purpose to the unity.

The sorriest thing about this resistance to the "victim" label is that when individuals feel as if they are acting out some independent, romanticized act of resistance, they are also joining forces with backlash critics who would deny that male victimization of women is widespread. The call "I am a survivor," comes from a belief that people *can* label themselves and that this is an empowering strategy in a world where others seek to label you. But this imagined power that we can label and create ourselves is deceptive and causes individuals to be blind to the places from which this power is derived. We must look at who has the power to label and not so readily assume it is an individual's choice. And we also must look at the kinds of cultural forces that support certain labels over others, and what function each label serves.

Where Have All the "Victims" Gone?

I present two stories of victims below. In the first story, the victim does not recognize what happened to her as victimization. In the second story, the victim recognizes that she was victimized but does not want to call herself a victim. Both women experienced abuse from their grandfathers.

In the first example, the story comes through a therapist friend of the victim:

This friend entered therapy as an adult and was asked if she had ever been sexually abused. In this story the woman replied, "No," when her therapist asked her the question. She then went on to report that from ages three to eight she had shared a bed with her "beloved grandfather," who regularly masturbated against her thighs. The therapist pointed out to her the discrepancy between her denial that she had been abused and her description of this five-year period. Only then did the woman begin to name this experience (which she had always remembered) as abuse. She then began to think how horrific it would be if someone were to abuse and exploit her own small daughter in such a way and finally was able to realize how horrific it had indeed been that she herself was forced to endure it. She is still assessing the repercussions of her betrayal by this man, whom she had loved so uncritically and trusted so much.

There are contradictions in this story. While the victim does not initially label the experience as "abuse," she actually brings up the experience in response to the question. She is ambivalent, as if saying, "I have not called this abuse, but you might." As she began to conceptualize her experience as abuse, was the "beloved" grandfather aspect of the experience made obsolete by what was now perceived as "horrific"? Were loving memories of her grandfather now called into question? The relater of the story then tells us that her friend began to "name the experience" as abuse, as if "abuse" would be the only name for it.

The grandfather's actions represented a betrayal of sorts, a seduction, a use of a child whom possibly he loved in so many other ways than as an object for sexual pleasure. He used her with reckless disregard for the effects his doing so might have on her. But what, then, were the effects? This is more complex to determine. We are told she is still assessing the repercussions. I wonder if it is possible that there were no severe repercussions after the woman and the therapist named the abuse. Are we afraid that by saying that she may not have had long-standing bad effects from this act, the act was not bad? The moral judgment of the act could exist apart from the harm it caused. Is it possible that this grandfather was so loving in other ways that it made up for the "bad" act? Maybe the child forgave him the discomfort, whereas the grown woman cannot.

And what if the woman and her therapist find together that the repercussions of this act include distrust of men or a passivity around men that makes her vulnerable to being taken advantage of? Who is to say this abuse specifically led to that distrust or passivity? Many women who have not been abused grow up in patriarchal situations in which distrust of men (or passivity around men) develops "naturally."

We can analyze the term *beloved* in the same way. Was he really beloved, or was this a construction that goes far beyond a little girl's denial? The television commercials of little girls on grandfathers' laps, the virtual bestowing of "belovedness" on grandparents—these are cultural constructions that create yearnings. Given the cultural construction of the grand-father/granddaughter relationship, we can also question her desire to see and experience a grandfather as beloved as internalized patriarchy.

I am not arguing here, as do so many backlash critics, that the "bad" therapist implanted the idea of "abuse" in this woman's head. There would be cultural consensus that this was abuse on the grandfather's part. But what is the crucial next step in making meaning of the event? Does the woman then search through her life history to explain every other problem as a result of this abuse? Does she then negate the humanity of the perpe-trator, or can she hold the ambivalence? Does she begin to see herself dif-ferently? Does she see herself now as more helpless and betrayed? Or does she look back in horror at her childish, innocent pleasure in the warmth of her grandfather? Does she punish herself for that pleasure? Does she pun-ish herself for her love of him by calling it "denial" or by calling herself "blind"? Does she see the event as primary or among many other male acts of violence; abuse; taking advantage of her youth, innocence, guilt, love, warmth? Does she call herself a "survivor"? Is her love for her grandfather now viewed as a false love—the love of a slave for a master, a prisoner for a jailer, a product of the Stockholm Syndrome—or as a love that was built from a false consciousness about men and women?

In the story, we move from the phrase "beloved grandfather" to the phrase "forced to endure it." Once the acts are exposed, neither by itself is any longer an adequate description. This example highlights the difficulties with the sterile, unnuanced version of victim as simply innocent and pure.

In the second example, a college student writes about a similar experience of abuse with her grandfather. While the first woman's story is one about the naming of abuse, the second story discusses both the difficulty of nam-ing abuse *as* abuse and the difficulty in naming oneself a "victim." (The ital-ics in her discussion of whether or not she is a victim are my own.)

> I was sexually abused by my grandfather when I was nine years old. While watching TV my grandfather had asked me to sit next to him on the couch. As we watched the eleven o'clock news he placed his hand on my lap. Later on his hand moved to my neck and then around to my shoulders. Soon it rested on my chest and began to touch and caress my nipples and very small breasts. After a few minutes he placed his hand on my lap again and began to unbutton my jeans. He then slipped his hand underneath my underwear. For the next twenty minutes or so he touched and prodded me, gently. The same act happened several times that summer, each time on the couch while

watching television. Sometimes we were alone, sometimes others sat in the room with us but noticed nothing. They were too enraptured in a movie or sitcom. Each time my grandfather patted the cushion next to him on the couch, I knew what would transpire if I gave in to his wishes. I sat there each time he asked.

One night as the ritual began once again, someone noticed, finally. My mother saw her "own father's" fingers reaching for and enveloping her daughter's small breast. She quickly announced that it was time for me to go to bed and ordered me to my room. In my room, my mother held me in her arms and in tears asked me how long this had been going on. Embarrassed, I answered that it had occurred just twice and begged my mother not to get angry. My mother was not angry but rather hurt and confused. She tried to explain that my grandfather was very sick and was taking a lot of medication for a heart condition. It was decided, in my room, that my grandfather's medication had altered his way of thinking and he had known little of his actions. It was also decided that these experiences would never be spoken about again. I was only reminded of it again years later when my mother told me that he had begun doing the same to my younger sister. . . . I remember having a deep sense that a wrongdoing was taking place but I had little understanding of how to define this offense. *I chose instead to interpret it as an acceptable and enjoyable experience.* This interpretation not only justified my grandfather's actions but it also justified the feelings of arousal I felt each time my grandfather touched me. This way of looking at the experience *allowed me to become an instigator of my own abuse.* In order to transgress [sic] from the frightening reality of my grandfather's actions, *I made myself believe that I was involved in a secret game with him.* This perception allowed me to believe that I was special. *Each time I chose to sit next to him, I assured my own agency, my own will to allow the actions to continue.* . . . During the abuse I feel like *I had "saved" my own sense of self by translating the experience as a game,* a game in which I was a willing participant. This gave me a sense of control over the situation. When my mother appeared on the scene, however, blame entered the scenario and two things happened to my sense of the experience. First I realized that a very bad thing had been done to me and it had happened because of my very own actions. . . . Later, as a result of my mother's actions, I realized that my grandfather was to blame. But by placing all the blame on my grandfather through her actions, my mother made me a helpless victim without any control over what had happened to me.

In this example, a woman looks back at her childhood resenting not her grandfather but her mother for *making her* a "victim." She sees herself as an "instigator" of her own abuse. She writes a story with an agentic voice, one that acknowledges choices made, even though she was young and immature—the choice being to continue to sit next to her grandfather on the couch. As she associates agency with a nonvictim status, this choice makes her less of a victim. But is this the choice of the child or the memory of the adult?

The cultural consensus would again be that this experience constitutes child sexual abuse and that the grandfather was wrong to do what he did. She was young, and regardless of her belief in her own agency and power, as adults we have to acknowledge that her grandfather might have been so imposing a figure that she couldn't say no to him. It may be that this experience did not have the forever-lasting, deep-suffering trauma that other, more severe betrayals of trust seem to induce. The woman, looking back, recognizes the small part she played in the continuation of the abuse and recognizes what was wrong with it. She does not elevate herself to a "survivor," for realistically, she did not survive anything but exploitation. We do not know if this experience affected her deeply the rest of her life. Research tends to indicate that if all else went fairly well in her life, if she had a supportive family and friends and talents, she probably has not been long-suffering.

The author of this second story brings up the excellent question of who gets to create the story that explains the event. Her mother's version is one that would probably protect her, and maybe did protect her, from further abuse by her grandfather. Her own story that it was a game, while leading to continued exploitation, was a valid way for a nine-year-old to see what was happening; it preserved her agency, preserved the wrongness of the act, but didn't elevate it to a trauma.

It is interesting to see how the woman deconstructs her memory. She writes that she actively chose to perceive the experience as a game and that her mother awoke her to the harsh reality of the "truth" of the event. Can her earlier perception of the experience be dismissed as a "defense"? It was a game for her. In a context of pervasive harassment, from irritation to physical violence against women, such small incidents need to be counted. Rather than arguing whether there was "abuse" or not, these incidents ought to be seen as existing on a continuum.

Why do this young women and others hate to be called "victims"? It is because the whole of their experience is not described by that word. The word speaks to only a part of the experience. The ambivalence for these two women is between the moral wrong and the pleasure or love felt.

Some victims also hate to be called "victims" because to do so revives the original feeling of helplessness and vulnerability. Our culture makes victims choose between the two aspects of strength and vulnerability. And as empathy for victims has been so fleeting a reaction, and as belief in individual responsibility has become a 1990s motto, victims have chosen in increasing numbers to not "be" victims unless resiliency, agency, and strength are part of the definition.

This seems right; why should the public begrudge victims the right to point out their strength, resistance, and resiliency? But we also might wish for a culture in which all aspects of victimization—the strength as well as the vulnerability—would be acceptable. If the culture overemphasizes the helpless victim, and if victims overemphasize the survivor victim, we are caught between two stereotypes that preclude a range of experiences and the unifying awareness that victimization is too frequently a part of every woman's life.

III. Reworking the Label and the Metaphors

The Problem of Agency

Researchers, therapists, and the general public lose track of the kinds of resistance victims employ. When such resistances are acknowledged, they are called "methods of survival," but they are also evidence that a smart, thinking woman (or girl) was doing what she could to avoid being abused. In our research on children who've been sexually abused, these victims report kicking, yelling, biting, and hiding—all sorts of active strategies. They also report a number of passive reactions, some of which could be called strategies (Lamb and Cuddy 1996).

The issue of agency is confusing for therapists and for victims. If we see the victim as a "victim," then it is fine to acknowledge that there might be times when she is just reacting. If we see the victim as a "survivor," then everything she does is given a "spin" that makes it active and assertive. For example, therapists may conclude that she "dissociates" on purpose, learning the cleverly practiced skill of self-hypnosis. She is thus seen not as helpless or frozen and paralyzed but as actively coping.

There are data to support the overwhelming amount of anger that victims feel (and rightly so) in response to their abuse. But it is difficult for the public to put up with an "angry woman" for long. This anger is not "pretty" and does not always fit with the image of the "good" victim. Thus, when angry feelings of a victim are presented to the public, as in a movie or to a therapist in an evaluation, they are put in a framework that describes the anger as unmanageable and overwhelming: "I don't know what to do with my anger."

The anger is sometimes written out of the story. For example, when we hear of battered women killing their husbands, it is almost always in the context of self-defense and rarely in the context of anger that had built up over so many years of abuse that it exploded in a violent act of her own. Some of this is framed by researchers and therapists in terms of the building up of the effects of trauma—the woman has lost herself after years of domination and abuse—but rarely is this expressed as the building up of *anger*. The public didn't know what to do with Lorena Bobbitt, who clearly cut off her husband's penis out of rage, because she was also a victim, also a battered wife. Categorized, as she soon was, as a battered woman, we came to understand her as "not right in the head," believing that this was her only choice to escape a battering husband. We alternately might have seen her as overwhelmed by her anger after years of mistreatment. There is a difference.

We understand so clearly how boys who have been abused grow up to be perpetrators; yet women seem exempt. After years of abuse, why could not women also do the abusive thing that they are accused of? It does not fit with being a female victim. Imagine the havoc that would erupt if the new version of victim were of a woman enraged and out for revenge, finding not just her voice but her legs, her arms, her whole self. This is the kind of agency/power that is not often acknowledged.

There is also literature to suggest that girls and women sometimes feel sexual pleasure when being abused. This pleasure is discounted as accidental and biological—a "physical reaction" and, once again, a "betrayal of the body." Sociologist Carol Rambo Ronai (1995) writes in a revolutionary way about the pleasure and "passive joy" she felt in fulfilling her horribly abusive father's needs. It is a memory that now "sickens her," because, she writes, it interferes with "the righteousness of my victim status."

Finding One's Voice: The Perfect Metaphor for the Victim

"Voice" and "silence" are probably the most important metaphors of the second-wave women's movement. The metaphor of "voice" is ubiquitous, from *In a Different Voice*, to *Silencing the Self*, to discourse about "listening to women's stories" and their "narratives." Works based on uncovering voice not only opened the culture to hearing about experiences of women but validated those experiences as authentic (Mahoney 1996). These works also came to elevate the stories in a way that allowed the public to hear victims' voices as voices from the battlefront, stories from survivors (Haaken 1998).

The metaphor of "voice" is particularly evocative in the area of victimization because it cuts across so many dimensions. It evokes the idea of a political agenda—as in raising voices together. It evokes a feeling of truth or authenticity. And it evokes an aura of specialness around the victim, a unique individuality that is precious and vulnerable.

With regard to the political agenda, the metaphor of "voice" can be used to refer to the silencing of a people; suppression, domination, participation, and power are all ideas that are expressed through the metaphor. The original work on voice and women's narratives did address a political agenda. Writers recognized that what had been accepted as truth in the past was merely white males' unchallenged right to tell stories from their position of dominance. Those who wrote originally about voice believed that forces of domination suppress voice and that acts of resistance begin with self-expression. Voice was and is an element of democracy, a means of equal participation. Women's voice, women's narratives, women's stories, as they were originally presented, became a way to access power and share in the understanding of present culture and history. Women's stories of rape and abuse rewrote the history of male domination and women's place in the history of heterosexual partnership.

With regard to voice as truth, the metaphor of "voice" has also been used in a way that suggests that finding one's voice or hearing the voices of women is a way to supplant earlier versions of the "truth" with a new truth. But stories of rape and abuse were told from a very unsophisticated position (see Scott 1988), as those doing the relating assumed that a single, suppressed truth that cut through the lies of dominant voices could be uncovered (see Haaken, Chap. 1 in this book).

To say that the stories of abuse were unsophisticated is not the same as saying they were false; it is more accurate to say that they speak to *a* truth, and not *the* truth. Chris Weedon (1997) writes that to speak is to assume "a subject position within a discourse and to become subjected to the power and regulation of the discourse" (p. 116). This is to say that when a woman or a victim speaks, there will be certain kinds of narratives that are "allowed," so to speak, and other narratives that are subversive or subterranean. All narratives are stories, in a sense, and as such, they are partial truths.

The "truth" about sexual abuse, many have argued, was silenced by Freud. Freud replaced his idea that girls were being sexually abused in great numbers with the idea that girls were not being abused but expressing repressed unconscious fantasies (Masson 1984; Rush 1974; 1980). Sexual abuse was covered up or ignored for so many decades of the twentieth century that it was almost accurate when researchers and clinicians spoke of "discovering" sexual abuse in the early 1970s (Gordon 1988; Rush 1974; 1980). The idea that there was a cover-up (not just Freudian but cultural) reproduced the dynamics of the single abuse situation, where a perpetrator often tells a child to not tell anyone or tells a child that what just happened did not take place. It also reproduced situations in which individual disclosures of rape and sexual abuse were not believed. "Voice" serves as the perfect metaphor to use in these discussions, because it evokes both the social and individual "silencing" of victims and a singular truth.

What are the dominant discourses about voice that victims tap into ("position themselves in") when they believe they are speaking from an "authentic" voice? One kind could be called "talk-show discourse" on voice. On talk shows, women speak and reveal as if in a public confessional. The truths allowed in such a discourse are therapeutic truths of harm, symptomatology, survivorship, lifelong suffering, and struggles to come to terms with abusive events. (They don't tend to focus on the abusers or institutionalized violence against women.) The metaphor of "finding one's voice" is one of finding one's self and freeing the self from the oppression of self-blame and self-loathing. The "authentic" voices that are freed from self-blame, however, are individual voices and no longer serve a transgressive purpose. That is, they no longer challenge the status quo; they do not lead to social change.

Another discourse about voice comes from the academic literature, where feminist research that is qualitative in nature depends on interviewing and representing people's, often victims', voices as authentically as possible. Here, voice is treated as some precious entity that the researcher tries her best not to sully or "rape" again. At a conference on qualitative research sponsored by the Graduate Center of the City University of New York in November 1997, I listened to many graduate students, researchers, and interviewers speak about their subjects in awed tones. They chided themselves for behaviors or questions that might have interfered with getting at the "truth" or hearing an "authentic voice." They spoke as if their subjects' words were virginal victims capable of being destroyed again through the researchers' misrepresentations. Some of this careful tone was most likely the tentativeness of graduate students speaking publicly for the first time, afraid to be "wrong." But some of them spoke of their subjects' words as if the actual words were something sacred, without any awareness that a subject might misrepresent herself or that the spoken version of an event may be only one version, one narrative.

The metaphor of "voice," for qualitative researchers, re-creates an individualized and therapeutic way of finding something special in each victim, each woman. Here, and when used as a metaphor in therapy, the idea of "finding one's voice" or "listening to the voices" serves to combat the historical objectification and stereotyping of women as a group. That is, to be special and unique—particular—combats objectification and stereotyping.

The academic discourse about the voices or experiences of victims also distances women academics from victims, implying that most of the interviewers and writers were not themselves victimized and that all of the interviewees and subjects who are studied were. The interviewers ironically participate in the silencing of their own voices, conforming as they do to rules of research and interviewing. Carol Rambo Ronai (1995), a sociologist and professor, writes that her academic friends warned her not to write about or analyze her own abuse in her methodological piece "Multiple Reflections of Child Sex Abuse: An Argument for a Layered Account." They told her that it might hurt her career and that her work would not be taken seriously. In her piece, she writes about some of the worst abuses imaginable, and this, coming from an intelligent and successful academic, is jarring and transgressive.

Although authors rarely disclose their own experiences of abuse, they typically—more frequently than the reader is likely to believe—revise the experiences of the victims they report. They rewrite the supposedly authentic voices to present them more professionally, removing positive messages and political aspects of their victimization (O'Dell 1997). Thus, voice becomes something of a dress that has been chosen from the cultural wardrobe according to the rules of fashion and decorum, which is then rewashed, pressed, and rehung on the victim by researchers, therapists, and authors according to similar but slightly different rules of fashion and decorum. What lies underneath the voice is not the naked truth but a body that also has been shaped by cultural rules and discourses. There is no concealed naked or unadorned truth.

Finally, there is some discourse about voice that considers it a fundamentally female metaphor. Being "revelatory" is a gendered role (LaFrance and Henley 1994). In our culture, women are better than men verbally and are said to be better at and to enjoy self-expression. Males report greater satisfaction with their dating relationships when the men disclose less to their female partners than the women disclose to the men (Millar and Millar 1988). Furthermore, males are more attracted to a highly expressive woman than to a woman who is less expressive (Sprecher 1989). Yet stereotypes abound of women being too chatty, too self-disclosing.

What is it about finding voice for women and abuse victims, what is it about talking and disclosing, that disrupts rather than supports the status quo of male domination and widespread abuse and harassment of women by men? Is there anything transgressive about disclosure at all? It has been argued that speaking about things that haven't been mentioned before is a transgression; but the very act of disclosing appears "natural" for women, and it has become even more natural to disclose stories of abuse. When these stories and their disclosures fit a pattern of victimization that is pat and neat and no longer uncomfortable to the public, then they are probably conforming to the status quo. Habituation swallows even the grossest violations of persons (Hare-Mustin, forthcoming).

Of course women and girls should continue to disclose incidents of abuse; however, there should be some awareness that such disclosures get co-opted into a discourse that renders them apolitical. Talk-show hosts, therapists, and researchers, by worshiping authentic voice for its own sake, have contributed to an essentializing of the feminine as victim and have participated in the loss of the political meaning once associated with voice.

Making Abuse Apolitical

I am not the first to have been dismayed at how abuse has become apolitical, that is, about individual mental health rather than about social problems. Many have spoken of this before (Armstrong 1994; 1996; Daly 1994; Simonds 1996). Several forces contributed to this current apolitical conceptualization. By focusing on pathology and ignoring resiliency, medical aspects of victimhood were emphasized, political aspects de-emphasized. The "professionalization" of the field of therapy assimilated feminists. When victim advocacy became "victim-centered advocacy" (Daly 1994), offenders were demonized and crimes were individualized (p. 780). And when the primary methods of dealing with abuse became individual therapy and individual redress through the law and the police, the political became personal; generalized culture became personalized culture

(Daly 1994; Simonds 1996, p. 6). Juliet Mitchell (1971) has written of the importance of voicing deeply personal problems or frustrations in groups as a way of making the personal political. She wrote of the phrase "speaking bitterness," which comes from the Chinese peasant revolution and which can provide the impetus for seeing a problem many share as belonging to the group, thus uniting people with one another. The purpose of early consciousness-raising groups was to show women that their personal problems had social causes and to create solidarity (Dean 1996; Haaken 1998).

Postmodernism has introduced the word *discourse* to describe how power and knowledge as social forces create "subjects"—who we are, who we think we are, how we think, how we act. I find interesting the notion from Michel Foucault that human beings are always incarcerated. Humans are prisoners of modern systems of thought and practice "which have become so intimately a part of them that they no longer experience these systems as a series of confinements but embrace them as the very structure of being human" (Bernauer 1988, p. 45). These modern systems of thought and practice are also called "discourses." But while we are bound by certain discourses, such as that of the helpless victim and the present-day discourse of the whining victim, there is still a way—at least in part—to transcend the notion that we are totally constructed by the dominant talk, the knowledge, and the social practices around us.

One resists power through "counterdiscourses" and builds meanings through questioning common discourses and challenging what is seen as "real" or "natural" (Hekman 1995; Weedon 1997). Susan Hekman argues that we needn't stop with an analysis that sees women, and victims for that matter, as "social dupes"; we can find some discourses that also provide a possibility of agency. By living out alternatives, women threaten the "naturalness" of the way things are (Weedon 1997, p. 108).

So what, finally, would a more politicized anti-abuse movement look like? Anti-media campaigns could attack the versions of victim that are currently accepted. Therapist education could emphasize a cultural rather than an individual approach. Movements could attempt to create solidarity among women while respecting the diversity of women's experiences of abuse and harassment. And public education could convey the diversity of these experiences of abuse and harassment in a way that is sensible and free of exaggeration and that doesn't elevate all experiences to trauma but is able to link them together as gendered. This would be a reasonable way to begin.

Victims Do Exist

Having a category of "abuse survivors" at all misleads the public from recognizing that a majority of women, not just a subgroup, have been victimized, abused, or harassed in some way. When we look at the lifetime incidence of some form of sexual abuse, however small, it is clear that abuse affects a majority of women (MacKinnon 1987). We do not need, however, to throw up our hands and say, "Accept it, it is a part of life." The commonness of it, even the "normality" of it, does not have to mean it is moral or acceptable.

Recently, the daughter of a friend of mine was raped by an acquaintance. My friend and her partner made considerable efforts to do the things one does for a victim. One reads the books and makes the recommended comments, such as "You mustn't blame yourself," and one gets the victim into therapy. When they asked me, a psychologist, how they might help this girl deal with her rape, I tongue-in-cheek suggested to them that they "welcome her to the world of women." I said she should know that just about every grown woman she knows has been raped, or abused, or harassed, or at the very least has a good friend to whom it occurred. I knew my friend's daughter was harmed and suffering from her rape, but I wasn't sure that merely addressing the harm was the approach to take. Talking about the world of women and the expectation of violence in the lives of women moves away from creating a separate category of "victim" that a mental health condition can nicely explain. Instead, it moves to a political stance: that the girl is a victim of something endemic in our culture—male violence.

To take such a stance would mean, perhaps, expressing less caretaking worry about many victims, in contrast to the extensive care we clinical psychologists, therapists, feminists have of late lavished on them. This approach might make some victim advocates uneasy, and it would risk angering backlash critics who think that the recognition of the violence that men do is "discrimination masquerading under the name of feminism" (Denfield 1995, p. 12). But if the problem were viewed from a more political stance, it would be that women can't go through life expecting not to be abused without some change in society. We would then take action to change perpetrators and change men, starting with the development of boys. In changing the focus, we would also no longer be interested merely in women telling their stories of abuse but rather would encourage their stories of everyday resistance.

This is an approach that could unite women, that sees victimization as a public health and safety issue and puts the responsibility for change on the party most likely to cause this problem: men. The focus on differences—victim, survivor, battered woman, sexually abused woman, those who can remember and those who cannot, those who falsely remember and those who rightfully do, those who have been harassed and lost their job because of it and those who are just mildly irritated at the *Penthouse* foldouts in the workplace—eclipses the fact that these are, *we* are, women who have a lot more in common than men and the media would have us believe. Seeing the commonalities among women and the ubiquity of abuse is not an exaggeration; it's simply recognition of a broad-based social problem. Throwing out the "victim" label is not the answer. If we broaden it so that small incidents count, we might produce greater solidarity among women with different backgrounds. Embracing women's everyday strength and resistance toward gendered hostilities as well as violence might help women reclaim a common understanding of victimization.

Finally, if preventing male violence becomes the focus of a new solidarity that replaces the current rhetoric on the development of women's individual power and voice, our power would come from action rather than expression; women would seize power rather than ask for it. Sick girls can't fight back. Empowered girls can.

NOTES

1. Prevalence studies of sexual abuse, rape, and harassment show about one-third to over one-half of women across a variety of samples have experienced abuse. A survey of North Dakota public schools (Stratton and Backes 1997) shows girls and boys reporting a high level of sexual harassment, with 93 percent of girls reporting that they have been harassed. Wyatt and Riederle (1995) find that most white and African American women report sexual harassment in the workplace. And Charney and Russell (1994), in their literature review, find around 42 percent of women in occupational settings, and 73 percent of women in medical training, report sexual harassment. Sixty-one percent of homeless and poor women report severe violence from a male partner (Browne and Bassuk 1997). Forty-eight percent of female patients in a family practice setting reported some form of contact sexual victimization in their life; and 57 percent of students going to a student health service clinic reported contact sexual victimization (Walch and Broadhead 1992). Nicola Gavey's survey (1991) of New Zealand university students showed over half of them had experienced some form of sexual victimization. These are just a few

prevalence studies, and some are based on survey instruments that have been criticized for being overly inclusive. But if we count minor incidents as well as traumatic incidents and understand that the women who were sexually abused were not always the women who were beaten (although there is some overlap), it is clear that a great number, well past half, have experienced some form of gendered victimization in their lives.

2. I suspect this idea is prevalent among those who treat sexual abuse victims; however, Norah Feeny, a researcher at the Medical College of Pennsylvania in Philadelphia and a feminist who treats and interviews victims of rape for Edna Foa's research projects on post-traumatic stress disorder, is the person who argued this point to me.

3. See *Loving to Survive: Sexual Terror, Men's Violence, and Women's Lives,* by Dee Graham (with Edna Rawlings and Roberta Rigsby; 1994). These authors turn what I am saying on its head by claiming that the characteristics we see as prevalent in females in general are characteristics that are expected and exhibited in captives or hostages, as in the Stockholm Syndrome.

REFERENCES

American Psychiatric Association (APA). 1994. *Diagnostic and statistical manual of mental disorders.* 4th ed. (DSM-IV). Washington, D.C.: American Psychiatric Association.

Anisfeld, L. S. 1997. Review of *The trouble with blame. Psychoanalytic books: A quarterly journal of reviews* 8, 343–345.

Armstrong, L. 1994. *Rocking the cradle of sexual politics: What happened when women said incest.* New York: Addison-Wesley.

———. 1996. In the footsteps of Doctor Freud and down the proverbial garden path. *Feminism and Psychology* 6, 298–303.

Becker, D. 1997. *Through the looking glass: Women and borderline personality disorder.* Boulder, CO: Westview Press.

Bender, L., and Blau, A. 1937. The reaction of children to sexual relations with adults. *American Journal of Orthopsychiatry* 7, 500–518.

Benedict, H. 1992. *Virgin or vamp.* New York: Oxford University Press.

Bernauer, J. 1988. Michel Foucault's ecstatic thinking. In J. Bernauer and D. Rasmussen (eds.), *The final Foucault* (pp. 45–82). Cambridge, MA: MIT Press.

Bordo, S. 1993. *Unbearable weight: Feminism, western culture, and the body.* Berkeley: University of California Press.

Browne, A., and Bassuk, S. S. 1997. Intimate violence in the lives of homeless and poor housed women: Prevalence and patterns in an ethnically diverse sample. *American Journal of Orthopsychiatry* 67, 261–278.

Charney, D. A., and Russell, R. C. 1994. An overview of sexual harassment. *American Journal of Psychiatry*, 151, 10–17.

Coons, P. M. 1994. Confirmation of childhood abuse in child and adolescent cases of multiple personality disorder and dissociative disorder not otherwise specified. *Journal of Nervous and Mental Disease*, 182, 461–464.

Daly, K. 1994. Men's violence, victim advocacy, and feminist redress. *Law and Society Review* 28, 777–786.

Dean, J. 1996. *Solidarity of strangers: Feminism after identity politics.* Berkeley: University of California Press.

Denfield, R. 1995. *The new Victorians: A young woman's challenge to the old feminist order.* New York: Warner Books.

Faith, K. 1994. Resistance: Lessons from Foucault and feminism. In H. L. Radtke and H. J. Stam (eds.), *Power/Gender: Social relations in theory and practice.* Thousand Oaks, CA: Sage.

Fillion, K. 1996. *Lip service: The truth about women's darker side in love, sex, and friendship.* New York: HarperCollins.

Finkelhor, D. 1990. Early and long-term effects of child sexual abuse: An update. *Professional Psychology: Research and Practice* 21, 325–330.

Gavey, N. 1991. Sexual victimization prevalence among New Zealand university students. *Journal of Consulting and Clinical Psychology* 59, 464–466.

Ginorio, A. B. 1998. Contextualizing violence in a participatory classroom: A socially defined identities approach. *Psychology of Women Quarterly* 22, 77–96.

Gordon, L. 1988. The politics of child sexual abuse: Notes from American history. *Feminist Review* 28, 57–64.

Graham, D. L. R. 1994. *Loving to survive: Sexual terror, men's violence, and women's lives.* New York: New York University Press.

Haaken, J. 1998. *Pillar of salt.* New Brunswick, NJ: Rutgers University Press.

Hare-Mustin, R. T. Forthcoming. Challenging traditional discourses in psychotherapy: Creating space for alternatives. *Journal of Feminist Family Therapy.*

Hekman, S. 1995. Subjects and agents: The question for feminism. In J. Kegan Gardiner (ed.), *Provoking agents: Gender and agency in theory and practice.* University Park: Penn State Press.

Herman, J. 1992. *Trauma and recovery.* New York: Basic Books.

Hochschild, A. 1988. *The managed heart: The commercialization of human feeling.* Berkeley: University of California Press.

Hollway, W. 1995. Feminist discourse and women's heterosexual desire. In S. Wilkinson and C. Kitzinger (eds.), *Feminism and discourse: Psychological perspectives.* London: Sage.

Kaminer, W. 1996. *True love waits: Essays and criticism.* Reading, MA: Addison-Wesley.

Keaney, J. C., and Farley, M. 1996. Dissociation in an outpatient sample of women reporting childhood sexual abuse. *Psychological Reports* 78, 59–65.

Kitzinger, C. 1994. Problematizing pleasure: Radical feminist deconstructions of sexuality and power. In H. L. Radtke and H. J. Stam (eds.), *Power/Gender: Social relations in theory and practice.* Thousand Oaks, CA: Sage.

Konradi, A. 1996. Preparing to testify: Rape survivors negotiating the criminal justice process. *Gender and Society* 10, 404–452.

LaFrance, M., and Henley, N. 1994. On oppressing hypotheses: Or differences in nonverbal sensitivity revisited. In H. L. Radtke and H. J. Stam (eds.), *Power/Gender: Social relations in theory and practice.* Thousand Oaks, CA: Sage.

Lamb, S. 1996. *The trouble with blame: Victims, perpetrators, and responsibility.* Cambridge, MA: Harvard University Press.

Lamb, S., and Cuddy, A. 1996. Coping and resilience in sexually abused children. Unpublished manuscript. Bryn Mawr College, Bryn Mawr, PA.

MacKinnon, C. 1987. A feminist political approach: Pleasure under patriarchy. In J. Geer and W. O'Donohue (eds.), *Theories of human sexuality* (pp. 135–152). New York: Plenum Press.

Madriz, E. 1997. *Nothing bad happens to good girls: Fear of crime in women's lives.* Berkeley: University of California Press.

Mahoney, M. 1996. The problem of silence in feminist theory. *Feminist Studies* 22, 603–625.

Masson, J. 1984. *The assault on truth: Freud's suppression of seduction theory.* Harmondsworth, England: Penguin.

McCarthy, T. 1997. Rethinking theories of victimology: Men's violence against women. In S. Cook and J. Bessant (eds.), *Women's encounters with violence: Australian experiences* (pp. 127–144). Thousand Oaks, CA: Sage.

Millar, K. U., and Millar, M. G. 1988. Sex differences in perceived self- and other-disclosure: A case where inequity increases satisfaction. *Social Behavior and Personality* 16, 59–64.

Mitchell, J. 1971. *Woman's estate.* New York: Pantheon.

O'Dell, L. 1997. Child sexual abuse and the academic construction of symptomatologies. *Feminism and Psychology* 7, 334–339.

Putnam, F. W.; Guroff, J. J.; Silberman, E. K.; et al. 1986. The clinical phenomenology of multiple personality disorder: Review of one hundred recent cases. *Journal of Clinical Psychiatry* 47, 285–293.

Rambo Ronai, C. 1995. Multiple reflections of child sex abuse: An argument for a layered account. *Journal of Contemporary Ethnography* 23, 395–426.

Ross, C. A.; Miller, S. D.; Reagor, P.; Bjornson, L.; et al. 1990. Structured interview data on 102 cases of multiple personality disorder from four centers. *American Journal of Psychiatry* 147, 596–601.

Rothbaum, B.; Foa, E.; Riggs, D.; Murdock, T.; and Walsh, W. 1992. A prospective examination of post traumatic stress disorder in rape victims. *Journal of Traumatic Stress* 5, 455–475.

Rush, F. 1974. Sexual abuse of children: A feminist perspective. In *Rape: The first sourcebook for women.* New York: New American Library.

————. 1980. *The best kept secret: Sexual abuse of children.* New York: McGraw-Hill.

Scott, A. 1988. Feminism and the seductiveness of the 'real event.' *Feminist Reviews* 28, 88–102.

Silver, S.; Boon, C.; and Stone, M. H. 1983. Looking for meaning in misfortune: Making sense of incest. *Journal of Social Issues* 39, 81–101.

Simonds, W. 1996. All-consuming selves: Self-help literature and women's identities. In D. Grodin and T. R. Lindlof (eds.), *Constructing the self in a mediated world.* Thousand Oaks, CA: Sage.

Sprecher, S. 1989. The importance to males and females of physical attractiveness, earning potential and expressiveness. *Sex Roles* 21, 591–607.

Stratton, S. D., and Backes, J. S. 1997. Sexual harassment in North Dakota public schools: A study of eight high schools. *High School Journal,* 80, 163–172.

Walch, A. and Broadhead, E. 1992. Prediction of lifetime sexual victimization among female patients. *Journal of Family Practice* 35, 511–516.

Weedon, C. 1997. *Feminist practice and poststructuralist theory.* Cambridge, MA: Blackwell.

Wyatt, G. E., and Riederle, M. 1995. The prevalence and context of sexual harassment among African American and white American women. *Journal of Interpersonal Violence* 10, 309–321.

Chapter Six

In the Line of Sight at *Public Eye*
In Search of a Victim

Carol Rambo Ronai

Recently, I found that I was tempted to view myself as a "victim"—of the news media. As I tried to write about it, I found the vocabulary of "victimology" inadequate for the task of describing what happened. Each time I cast myself as the innocent victim and CBS as the big, bully perpetrator, it felt like I was lying. The language of victimhood created an artificial space for my identity that ignored how I benefited and how I resisted. It is these qualities that I wish to capture and represent for the reader in this "layered account" (Ronai 1998; 1997a; 1997b; 1996; 1995; 1992) of my experience with CBS's *Public Eye with Bryant Gumbel.* I write this chapter from a multitude of identities: academic, daughter of a mentally retarded mother, opportunist, and victim, among others. Each identity contaminates the others, throwing the others into a play of ambiguity. Let each of these textual breaks denote a shift to a different time, space, or attitudinal realm.

Perched on the threshold of a new millennium, wedged in the margins of the past and the future, postmodernism can be regarded as both a "moment" and a "position" from which to reconsider the impact of many taken-for-granted, tacit notions about identity and everyday life. Concepts such as "victim," "perpetrator," and "blame" have served both to enable and to constrain the lived experiences of women and men in the nineteenth and twentieth centuries. In the 1860s, the American Society for the Prevention of Cruelty to Animals (ASPCA) was founded, codifying that the status "victim" could be applied to animals. Ten years later, the creation of the American Society for the Prevention of Cruelty to Children (ASPCC) accorded the same potential to children. The financial resources and interventions these institutions provided helped many in need. Perhaps of greater significance, however, is the symbolic capital these organizations wielded. Knowledge of the existence of an ASPCA and an ASPCC affirmed for the public that the experience of neglect and abuse was pervasive and may have yielded more leverage for social change than the actual activities of either society's members.

Early in the twentieth century, the attention that was focused on victims primarily aimed to determine what it was about their character and disposition that brought on their problems. In one example from the childhood sex abuse literature at the time, Loretta Bender and Abram Blau (1937) developed a typology of children who had been abused, openly referring to some of them as attractive, alluring, or provocative. As the decades passed, an inversion of the binary construct victim/perpetrator took place by shifting "blame" more squarely onto the shoulders of perpetrators (Lamb 1996).

On the face of it, the new discourse of the "innocent victim" and the "total perpetrator" put forth in self-help guides such as *The Courage to Heal* (Bass and Davis 1988) created a new, liberated space where people could talk about their experiences without having their selves and their legitimacy called into question. (See chapter 1 by Janice Haaken in this volume.) It was now "okay" to tell stories about abuse and mistreatment, as long as the person was willing to take on the identity of victim and conform to the attendant role expectations.

A quick survey of mainstream media, a mere click of the television remote control, reveals that the idea of victim and perpetrator are alive and well in made-for-television movies, talk shows, and newscasts. Given the complexities of modern life, a good victim and an obvious perpetrator are very appealing; there is no uncertainty and no second-guessing, as is typically the case in everyday life. A morality play in which the known boundaries of right and wrong are reaffirmed and everyone knows who to root for and who to hate garners market shares and advertising dollars.

Postmodernism focuses attention on how discourses are locally generated at particular times and in particular contexts (Lyotard 1977). The discourse of victim/perpetrator has changed over the years, but not enough to transcend its effects. A simple inversion of a power dichotomy that still makes use of the same terms does not constitute a real change, just a reassignment of power within the set. Many scholars have commented on the negative effects the language of victimhood has had on individuals who have been the targets of abuse (Daly 1994; Kahn and Mathie, forthcoming;

Lamb 1996; McCarthy 1997; O'Dell 1997; Shilling and Fuehrer 1993; Simonds 1996), as well as the larger political scene where it intersects and has consequences for policy-making decisions (Daly 1994; McCarthy 1997).

The language of victim/perpetrator has become an oppressive "metanarrative" (Lyotard 1977) that continues to inform the identity construction and narrative practices of academics, clinicians, and the media. The terms used have become *the* terms framing the ongoing dialogues many feminists, civil rights leaders, and other activist storytellers engage in. These categories fail to encompass the ambiguous nature of the thoughts and feelings of those in question. This hyper-polarized dichotomy has become more constraining than enabling, forcing many individuals' narratives into suffocating, rigid, reductionist categories that leave much of the information pertaining to their lived experience on the "cutting room floor" because it cannot be made to fit in the confines of the existing terms. When nothing new results from an ongoing conversation, the terms of that dialogue should be reconsidered. This book, this chapter, this writing format, and my story about my involvement with the media are all efforts aimed toward these goals: to reclaim what previously has been left on the cutting room floor and to encompass the ambiguous and often conflicting thoughts and feelings of a victim.

I shopped three afternoons trying to find the right clothes, but I was unable to find an outfit that I really liked. I settled on a scoop-necked, long-sleeved, drop-waisted denim dress with slightly padded shoulders and a full, shin-length skirt that I already owned. It was neither too uptight nor too "sexy," figure-flattering without being vulgar. I got my hair cut, highlighted, and styled, something I had not done for almost three years. I went so far as to consider a professional makeup consultation but decided that was over the top. Some days I wear eyeliner below my lower lashes, a bit of blush, and lip gloss; on others I wear no makeup at all. For this, I decided I would do the whole regalia—eye shadow, mascara, liner, foundation, blush, lipstick, all of it—but I would apply it modestly. Again, I wanted to look nice, not trashy. How I looked, the impression I made—these were things I had control over, or so I was naive enough to think.

I had called my family, friends, and colleagues to get their opinions. It seemed exciting yet potentially dangerous, an intoxicating combination.

"They all have a bad reputation, you know, just out for themselves," one friend suggested.

"They'll say anything to get you there, then do with you what they want. You won't have any control of what happens after you walk in the door," warned my sister-in-law, who is in broadcasting.

"You'll just end up being used, I trust none of them, none of them," a colleague stated flatly.

But others had more positive feedback:

"Going could be good for your career."

"Going will be good experience for you."

And from a social worker: "Going could mean getting attention for a very important issue which has been ignored. Now I don't want to say you *have* to do it, but one way of reading it is that you owe it to the community to help if you possibly can."

Ultimately, I had to face myself in the mirror. It was flattering to have been asked, a marker for a particular kind of "success" in my work world, but ego gratification was a deadly reason to go; it lacked integrity; it was a sure way to make me vulnerable and useless to anyone. The bottom line was that I was curious, I wanted the experience and the exposure; and I hoped I could use the exposure, later, to help get a book contract.

Did I ask for it? Was this a metaphorical "date rape"? My motives for being there were self-serving. Does that mean I am stupid to be sitting here at this computer, exposing this, writing it all down to be read? How he hurt me? How he forced me to stay in my seat and take it, against my will? Should I just get over it, take it in stride and move on? Maybe if he doesn't say anything about what happened, I'm obligated not to as well. If I tell, am I taking the chance of stirring up trouble I'm not ready to deal with? Am I being like him, looking for the sensational components of the story? Maybe, I should just walk away.

As with a rape, it is difficult for an outsider to determine if a violation took place. The first line of defense is to deny the act happened. The second line of defense, provided both parties acknowledge the act took place, focuses on consent. Did the accused believe there was consent? With no visible sign of physical violence, it is often difficult to decide what happened.

I'm the daughter of a mother with mental retardation and a father who was diagnosed as a sexual psychopath. I have written about those experiences in various academic contexts (see Ronai 1997a; 1997b; 1996; 1995). I have carved for myself a rather peculiar postmodern niche as someone who is a researcher and who *is* the phenomenon under consideration, including the areas of childhood sexual abuse, exotic dancing, and having a parent with mental retardation. I was cited in the *New York Times Magazine* in March 1998. Subsequently, a CBS news show invited me to come to New York for an interview. They were doing a piece on children of parents with mental retardation.

How I was treated was normal. He wanted a reaction from me. I needed to be stronger in standing up to him, standing up for the message I was trying to deliver and for my rights. He smelled my doubt and went in for a "kill" because of his training. I am blowing it all out of proportion, and it really wasn't as bad as I thought it was.

The following quotations and statements are paraphrased from my best recollections of these discussions and the interview. None of the quotes that follows is verbatim. All are inexact, based on my memory. CBS refused to give me a copy of my interview in any form when I requested it, repeatedly, from an assistant producer and others. I was told I could get a copy only of what aired, after it aired. As of this time (August 1998), the show has not aired and an airdate has not been scheduled.

"Hi, I'm Karen Palmer, a producer with the CBS news planning unit. I saw your name in the [Rene] Denfeld article in the *New York Times Magazine*. That child's story is really something," she says.

"It's amazing," I agree, tentative, cautious, yet curious. This whole thing has been a small barrage. I have been contacted by several production companies that make documentaries or made-for-television movies, a newspaper magazine in Brazil, a radio talk show, and I've been asked to do some local speaking engagements as a result of that *New York Times* citation.

"But what struck me was you. You are an adult who has been through this experience, and well, that is quite a story in itself, a unique perspective," she adds.

"I have written on the topic, it is a story, you are right," I answer, fumbling, already suspecting that she is going to ask me to be on the show. There is a lot at stake. My mind is racing.

"Oh really? I'd love to see those materials. Do you have copies?" She gives me CBS's Fed-Ex billing account number and asks me to send the materials as soon as possible.

We talk for a while about the Denfeld article, the little girl who was featured there, and my experiences with that reporter. Finally I ask, "What can I do for you?"

"Well, we were wondering if you could just talk to us for a while, you know, off the record, and see if some kind of participation on your part would be appropriate, something good for everyone. I know that when someone is asked to do something like this they are suspicious right off. That is totally natural and understandable as a reaction. The thing is, we are a hard news show; we strive for integrity. Maybe after we talk some we can both figure out if it would be a good thing," she says.

There it is. If this had been about my father, I'd volunteer to be there in a second. The child molester is dead, and no one could be hurt; but my mother—she's still alive. She manages very nicely within a delicate network of family, friends, and church. I would not want to hurt her by doing this.

I answer, "My mother is alive, and here is the kicker—no one has ever told her she is mentally retarded. I don't know about this." I ask for Karen's E-mail address and offer to go through my list of adults whose parents had mental retardation and give them her E-mail address. She thanks me, and I do not hear from CBS again for almost two months.

"Hi, my name is Mariana Barzun, I'm an assistant producer with CBS, for Bryant Gumbel's show, *Public Eye*. I believe you were contacted by our producer, earlier?" her youthful, enthusiastic voice sings out over the phone.

"Yes, I was," I answer, my pulse up a bit. I thought this was resolved, that this wasn't an issue anymore.

"Well we were wondering if you had time to consider coming on the show?" she asks point-blank.

I am flustered, stumbling over my words, "My mother is still alive and I just don't know about that. She could be hurt in all of this. I don't want her involved."

"It's not necessary to involve her, we just want to talk to you," she answers.

"I would need to talk with my family before I agreed to anything. I just haven't had the time to think through the ramifications of this," I return.

"It is perfectly normal to be concerned about this. I understand. We would not need to involve your mother at all."

"I wouldn't want her name used, in fact, maybe you wouldn't use my real name either," I counter.

"We will protect you to whatever level of anonymity you want. The story would be better if you used your real identity, but we don't need your mother's," Mariana says.

"I don't even want you to mention the state she resides in. I would want as little as possible to connect her with the show. I still have to check with a lot of people before I agree to anything."

"So just think about it, we will call you back. Maybe I can get the producer to call you and reassure you."

I backpedal rapidly. "You know, because there are so many things involved with my story, I may not even be appropriate or representative of the typical experience. Have you read my articles?"

"What articles?"

"The ones I sent using your Fed-Ex number," I say, fishing through my memory, sure I mailed it, and annoyed at being contacted when they hadn't read my articles. Like my students, they haven't done the reading. I go on a diatribe about how, recently, when my story was featured in a Brazilian news magazine, they had also not read the articles I sent before the interview. All the questions they asked over the phone were addressed in the article.

"I'll bet you sent your articles to the producer and that's why I haven't seen them," she states defensively.

I respond to save her; there is no use in treating her this way. "I did send them to her. Unless she gave them to you, how were you to know? In all seriousness, you need to read that stuff and then see, okay?"

I am an academic. I am also the daughter of a mother who is mentally retarded. I am both of those identities, and yet they seem to want more of one.

"Hi, I'm Vicki Samuels, a producer with CBS news, *Public Eye with Bryant Gumbel.* You've been in touch with my assistant?" Vicki asks.

"Yes, I have," I respond. I am more ready for this now. I have conferred with, written, phoned, and E-mailed a good number of people, including some family members.

"Well, I've read your work and it's great. You offer a great deal of insight into what it is like to be the child of a mentally retarded parent. After looking around a bit I have to agree with you that no one is really doing this issue justice in terms of publicizing it and the debates around it."

I relay to her my concerns about protecting my mother's anonymity. I also say, "I don't want any discussion about her involvement with my sexual abuse, on national television."

"I don't think we need to talk about any of that, I don't see the need. That part of your experience is not representative of the experience of all children with mentally retarded parents. We are more interested in the reflections of an adult who remembers how it felt as a child to have a mentally retarded mother," Vicki says.

I feel comforted by this. I'm thinking, yes, *that* I can speak to, that I can do. I can talk about how all of that felt, without talking about her involvement in my sexual abuse. I say, "And something else, I'm not an expert. I know the literature, but I have not spent any time in the field per se."

"We have plenty of experts to speak about the statistics and the programs; we are interested in hearing about your experiences, your perspective as a child of a mentally retarded parent," Vicki responds. Then she adds, "Many of the Pittsburgh people are familiar with your work. They are very excited to hear what you might say on the topic."

I tell her I still have a few more people to talk to before I can answer her. She tells me her assistant will be in contact with me, and she will be happy to talk to me some more if I want to call.

My aunt is on the phone. "I just talked to your mother and she is very upset," she says. I am amazed. I thought that my mother and I had a great conversation, where she was at first scared and then okay with the whole thing. She was given the opportunity to voice fears about things that had happened years ago that she could never explain to herself. I thought we had a fantastic, cleansing exchange. Did I just hear what I wanted to? I ask myself.

A week or so after our second conversation, where again, I believe that my mother is okay with me doing some kind of public appearance regarding "our past," I receive this note:

Dear Carol,
    Please Do Not Dig Up The Pass If you I Well Not take to you at All live the pass also.

                                                                    Love Suzanne

Isn't it ironic? She is the one who is mentally retarded, yet I am the one who can't understand her meaning in these conversations over the phone.

I call the producer in a panic, three nights before the flight to New York. "Tell me how, exactly, you plan to use me in this. I've had feedback from people recently that is making me think I'm making a huge mistake here. You know, people might, for instance, hear my story and say, 'Mentally re-tarded people should not be allowed to parent.' They might use my story as an example of all the bad things that can happen."

Vicki reassures me, "We are looking to give a balanced report in this piece; perhaps you could even say 'uplifting.' We are not interested in any-thing sensational. Bernie Goldberg is going to be the correspondent on this, and I talked to him about it and he has reassured me that he is not inter-ested in all of the other details of your biography. As he put it, 'That would be too Jerry Springer.' We don't need to attack you; it's not like you are a public figure, or that you are hiding something awful."

I say, "I don't really know if I'm doing the right thing because of my mother. What if she should flip channels and see it, see me sitting there talk-ing about her mental retardation? She doesn't know about it, though some say she must suspect."

Again Vicki reassures me, "I understand what you are saying. Many of the women in the Pittsburgh, Pennsylvania, program did not know they were mentally retarded either. They were labeled as 'learning disabled' or something else."

I am excited by this; she *does* understand the situation. That my mother does not "know" sounds peculiar to outsiders. With Vicki's remark, she starts to take on a trustable "insider" status with me. I answer, "Yes, they pass, with themselves and others." I see an image of her crew spending time talking and visiting with people. Perhaps they really do understand and I am being overly anxious. Why should anyone want to ambush me, as some have suggested?

I'm at the CBS studio in New York City on the morning of June 10 at 9:45. The day before, I had an exciting afternoon and night walking around town, drinking in coffee and the streets while munching on a nine-dollar corned beef sandwich and dill pickles. This morning I am infused with the enthusi-asm and delight of a child at Disney World. New York is spectacular.

The sixth floor of 555 West Fifty-seventh Street is starkly appointed, with white walls; industrial office carpeting; a front counter; a small sofa, chair, and table in the waiting area; and a picture of the *Public Eye* team mounted on the wall. I wonder which one is Bernie. Except for the black, jagged metal ceiling, there is nothing distinctive about this room; everything feels im-permanent, like props, rather than a "lived-in" space.

I am met by Mariana. She greets me warmly, flattering me, as if she is surprised by my appearance. I have to laugh at her response. I spent a good deal of time discussing clothes, hair, and makeup with both Vicki and Mariana, as well as with my sister-in-law, who has been the "talent" for several broadcasting ventures. Mariana tells me how nice I look as she guides me into a room with chairs, bright lights, a bookcase, and other items. In the room are two cameramen, a soundman, another man, and Vicki, who introduces me around.

Vicki talks to me a minute before the other man bellows, "Don't worry about leaving me standing here in the bright light or anything." Vicki smiles as she introduces me to Bernie Goldberg, as if sharing a joke, but I can see he is aggravated for a good reason. He has been left, half crouched, with a light shining two inches from his face, with his hand slightly extended, waiting to be introduced to me.

They direct me to a chair across from him. I say, "So this is it, we're going to start filming now?"

"Unless you want a minute," Vicki responds.

"I would," I say, as I pick up my purse and leave my jacket and folio.

When I return, the soundman awkwardly asks me to run a microphone wire down the front of my dress. He clips it to my collar. As I am seated and reseated and reseated again on the chair, Bernie asks me, "So Carol, where are you originally from?" I am startled. I try to make it sound like I'm joking with him, as I say, shaking my finger at him, "Now remember, some topics are off limits."

Bernie's head tilts downward as he glances up at me for an instant, his face a slight scowl, and says, "I'm just trying to get us comfortable with each other while they set up." I realize, sheepishly, he is right to do so and start telling him a bit about my background. We discuss several topics, including the news industry. He informs me that age is a major issue in broadcasting, for both men and women; that even he is sensitive about it. This information somehow reassures me for a second that he understands vulnerability and that he will be okay to deal with in this interview. I tell Bernie I venerate elder broadcasters for their experience. He informs me that my point of view is not typical for the age demographic I represent.

The cameras are rolling, and he starts the interview. He covers many topics—my being stigmatized by other children while growing up, parents of other children not wanting me to play with their kids, my emotions about having a mentally retarded mother, my mother's physical abuse of me. All of the topics are negative. I start to feel as if the interview is negatively slanted, and I can feel myself stiffen up. I concentrate on standing my ground. He focuses for a while on her physical abuse of me, describing it in graphic terms; I find myself trying to minimize it. It is neither what he is representing or what I am representing. Or it is both. He says, "But didn't she just beat the heck out of you?" I say, "Something like 70 percent of mainstream America believes in corporal punishment. Sometimes it goes too far. I don't know if it was necessarily a function of her mental retardation." Many of my answers to his questions seem to be patterned this way: he asserts how bad she was as a mother on some dimension, and I reassert that we can't know if it was about her mental retardation or not.

It is common knowledge among clinicians and researchers that targets of sexual, physical, and emotional abuse tend to minimize the situation in their own accounts of it. Confronted with choosing the discourse of victim versus agent, people "can be either a victim or an active subject; but not both" (Kahn and Mathie, forthcoming, p. 25). Acknowledging either status forfeits the other. For the agent to acknowledge a victim status with herself or himself is to give up the autonomy accorded those who have control. Contrariwise, for victims to acknowledge any agency in the situation is to complicate the account and their status; thus they are not "genuine victims." Given these choices, both silence and minimizing one's victimization makes sense.

This guy is trying to make it look like all mentally retarded parents beat their kids! *Pleeease* don't do this. This is not just a story.

He reads a quote from one of my articles out loud: "I am disgusted that this creature is my mother. She is horrifying, vile, potentially defective genetic material, someone I or my child might take after." Then he asks, "What did you mean by that?"

I sit for several seconds in a stunned silence. I see before my eyes my mother, hearing that about herself on national television. The poor woman. What does he want from me? What is he looking for? This is one statement which, in a layered account format, represents a pose or a moment in the experience of having a mentally retarded mother. There were happy times, too. It does not sum up the entire experience. I cannot conceive of what he could possibly be doing, asking me to respond to this on national television.

"I don't understand what you are looking for," I respond.

"You wrote it, you tell me," he states.

Again I am inarticulate, trapped in a vertiginous free fall; I don't know what to say or do. I can't make what he is saying make sense to me. I ask again, "I don't know where you are going with this, could you rephrase your question different?"

"You wrote it, you tell me what you meant by it," he answers. He continues after more silence, "You know what I think. I think you regret you ever wrote that, that's what I think."

I cannot move. I brought this on myself. What the hell was I thinking, showing up to do this? Why can't I make sense of this and see where he is going? I feel panic, which I know I must control. Images of taking off my microphone and walking away cross my mind, but I cannot, must not. I think to myself, I am here representing my family, my department, my university, my profession, and all the people who are dealing with the issue of mentally retarded parenting. I cannot walk away. I cannot look weak. To break down, to look like I can't handle this, is to betray everyone (and myself). I must keep my composure. My heart is pounding, every sense is aroused, the lights are too bright, and I cannot let him do this to me.

I resist. "I was told this was possible, but I can't believe it is actually happening. I was told this might be an ambush, that you would say whatever it took to get me in here and then use me however you wanted to, but I can't believe it is really happening. Your producers promised me that the slant of this report would be uplifting, balanced. That is not what is happening here." The cameras are still rolling. I look over at Vicki, who is behind some equipment. Her face reflects no emotion.

He says, "You're being paranoid. I think you could talk to everyone in this room and find that all of the questions I am asking here are reasonable. The producers, the camera people, everyone. No one would say that anything was done unprofessionally here or carried out under false pretenses. You shouldn't feel uncomfortable here."

I fire back with controlled venom, "But that is exactly what you have accomplished. I do feel uncomfortable now, and you are going to have to deal with that the rest of this interview."

A signal passes between Bernie and the cameramen—the audience that is there but not there. Bernie informs me the camera is off, for now, to reload film.

Bernie says, "You know, I don't know who your colleagues are, and I don't mean any disrespect, but I mean, let's be honest. Let's face it. It's not like we invite people from, where? University of Memphis? to come on the air and speak. We don't. I mean no offense, but you do know that, don't you? Whoever is advising you, they don't know anything about this, they don't know what they are talking about. No one is asking them to do anything on the air. We have asked you, not them. Whoever told you we were going to ambush you, they don't know what they are talking about."

Again I am stunned. Am I supposed to be reassured by this? flattered? exactly what? Again, I don't understand his motives.

Who does he think I am? It's clear that my academic credentials are meaningless to him. Could it be that he wants to see me only as a victim daughter and nothing more?

Actually, it was my sister-in-law who issued the firmest warning about the possibility of being ambushed by CBS. The University of Memphis has one of the top programs in social psychology in the United States, one of the premiere philosophy departments, as well as a top-notch crew of seismologists who are frequently interviewed for national television news shows, given that Memphis is on a fault line. To have said any of this would have sounded defensive.

The cameras are back on. "But really, should mentally retarded parents be allowed to parent?" Bernie asks.

This I am ready for; this is *the* issue. I answer, smiling and nodding, "That is a typical question, I know why you asked it, but it's not a good question. It implies that somehow we have a choice in the matter, that we have control. The mentally retarded will have sex; they will be parents. It becomes an equation where we need to educate them on the front end, have frank discussions with them about sex and birth control. You know how some high schools have baby dolls that cry and wet and need feeding? Let the mentally retarded carry those around for a while, or even a sack of flour if there are not the resources for a doll. On the other end, we need services to help mentally retarded parents parent."

Bernie says, "Okay, I understand what you are saying, but putting that aside, wouldn't it be better if the mentally retarded weren't parents?"

I am surprised he is asking this again but I'm game. "I have friends who are orphans and as hard as it has been for me, I would much rather be connected to my mother and know her and who she is than be an orphan. The people I know who are orphans seem like they crave connection to something in the world. I at least have that connection rather than a void."

He replies, "Okay, I understand that. But in an ideal world, let's talk about an ideal world, wouldn't it be better if they didn't have children?"

Again, I am being pressed in a way that I don't understand. I cannot fathom what he is about, but I am not about to be responsible for suggesting that children get pulled away from their homes. "You are asking me to say that I should not have been born, it would be better if I never existed. I can't support that. I can't go there," I say, grinning, trying to defuse him. I continue, "Look, all of us have things that happen in our lives that shape our character. This one is mine. I see us all on this planet as individual social experiments, and each of us is given something to deal with. Mine is having a mentally retarded mother."

Bernie says, "Okay, I know that you don't want to say you should not exist, but let's put that aside and talk about an ideal world. Let's go at this another way; see if you understand this. Let's say that we have an alcoholic, we're talking about an alcoholic, should alcoholics be allowed to parent, in an ideal world?" He thinks I am not understanding him, or I would respond the way he wants me to.

"Of course they should; of course they need services; they need help, like the mentally retarded," I say adamantly, as Bernie smiles. What was he looking for?

On reflection, it is very clear what he was looking for—a good victim. Every time I refused to cave in and confess to how horrible it was to have a mentally retarded mother, I was failing to take on the role of victim and co-construct with Bernie a narrative of victimhood. The language of victimhood—even survivorhood—is disempowering. For Bernie to fulfill his role as an authority figure, it was necessary that he disregard the complexity of what I was trying to convey about the experience of being the daughter of a mother with mental retardation. To fulfill the journalist's role as the culturally prescribed protector and bearer of truth, he needed me to be a concomitant, appropriate, culturally prescribed victim.

I believe, in his own way, Bernie meant well and saw himself as an advocate, getting out the "story" for me and for all children of parents with mental retardation. He was eager to feel sorry for me. Bernie engages in a victim discourse, ostensibly trying to appear objective or unbiased about the topic of parents with mental retardation, when in fact, he is inherently biased, unquestioningly accepting the victim/perpetrator construct (Shilling and Fuehrer 1993).

By engaging in the discourse of victimhood, however, he perpetuates a rhetorical stance that the authority, indeed, the author of experience itself must be a privileged "other." How can I respond except to be that privileged other and argue my privilege to define the experience my own way? But authority implies some unitary view, and as he presses one view forward, I argue an opposing one, neither of which is complete.

It is the end of the taping session. They turn the sound off and film Bernie talking to me while I listen. He says, "Now you have to listen to me. I get to talk for thirty seconds and you have to sit there and listen to me without talking." I am stunned by the intensity of his manner as he says this, as if I had been rude to him, as if I had been interrupting him the whole interview, as if I had invalidated him or his identity somehow. "The uplift of this story is that you exist at all. Don't you understand that? That you are a professor. Let's face it, your father was a pervert, your mother was retarded, and your grandmother was an abominable character. That you made it at all, that is the uplift of this story. I want you to walk away from here understanding that." He talks on as I listen, "You wrote this article, and to tell you the truth, it depressed me. You wanted to reach someone and you did, you reached me. I was very moved."

There is an expression: "It's not that the horse can sing well; it can't. It's that the horse sings at all." Bernie's response informs me that no matter what I accomplish, no matter what I do, I will always be seen by him as interesting "because I exist," or because "I can sing at all." I am a guest here, an oddity in the palace, and clearly one who is not good enough, coming as I do from the University of Memphis, and clearly not grateful enough for the scraps she has received from the table.

Vicki interrupts my thoughts: "Okay Bernie, now you gotta shut your mouth for thirty seconds and listen to her." She is grinning, along with several others in the room.

I say, "What you have done is pick out the negative elements in my article, taken them out of context. . . . "

Bernie interrupts me, "No I didn't, I. . . . "

Vicki says, "Bernie, we have to start over again, we need you to be quiet." Everyone smirks.

We go through this several times, the last one my fault, before the camera crew can get their footage.

After Bernie shakes my hand and leaves, I sit on the chair watching the crew pack up, and Vicki comes over and asks, "Are you okay?"

Tears leak out of my eyes as I try desperately to contain myself. Her offer of comfort is all it took to break me. I say, "I hate this; I hate that I'm crying; I hate that he got to me. I'll get it under control in a minute." After a minute, I ask Vicki, "Was I being paranoid, like he said, was I?"

She answers, slowly, "Well, yes, but it was understandable that you would be."

Later I ask, "Don't you find this sexist, that you get to do his emotional scut work."

Vicki is defensive; her words take on a harder, more measured tone. "No, it's not sexist, this is the job of a producer. If that were a woman who had just walked away, I'd still be over here doing this. Man, woman, when they are done, they walk."

Tears continue to fall for a moment, then I get it under control. I never express more affect than this in their presence. I cling to this as a small triumph.

Like Arlie Hochschild's (1983) stewardesses, Vicki cannot afford to see herself as an emotion worker; yet that has been the defining component of our relationship to each other and to the corporation, CBS. Vicki calls me and reassures me that everything will be safe at the interview. Vicki flatters me so that I will feel good about coming. Vicki listens to my anxiety attack over the phone about doing the interview. Vicki sits with me while tears spill and Bernie gets to leave. She is positioned as a middle-management emotion worker, doing emotion work with her superiors, her subordinates, as well as outsiders whom CBS needs something from. Vicki is very good at her job.

Back at the hotel, I have already been checked out. The desk has my luggage. I take my luggage upstairs to the spa, unpack so that I may change, and find myself gasping for air. I am so scared and so alone. I think, What did I want out of this? Was anything I could get worth how I feel right now?

I weep outright as my knees buckle, falling to the ground with the weight of my emotion. I feel so profoundly helpless and humiliated that suicide crosses my mind as a humorous option. I laugh and snort, realize that I am being melodramatic and that I must blow my nose. I walk in my bra and hose to the tissue dispenser. Is my career ruined? Why aren't I calloused enough to be able to handle this? If I want to write a book, and if it were to receive some attention, then I'd damn well better grow up and get used to the beating. If I am ever interviewed like that again, I should expect the same.

Will that exchange between us air? Vicki said that if it makes Bernie and them look bad, they will not air it. But at the end, Vicki also told me Bernie writes the text and has the final say on the footage.

I pace back and forth, one moment racked by sobs, the next moment wrestling with getting myself under control in case someone walks in. I turn and pace and turn and pace. There is nowhere to go with this feeling.

In my mind, Frank Sinatra serenades me sarcastically, "CBS is spreading the news, it's coming your way, you want to be a part of it, New York, New York. If you can't make it there, you won't make it anywhere, it's up to you, New York, New *Yooork*." I laugh and weep at the same time. It's all too messed up. Bernie doesn't know any more regarding what he is about than I do! We are all blindly trying to construct our realities by the seats of our pants, all using the resources we have to the best of our abilities. I will scrape the crap off my shoes and go on and live with the consequences.

At first I thought I would tell no one what happened, but that was not possible, as I had told too many people I was going. Everyone wanted to hear what happened. As I told and retold the story, I got responses like these:

"All they want are ratings, they just wanted to do some shock theater and see what you would do."

"CBS hasn't been doing too well lately. They paid Bryant Gumbel a lot and the show has not been picked up for the next season. Maybe they are going *Jerry Springer* on us."

"Maybe you weren't giving them enough emotion and that was why he was pressing you so hard."

"Perhaps your answers were too pre-canned and you were being boring."

"What did you expect? What should anyone expect?"

"You were used, too bad."

There is another take on what happened in the line of sight at *Public Eye.* Bernard Goldberg has a distinguished record, including six Emmy Awards, an Ohio State Award, and a Sigma Delta Chi Award. He has been a correspondent for *Eye to Eye with Connie Chung, 48 Hours, Verdict, Street Stories,* and the *CBS Evening News with Dan Rather.* One of his reports resulted in an innocent man being set free from a life sentence in prison. In a special he hosted for *Eye to Eye,* he received critical acclaim for exploring the movement in American culture toward not accepting responsibility for one's actions.

Bernie is a good guy. It is not his fault that he tried to construct me as a victim. This particular meta-narrative has spilled out of the boundaries of the academy and clinical practice and into our everyday conversations. Situated in a larger context, the discourse of victimology and symptomology, on the face of it, appears rational and scientific, but on closer examination, it serves to regulate appropriate childhoods (O'Dell 1997). Thus, a childhood with a mentally retarded parent can never be a story of an "appropriate," happy, or well-adjusted childhood; it must be a victim's story.

My experiences as a child and at *Public Eye* were ambiguous and complicated. Bernie is and is not a perpetrator of abuse. He was "doing his job." He is also a victim of a larger social context he is unaware of and is passively reproducing. I am and am not a victim. I went to *Public Eye* knowing what was possible. Bernie certainly believed he had my consent, yet I do not believe I consented to what happened. In one moment of reflection I thought of my mother as "vile," while in others I thought she was the best mom a kid could have. She abused me physically and sexually, yet she often protected me from my father, who was far worse. In writing about her, there is a way in which I victimize her by telling our secrets against her will, yet I have also worked to protect her.

"Victim" is a moment in the dialectic of identity, one pose among many that constitute parts of who we all are as long as we engage in this discourse. To construct myself here as a "concrete," "absolute," or "innocent" victim is problematic and would be to fall into the old meta-narrative regarding victims and abusers. This was my "date," the one I made up for, the one in which I made small talk initially, the one in which I was victimized and in which I resisted, the one after which I cleaned up. I subvert this construction of self that I wrote by also writing reflexively and transgressively, with a layered-account format, making as many resources as possible available for the readers for the purposes of constructing, through the filter of their own experiences, their interpretations of who I was and who Bernie was in the line of sight at *Public Eye*.

REFERENCES

Bass, E., and Davis, L. 1988. *The courage to heal.* New York: Harper Perennial.
Bender, L., and Blau, A. 1937. The reaction of children to sexual relations with adults. *American Journal of Orthopsychiatry* 7, 500–518.
Daly, K. 1994. Men's violence, victim's advocacy, and feminist redress. *Law and Society Review* 28, 777–786.

Hochschild, A. 1983. *The managed heart: The commercialization of emotion.* Newbury Park, CA: Sage.

Kahn, A. S., and Mathie, V. A. Forthcoming. Understanding the unacknowledged rape victim. In C. B. Travis and J. W. White (eds.), *Sexuality, society, and feminism: Psychological perspectives on women.* APA Press.

Lamb, S. 1996. *The trouble with blame: Victims, perpetrators, and responsibility.* Cambridge, MA: Harvard University Press.

Lyotard, J. 1977. *The postmodern condition: A report on knowledge.* Minneapolis: University of Minnesota Press.

McCarthy, T. 1997. Rethinking theories of victimology: Men's violence against women. In S. Cook and J. Bessant (eds.), *Women's encounters with violence: Australian experiences* (pp. 127–144). Thousand Oaks, CA: Sage.

O'Dell, L. 1997. Child sexual abuse and the academic construction of symptomologies. *Feminism and Psychology* 7, 334–339.

Ronai, C. R. 1998. Sketching with Derrida: An ethnography of a researcher/dancer. *Qualitative Inquiry* 4, 403–418.

———. 1997a. On loving and hating my mentally retarded mother. *Mental Retardation* 35, 417–432.

———. 1997b. Discursive constraint in the narrated identities of childhood sex abuse survivors. In C. R. Ronai, B. Zsembik, and J. R. Feagin (eds.), *Everyday sexism in the third millennium* (pp. 123–136). New York: Routledge.

———. 1996. My mother is mentally retarded. In C. Ellis and A. Bochner (eds.), *Composing ethnography* (pp. 109–131). Newbury Park, CA: Altimira Press.

———. 1995. Multiple reflections of child sex abuse: An argument for a layered account. *Journal of Contemporary Ethnography* 23, 395–426.

———. 1992. The reflexive self through narrative: A night in the life of an exotic dancer/researcher. In C. Ellis and M. Flaherty (eds.), *Investigating subjectivity: Research on lived experience* (pp. 102–124). Newbury Park, CA: Sage.

Shilling, M., and Fuehrer, A. 1993. The politics of women's self-help books. *Feminism and Psychology* 3, 418–422.

Simonds, W. 1996. All consuming selves: Self help literature and women's identities. In D. Grodin and T. R. Lindlof (eds.), *Constructing the self in a mediated world* (pp. 15–29). Thousand Oaks, CA: Sage.

Chapter Seven

Trauma Talk in Feminist Clinical Practice

Jeanne Marecek

> Both client and therapist use their skills as novelists as
> well as historians or detectives as they labor to get a story
> to work right and to feel right. . . . The therapist as histo-
> rian, humbled by the new understanding that any ac-
> count of a client's life . . . is but one of a hundred possible
> versions, . . . collaborates with the eyewitness.
>
> (Baur 1995)

> I'm haunted by the questions I didn't ask in the late '70s
> where I now know that those were women who were sex-
> ually abused as kids.
>
> (Therapist #159)

Male violence against women—rape, battering, and childhood sexual
abuse—has been a major focus of the second wave of feminism. From
the early 1970s onward, feminists initiated shelters and crisis services for
victims, advocated for changes in legal and criminal justice institutions,
and spearheaded scholarly research and theory. As women voiced what
had gone unsaid, a new lexicon for speaking about the sexual and physical violation of women, along with a narrative framework for explaining women's problems, developed. This lexicon circulates freely not
only among feminists but also in the mental health professions and the
mass media. I call this lexicon *trauma talk*. To say that trauma talk is a
set of linguistic practices for narrating a woman's problems is not to
question whether abuse occurred. Nor is it to deny victims' suffering.
Instead, trauma talk refers to the system of terms, metaphors, and

modes of representation for talking about the physical and sexual abuse of women.

In this chapter, I listen to the words of some forty feminist therapists. How, I ask, does trauma talk enter the everyday work of these therapists? Which meanings of experience does trauma talk bring to light? Which ones does it submerge? Descriptions are never just descriptions; they are also explanations. How does trauma talk shape therapists' understandings of their clients' lives and of therapy itself? What narratives about women, therapy, and feminism are possible when trauma talk is the medium for telling them?

The form of my questions intimates my approach, that of a social constructionist. For social constructionists, language is not a transparent medium through which reality can be seen; rather, language creates the reality of which we speak. Language practices shape what we can see and think. Moreover, language is not a vehicle for expressing private thoughts formulated inside a speaker's head; it is a social practice. Trauma, with all its attributes and associations, exists by virtue of cultural agreements to package it in this particular way. As Jonathan Potter (1996, p. 126) has said, "The terms and forms by which we achieve an understanding of the world and ourselves are . . . products of historically and culturally situated interchanges among people." These terms and forms—variously called "discourses," "interpretative repertoires," or "consensual discursive practices"—are systems of meanings so habitual and so familiar that they are taken for granted, if not invisible. In the interviews I analyze below, trauma was a central theme, even though not a single interview question asked about it. Moreover, although we did not recruit therapists who worked with trauma, over 70 percent of the respondents identified sexual or physical abuse of women as one of their clinical specialties.

Interviews

In spring and summer of 1996, Diane Kravetz and I, with the help of student interviewers, gathered a set of interviews with feminist therapists. The therapists were recruited from a variety of work sites, including state and private agencies, solo and group private practices, and college counseling centers. All were from the state of Wisconsin; most were located near the university town of Madison. We located our respondents by a variety of means, including peer nomination, utilizing the work and friendship networks of the student interviewers, and inquiring at agencies specializing in therapy for women.

Potential participants were contacted initially by telephone. This contact served both as an invitation to participate in the study and as a screening interview. In the screening interview, therapists were asked if they considered themselves to be feminists and if they brought a feminist perspective to therapy. In accord with long-standing custom in such research, we let potential participants define *feminism* for themselves. As Shulamit Reinharz (1992) has pointed out, feminism takes so many forms that it is impossible to impose a single definition on it.

Advanced social work graduate students carried out the interviews as part of a class on qualitative research methods.[1] Interviews lasted between ninety minutes and two hours; they consisted of nineteen open-ended questions about feminism in therapy, with probes for specific incidents and case examples. None of the questions concerned abuse, trauma, post-traumatic stress disorder (PTSD), and the like. All interviews were conducted in private; they were recorded on audiotape with the therapist's permission. Therapists' names were not given on the tapes, and all other names were removed from the transcripts, except for references to theorists, authors of books and articles, professional lecturers, and the like. Respondents indicated if they were willing to have verbatim quotations published and how much descriptive information could be attached to a quoted remark. Only one therapist did not give permission to publish verbatim material; her tape was erased.

We have transcribed the interviews of forty-four therapists to date, proceeding as funds allow. All were currently working; clinical work was their primary or sole paid occupation. Only those respondents who had some advanced training (i.e., beyond the bachelor's degree) in a mental health profession were kept in the sample. As a group, the respondents represent different schools of therapy, different professional backgrounds, different personal backgrounds, and different levels of training. All but two are women. Their ages range from thirty-one to fifty-seven. Eight identified themselves as lesbians, two as bisexual. All but three are white. All are experienced, with an average of nearly fifteen years in practice (range = five to twenty-eight years). Three are psychiatrists, twenty-eight are psychologists (seventeen with doctorates and eleven with master's degrees), and thirteen are social workers.

The interviews were transcribed verbatim. The transcripts were punctuated and paragraphed first by the transcribers and then by me, using our best judgment as to the intended meaning. The raw transcripts contain many sentence fragments, false starts, and digressions. The extracts presented below are not the verbatim transcriptions; in the interests of brevity and ease of reading, the dysfluencies and digressions have been edited out.

Analysis

Discourse analysis is a family of approaches to working with language. Discourse analytic approaches all focus on language and the way in which meanings are made. This form of analysis is different from customary academic reading practices, in which one reads quickly to get the gist of a passage. A discourse analyst attends to the details of the talk, to the process—the twists and turns of language—by which meanings get made. Clinicians who work in interpretive modes of therapy may see a resemblance to therapeutic listening processes. It is true that the mode of listening (or reading) is similar, but there is a key difference. In discourse analysis, the goal is not to infer mental states, defensive operations, or inner thoughts and beliefs but to identify the repertory of concepts and categories, the systems of statements, and the narrative frameworks that speakers rely on to make themselves intelligible.

I used two main strategies to help me see the practices that trauma talk entails. The first involved examining and contrasting the dominant and marginal discourses in the interviews. Dominant discourses are the ones that are granted the status of truth, the agreed-upon frameworks of language and meaning. Marginal discourses, in contrast, are counterhegemonic; they refuse or challenge received wisdom. Only a few therapists ventured such thoughts; they often spoke hesitantly or with trepidation. In our interviews, for example, respondents prefaced such statements with phrases such as "Most feminists might not agree" or "You'll probably be surprised by this" or "I guess I'm not what you call a politically correct feminist." In one instance, a respondent broke off abruptly in mid-sentence and asked nervously, "You said you're not going to use any names, right?" In my interpretive analysis, I focus on the points of contradiction, tension, and paradox inside the dominant discourses and between the dominant and marginal discourses.

My second interpretive strategy focuses on dichotomies, especially those related to gender. This strategy draws loosely on feminist deconstructive literary analysis and the ideas of Jacques Derrida. In Derrida's linguistic philosophy, words do not have single, immutable meanings; instead, they take their meanings from the systems of oppositions in which they are embedded (Hare-Mustin and Marecek 1990). In trauma talk, the dichotomy male–female is aligned with a set of other dichotomies, such as predator–victim and innocent–evil. I trace how this system of gendered oppositions produces the gendered identities of the respondents, their clients, and men who abuse women, as well as the meanings it lends to feminism and feminist therapy.

Trauma Talk in the Office

I use the term *trauma talk* to refer to a widely shared lexicon for speaking about the problems women bring to therapy. Trauma talk includes a particular vocabulary of distress, consisting of terms such as *trauma, wound, injury, emotional pain, brokenness,* and *damage,* to describe clients' problems. It supplies a diagnostic category for these experiences: post-traumatic stress disorder, or PTSD. It invokes highly charged language for men who have engaged in abusive behavior—*abusers, predators, perpetrators* (or *perps*), *batterers*—that unambiguously brands them as morally reprehensible. It figures therapy as a process of healing or recovery. Not all our respondents used every idiom of trauma talk, but few eschewed trauma talk entirely. Trauma talk produces new meanings of assessment, diagnosis, therapy, and feminism in therapy. In what follows, I examine these meanings.

For many respondents, trauma talk served as a rhetorical resource for voicing their objections, as feminists, to conventional diagnoses and the medical model.[2] Many saw diagnostic categories (except for PTSD) as stigmatizing and pathologizing "normal" women. Others saw labeling a woman as scapegoating, blaming the victim for the maltreatment she has suffered. For others, imposing any label (again, except PTSD) was an abuse of the therapist's power.

> There's lots of women who get labeled as borderline who have those characteristics but it comes out of twenty years of being beaten by their husbands or a severe incest. If you treat that as borderline personality disorder versus PTSD, [laughs] you get really different outcomes.... There's a continuum of sexual violence, and most women have experienced some amount by the time they're eighteen, and so I recognize that, and I recognize how it con-

stricts their lives that way, in terms of how they have to keep themselves safe, that may be what, that is the case in most inner cities or Detroit or South Chicago. . . . If we hadn't taken that step, we would have just said, "Oh, borderline personality."   (Therapist #67)

The whole category of borderline personality sort of bothers me—it's very much blaming the victim or blaming the individual for what would be a real normal response to a lot of the situations they've been in.

(Therapist #123)

Almost all my clients have PTSD and I tell them what it means. I say, "This means you are having a normal reaction to trauma. You're not having a sick reaction to trauma. You're having a normal reaction to trauma." The reason I like PTSD as a diagnosis and I'm glad it's there is that it says right in the definition that this is a normal response to trauma that most people would have.   (Therapist #121)

In sum, trauma talk in the interviews positioned women clients as the victims of catastrophic events that are undeserved and beyond their control. It insisted that, whatever problems bring such women to therapy, the women are normal. Trauma talk thus affirms a number of core tenets of feminist therapy (Ballou and Hill 1998; Wyche and Rice 1997). It takes an unequivocal stand that women are not responsible for male violence; it insists that oppressive social and cultural circumstances are causes of women's distress; and it seeks to empower women, bolstering their confidence and self-esteem.

In some ways, however, trauma talk runs the risk of constructing women exclusively as objects of oppression. It did not stop with exculpating women from responsibility for male abuse but went further to exonerate them from responsibility for the effects of abuse on their lives. A counterdiscourse emerged in a few interviews, suggesting that trauma talk, by positioning women as victims, can rob them of responsibility and agency. As one therapist put it:

I do think in spite of being victimized by husbands and society and all of that, women bring their own problems and their own difficulties to the situation and need help with that. Sometimes just saying, "OK, you've been victimized by this abusive guy. That's all that's wrong; you don't have to look at anything else; it just isn't helpful."   (Therapist #20)

For another therapist, a clinical psychologist with ten years of experience as feminist therapist, giving a PTSD (or any) diagnosis deflected attention from the work of therapy:

I would much rather talk about . . . how in context with me or with other people is this person. How fulfilling is their life? What are their goals? What are they hoping for? Where do they get blocked? What are the old patterns of thought that keep them locked in a behavior, locked in a certain position? Where are they stuck? That is much more interesting to me than what their diagnosis is. Much more interesting! And I think much more productive. And it may come out in the diagnosis in part; but somewhere in those descriptions and diagnoses . . . they seem like they're patterns in and of themselves. They don't lead to logical things that you could do. . . . "Oh! So this person has Post-Traumatic Stress Disorder." It's much more interesting to say, well, every time they try to do their creative writing, they run up against this wall of "No, you can't get enough" and all those patterned ways of thinking. That to me is much more interesting. . . . What's the key to unlock that? What's the key to changing it? Rather than "Oh, yeah, you've got Post-Traumatic Stress Disorder."   (Therapist #205)

Trauma Talk and the Medical Model: Against or Within?

Many respondents voiced further objections to what they termed the *medical model*. They rejected the authority of experts to judge and label women. They opposed psychological or psychobiological explanations for problems created by oppressive life circumstances. They regarded medicalized mental health care as de-humanizing and anti-feminist.

> Like the medical model is very nonfeminist, where the doctor is the expert. . . . So, there are some essential things about the medical model that put power in the hands of the expert. The other thing it does is pathologizes the individual. Often in an abusive or a negative situation, it used to penalize the woman. There was something wrong with the woman that she couldn't live in that abusive situation, as opposed to saying the context is crazy. So, there's that stigmatizing or scapegoating the individual for having the problem.
> (Therapist #158)

> The HMOs and the medical model go against the very essence of, certainly, feminist therapy, as I define it, but therapy in general. The humanness, the nurturing, the support, those things.   (Therapist #69)

In sum, respondents extolled the trauma model as not only opposite to the medical model but far superior. When we probe trauma talk in close detail, however, what had looked like clear differences between the two evaporate; many of the grounds for superiority disappear before our eyes. I begin by noting that the trauma lexicon describes clients' problems using medical and bodily metaphors: trauma, injury, insult, wound, brokenness, and pain. It also frames the action of therapy in medical metaphors: relieving pain, facilitating recovery, setting "healing processes" in motion. Some respondents, such as Therapist #106, figured the effects of trauma as bodily experiences. Blurring the distinction between emotional pain and physical pain, she recommended the same pain control techniques for both:

> A lot of people who've been through trauma, it's emotional pain instead of physical pain. . . . [A lengthy description of pain control techniques developed by Jon Kabat-Zinn ensues.] He's teaching mindfulness meditation and a form of yoga. . . . A lot of these people have back problems, neck problems, multiple injuries, surgeries, chronic pain. . . . I think this technique has implications for trauma people.

Ironically, trauma talk, far from countering the medicalized idiom of conventional psychiatry, has merely replaced one form of this idiom with another.

What is accomplished by this linguistic blurring of emotional and physical pain and the representation of women's suffering as (metaphorically and even literally) bodily pain? Feminists may couch the suffering of women in physical rather than emotional terms because physical suffering seems more real and therefore harder to dismiss. It is also true that biomedical practitioners and theories hold the highest status in the mental health field. Feminist therapists—who are, after all, part of that field—may consciously or unconsciously model their discourse on the privileged one.

It is not only at the level of vocabulary that respondents' trauma talk mirrored the conventional, medicalized model of psychopathology. Trauma talk operates within much the same logic as that model. It subsumes the particularities of a woman's experience into abstractions (e.g., "trauma," "abuse") and reduces experience into discrete, encapsulated symptoms (flashbacks; revictimization). It offers cause-and-effect explanations that are linear, mechanistic, and mono-causal. It sets aside a client's understanding of her own experience in favor of a uniform narrative: a single cause reliably (even invariably) produces a fixed set of symptoms. Furthermore, the goal of therapy is to produce healing. In trauma talk, both the verb *to heal* and the noun *healing* are in passive voice. Thus, clients "heal from" abusive relationships; women "do their healing" in therapy. This language practice implies a process that unfolds without an active agent. It risks transforming clients to patients, that is, those who wait passively while processes of repair and restoration take their course.

The respondents who were enthusiasts of EMDR (eye movement desensitization and reprocessing; Shapiro 1995) produced the most extreme examples of reinscribing trauma within a medicalized framework.[3] Locating PTSD in the brain, they narrowed their sights to trauma memories, which they construed in pseudo-neurological terms. Their descriptions of the EMDR procedure, which involves rapid eye movements and visualization of traumatic events, constituted highly mechanistic models of trauma and its treatment. The effects of the procedure were described as instantaneous, dissipating troubling emotions and magically restoring the victim to her or his (or its: one therapist claimed to use the procedure successfully on her cat) "healthy" self.

> She was abused sexually and physically by her father, and then her husband, her ex-husband, actually her two ex-husbands. And [I] help[ed] her in many different ways, using EMDR, using visualization to remember what she used to be like, and kind of allowing herself, or helping her become that person again. (Therapist #133)

> I'm going to throw my pitch in here because I think it's absolutely wonderful. . . . In the last two years I have learned about EMDR, which is Eye Movement Desensitization Reprocessing. It's trauma recovery. . . . It's a procedure that . . . actually helps your brain kind of reshuffle the deck. So you walk away from an EMDR session where the trauma feels like it happened in the past. And why I think that's so important as a feminist therapist is that the goal of feminist therapy is to work yourself out of a job. You're trying to get people to not be in your office for ten years. You want people to be able to do their healing and it's just phenomenal how it's stepped up the pace of healing. (Therapist #95)

> What happens during the EMDR therapy is that we process the abuse, all the different abuse they've experienced, and essentially it's just a sense of being able to deal with the situation, to access their adult coping mechanisms and skills. They may still remember the abuse, but it doesn't affect them as much emotionally any longer. So it's basically healing from old experiences. (Therapist #41)

It is deeply ironic that EMDR, which seems a caricature of the medical model, could be construed as its antithesis. The EMDR procedures are couched in mystifying mumbo jumbo. The therapist administers the procedure to a client who passively awaits the obscure processes of brain rearrangement to take place. EMDR promises instantaneous cure through a focalized, formulaic treatment. Indeed, in all these respects, EMDR serves up precisely the standardized quick fix that managed care demands; moreover, clients in EMDR are constructed as exactly the docile selves that managed care requires (Guilford 1996).

Several respondents favored the diagnostic category PTSD because it embeds the idea that the woman to whom it is applied is normal. This is a paradox that warrants further examination. We need to consider some features of the medical model of psychopathology on which diagnostic categorization is based. One feature of the medical model is that it is a discrete model, rather than a continuous one, with "normal" and "abnormal" regarded as qualitatively different states (Siegler and Osmond 1974). Moreover, the term *normal* has multiple meanings when applied to psychological conditions. It can mean "average," that is, lying within a statistical range of the mean—for example, normal height or normal blood sugar. It can also mean normal according to an absolute criterion. It can also mean "not deviant." This often boils down to whether or not the speaker approves of the behavior in question, for example, "People who pierce their eyelids aren't normal."

In trauma talk, the diagnostic category PTSD slides between different meanings of "normal." It asserts that a woman is normal even though she face difficulties severe enough to warrant psychiatric diagnosis and problematic enough that she seeks treatment. Here it seems as if the third meaning of *normal* is the relevant one. Therapists use the label "normal" to reassure clients of their approval, to relieve their shame.

Clinically speaking, one can question whether such preemptive reassurances are helpful. They seem to contradict a client's felt experience or, at the least, fail to understand it. It seems contradictory that feminist therapists, for whom (as we shall see later) empathy is a key therapeutic process, would assert their view of a client's state of being over the client's own. Moreover, such reassurances foreclose opportunities for clients to explore and resolve issues of shame.

For our respondents, the linguistic practice of declaring women with PTSD "normal" achieved an additional clinical aim. As feminists, they strove for therapy relationships that were collaborative, egalitarian, and nonauthoritarian (Wyche and Rice 1997). They objected to diagnostic labels as disempowering, stigmatizing, and victim-blaming. Moreover, they believed that the labeling process set up an expert doctor–sick patient hierarchy. For them, insisting on clients' normalcy seemed to suspend the therapist's power to judge and thus to dismantle that hierarchy. However, as Laura Anderson and Karen Gold (1994) have argued, the diagnostic process replicates the traditional mental health paradigm, whatever diagnosis is given. "Normal" is a diagnostic category; declaring a client "normal" reaffirms therapist's power to judge, as well as the hierarchy built into the therapy relationship.

The trauma model and the medical model are close cousins. Why, then, did trauma talk *seem* so radically different and so politically congenial to so many respondents? One difference seems key: trauma talk identifies clients as injured rather than sick. Trauma (or the trauma memories), like a fish bone lodged in the throat, merely needs to be excised. There is no question of whether the psyche is diseased or malfunctioning. In other significant respects, trauma talk is not opposed to the medical model but merely a variant of it. Why are the similarities so hard to see? Why is it so hard to move outside the medical model, even for those who vehemently reject it? Perhaps we should not be surprised by our difficulty. After all, the medical model is part and parcel of the professional culture of psychotherapy. Therapists, feminist or not, are part of that culture. Thus, paradoxically, trauma talk seeks to oppose a system of which it is part.

Abuse: Unbound and Unbounded

In trauma talk, categories such as "abuse," "trauma," "violence," and "battering" have ballooned to encompass virtually any negative encounter with another person or an institution. In our respondents' view, this often included therapy encounters.

> I think therapists abuse clients, obviously in the more overt ways, by becoming sexually involved or personally involved. I think therapists abuse clients by not listening to clients, not believing them. That doesn't mean that you shouldn't be skeptical, but to out-of-hand discount what people are saying because it doesn't meet with your reality is an abuse of power. I think to not support clients in their own search for help is abusive. As a general rule, for the therapist to impose the treatment on the client without working with the client to design that treatment and taking into account her unique stuff is abusive.   (Therapist #159)

For Therapist #24, "imposing my goals" on women in therapy was "abuse." She goes on:

> I think a potential exists for even well-meaning and well-intentioned and really skillful therapy to inadvertently abuse a client just through the relationship's power dynamics.

Therapist #51 sees therapists who impose their values on clients as akin to husbands who batter their wives:

> I think staying in a battering relationship by and large is not [healthy]. Maybe on very rare occasions there theoretically may be a reason why that was healthy, but I think you can also beat somebody up in the position of therapist by trying to invalidate them and disempower them.

For Therapist #120, the medical model itself perpetuates violence:

> I guess we could go maybe to the top of the list, the medical model, of pathologizing women's experience and labeling [that] as mental illness. Having grown up in a world of violence and anything that perpetuates that. And that a lot of people practice in ways that perpetuate that.

For Therapist #98, working with male clients who had abused women would constitute victimization for a woman therapist:

> It just seems like almost another element of perpetration if the woman [therapist] is working with abusers day in and day out when she is a member of the group that they have targeted. She's grown up with her own experiences of abuse or assault or attempted abuse or assault, as most of us have.

When *abuse, battering,* and *violence* become portmanteau words, that is, words into which we pack many disparate meanings, then they lose all meaning. We speakers lose the ability to make distinctions. When "not listening" becomes equivalent to physical violence or to forcing sex on a child, we run the risk of trivializing those severe transgressions. Mona Eliasson (1998) raises a parallel objection:

> Is the violence and are the humiliations experienced by battered women at the hands of men they live(d) with and love(d) similar enough to the injustices of economic discrimination, or being forced to give one's baby up for adoption, to justify the same label without removing meaning from the word "violence"?   (p. 229)

When the category of "abuse" is enlarged to encompass *any* negative, coercive, or uncomfortable encounter with the world, then trauma talk threatens to impose a totalizing psychology of personal development:

> It's my own belief that there are other equally terrible things that happen to children in addition to childhood sexual assault—the wearing away of the child by inconsistently effective or neglectful parenting or critical parenting. And those terrible events certainly have awful consequences for children . . .

that leave people damaged, leave people developing with wounds they carry into adulthood. (Therapist #3)

Moreover, as we shall see later, terms such as *abuse* and *trauma* are laced with gender meanings. Thus, trauma talk is also a way of producing male-female relations, imposing a highly charged set of meanings on them.

Trauma Talk as Feminism

After several months of hearing all of these stories of women being physically abused and sexually abused and emotionally abused, all of a sudden I can remember it just hitting me at one point. I thought, "Oh my God, this is the way the world is for women." I had never known that depth of pain or that kind of pain. . . . That epitomized my transformation into a feminist therapist.
(Therapist #121)

Over the past thirty years, feminist therapists of every theoretical persuasion have assembled a rich and vital array of clinical theories, practice innovations, empirical studies, and ethical reflections (cf. Brown 1994; Enns 1997; Lerman and Porter 1990; Marecek and Hare-Mustin 1991). Yet, for some respondents in our study, trauma talk eclipsed feminist therapy's rich intellectual history. They saw the trauma model as the *sine qua non* of feminism in therapy. Assessment, clinical formulation, and treatment all were reconceived within the trauma framework.

[Is there a feminist approach to assessment?] It's helping to construct a little history in terms of some of these [abuse] experiences and helping her understand what she's been through. Most women who come here often have a collection of various abuse experiences, from mild to sometimes horrendous. (Therapist #121)

[Can you tell me how your feminist perspective is reflected in your therapy?] OK, I screen very early for [abuse]. A lot of times people come in with a whole cluster of symptoms, but the assessment is always for trauma and abuse in the background. To be able to recognize that as a part of the wounds they carry and to address those and give them their due in terms of how we try to work with the healing process. (Therapist #12)

Post-Traumatic Stress Disorder comes probably closer than any diagnosis to recognizing the reality of women's lives. When women come in a nervous wreck, they may fit the criteria for a dysthymic disorder or some of the other mood disorders or such. But often you're also working with a Post-Traumatic Stress Disorder. (Therapist #69)

Thus, for some respondents, retelling a woman's life as a trauma narrative was both the feminist way and the one true way to tell a life. Yet, even though a woman has experienced abuse, narrating her life in terms of that experience produces only one of many possible stories. There is no single life story, nor one correct feminist version. Many versions are true; many are feminist. The constructionist's question is "Which ones are useful?" One therapist, carefully verifying her feminist credentials as she spoke, ventured the point of view that trauma narratives were not helpful to women:

> I think that one of the ways that things have shifted for me is that I still very much hold the cultural, societal perspective that we live in a very patriarchal society, but I don't think it's helpful that women just view themselves as victims of this society. I think it is just not a psychologically healthy position. I think we need to view ourselves as responsible adult human beings who are learning hopefully to make choices and figure things out for ourselves a little better. Now I know that there are women who are in very much victimized places. I'm not saying that's not a reality. But I get a little leery of some women just never having ever to be responsible for their own behavior, because they've been victimized. (Therapist #205)

Taking these therapists' voices together, we can see how different angles of vision yield different views. On the one hand, trauma stories respect and acknowledge women's experiences of violation, "recognizing the reality of women's lives." On the other hand, they run the risk of reducing women clients to nothing more than those experiences. Life histories do not merely tell about the past; they create possibilities for the present and future. Plotting a woman as a victim may leave her "never having ever to be responsible for her own behavior." Reflecting on these ideas, we can appreciate how many layers of complexity lie within our feminist commitment to empower women.

For therapists like #121 and #12, feminism dictates that the therapeutic task is reconstructing the client's history into a trauma narrative. But the practice of constructing a trauma history raises issues about the influence of the therapist and the power dynamics involved in constructing a clinical narrative (Haaken 1998). Respondents in this study were deeply committed to monitoring the power dynamics of therapy and determined to foster egalitarian relationships. But they seemed unaware of the power involved in seizing interpretive authority over a client's life.

When women clients are construed as "wounded," "damaged," or "broken" victims, therapy becomes refocused around the goal of healing their pain. Therapists become caregivers whose most important (or only?) actions are providing compassion, support, empathic acceptance, and nurture. For some respondents, these qualities had become the essence of feminist therapy.

> [What does it mean to you to say that your therapy is feminist?] It's softer . . . less critical, . . . less dualistic . . . less judgmental. It's a more open way of looking at an individual. (Therapist #64)

> I guess I would say the personal empathy. (Therapist #133)

> I think it means a consciousness of the relational model that is so important to women. . . . It means collaboration, and valuing connectedness and empathy. (Therapist #53)

> That all people who come through the door would be treated with dignity and respect, and compassion and equality. That's the essence of it. Safety. I would add safety to that. (Therapist #72)

> The humanness, the nurturing, the support, those things. (Therapist #69)

> Say a woman has been in a particularly abusive relationship and she comes in and she tells this to the therapist. She can either get understanding and compassion about what she has been through, or she might get the therapist questioning her and assuming that she possibly did something to provoke the physical abuse. Which is very different from a feminist orientation or even a nonfeminist orientation that there is never ever any justification for someone abusing you. (Therapist #121)

Do gentle compassion, support, and empathy constitute therapy? Or feminism? Framing therapy as "healing" submerges other goals, such as change, self-knowledge, and personal growth.

A subterranean stream of dissenting views ran through the interviews. In the excavation of these counterdiscourses, a variety of reservations come to light:

> [How have your ideas about feminist therapy changed over time?] I've probably become more aware of some need for boundaries as I come in more contact with more and more difficult clients. . . . From a feminist perspective, [we have] a continual awareness—especially with women—of how much they come into our offices and kind of hand over power. We have to continually empower and empower and give that message very strongly. [But] I think that particularly with borderline folks, . . . you have to work counterintuitively. Certainly I still think it's important to empower folks but that population has been real challenging, so caution for the therapist. [She speaks about her feminist training that emphasized creating relationships that feel respectful.] With that population, I have been more challenged. I

don't know that it's particularly helpful. I think it's a more boundaried stance, some need to be more cautious, not as free.   (Therapist #226)

I'm actually in [a network for treating sexual offenders]. I've always treated sex offenders. Here's my bias, which a lot of feminists probably won't like to hear. I don't think you should work with victims unless you work with offenders. I think that if you're so emotional that you are upset with being in vicinity of a sexual offender, then you should not be treating the victims. That it's going to get in the way of your work. The job of the therapist is not to be the best friend; it's to be an objective professional. If you can't do that, then you shouldn't be doing that specific kind of work.   (Therapist #12)

[Women don't] know how to do anything else. I'm currently spending a lot of time talking with clients and thinking about how women join together in suffering. There's an enormous amount of pressure, peer pressure to do that. And there's not a whole lot of pressure to necessarily be proactive. So, you hear it in teachers' lounges and you hear it in meetings. And it's a joining strategy for women, much like playing sports is a joining strategy for men, but how we stay locked in it! There's some good stuff about "let's talk about feelings, let's talk about feelings," but at some point you gotta take action.
(Therapist #64)

Additionally, some therapists worried that trauma talk, far from epitomizing feminism, was a dilution or even a betrayal of it:

I have a twenty-year perspective. I started as part of, not a therapy movement, but a political movement. What we were doing was early intervention, education about sexual assault, connecting people with natural support systems, setting up groups, and that kind of stuff. . . . Now, I wouldn't say that nobody needs therapy having been sexually assaulted, and it's probably true that more incest survivors and typically people who have been severely abused could benefit from therapy. But what I'm a little concerned about is it seems like that experience has gone from being a political experience. That one out of every three females and one out of every five males are sexually abused before age eighteen is a political issue. And instead [it's] pathologized so that every rape victim gets her turn for individual therapy and then they all go off and deal with it as if it's their individual pathology.   (Therapist #5)

Masculine Subjectivity and Feminist Identity in Trauma Talk

Trauma talk tells gendered stories, ones that encode male and female as opposites. These stories restrict the possibilities for each sex: woman, the injured party, is produced as innocent of responsibility, blameless, and powerless; man, the perpetrator, is her dark complement—coercive, domineering, unrepentant, even evil. Therapist #44, a man who treats male batterers, enunciated such a view:

> So my model of mental health is to teach men . . . to give up the need to have power and control over other people for their own happiness and well being. For women, it is to not accept that kind of control. . . . I just finished a group a few minutes ago with women, an orientation group for women whose battering and abusive partners are coming into the program. The message to them is that they don't have to change in order for their partner to change.

Another therapist related how she "cooked" her clinical assessment techniques to reproduce her beliefs about male batterers and female victims:

> [I was wondering, what are some of the issues with assessment tools that you're finding?] What I did was I just took the assessment instruments that had been used for a lot of years with batterers. So I just took the same ones, except I pulled out the ones on anger and hostility because . . . I didn't want to measure that because I didn't want to send that message, that [women] needed to have that measured. (Therapist #101)

Themes of male malevolence saturated respondents' trauma talk. We asked if there were "any individuals or types of problems that you do not work with for reasons connected to your feminism." With only a few exceptions, women told us they would not see abusive or violent clients (a category assumed to be composed entirely of men). Men involved in abuse were branded as predators, scary, evil. Indeed, the ubiquitous term *abuser* shrinks a man's identity to a single dimension, just as the term *victim* shrinks a woman's identity (cf. hooks 1989). Even though many respondents had no actual experience treating abusers, they believed that such clients could not be helped and did not want to change.

> I think it's harder because the rapists and the abusers and batterers and all tend to come from a very different frame of mind and often don't want to change. (Therapist #203)

> In order to be a good therapist I think you have to be able to understand the person's world view. And, I'm not sure because of my perspective on the world, that I could get my mind around into a space that I could say, "Yes, this person has an honorable intention" or find a rationalization for the behavior or whatever. And I'm not sure that I want to take the time to stretch myself in that direction. I couldn't do justice to them. And I'm not sure that I want to. (Therapist #158)

It [an experience of working with perpetrators] actually gave me a different perspective: that the men going through those treatment programs are individuals and are not complete evil people. You know, [that they] could be in some cases worked with and helped. But not in all cases.   (Therapist #205)

Rachel Hare-Mustin and I have warned that

when the emotionally fraught issues of intimate violence and sexual abuse are under discussion, the slide into unreflective male-female dichotomies becomes all too easy. . . . If women are victims, men must be oppressors. Although this formula serves to simplify a complex reality, it does so at the cost of ignoring the diversity of experiences of both men and women.
                                        (Hare-Mustin and Marecek 1994, p. 16)

Cruel, manipulative, brutal men; vulnerable and suffering women—these dichotomies spilled over into the therapists' own identities, as women and as therapists. Many, seeing themselves in terms of feminine powerlessness, held that they were not confrontational enough, not strong enough to withstand the anger and resistance of abusive men. Some argued that doing therapy with abusive men constituted a form of victimization for a woman therapist. Many assumed automatically that working with abusive men was a man's job.

I think that for the woman it's going to be really hard to come home [and] take it in, in some ways that really tie in to what it's like growing up female in this culture. If this were a culture in which women were not in danger every day, it would feel different to work with the occasional abuser or rapist, but as long as my choices and my mobility are limited and constricted in a lot of ways because of my concern for my personal safety from men, it's not good for me, as a woman, to work with men who perpetrate violence.
                                                                (Therapist #98)

I do not work with violent offenders because I'm afraid.   (Therapist #159)

It seems like another element of perpetration if a woman is working with abusers day in and day out; she is a member of the group they have targeted.
                                                                (Therapist #95)

I learned a lot about confrontation and I did some successful work, but I don't enjoy it. Taking power in a way that I don't enjoy, and the confrontation . . . it really doesn't suit my personality.   (Therapist #22)

I will not work in isolation with an abuser. . . . I don't think I've got enough power usually to really take that on. I'm talking physical abuse. Emotional or verbal abuse, I have no problem. But if there's ongoing physical or sexual abuse, usually with those particular individuals, it takes such harsh confrontation and I think it needs a different style than what I have. I'm not afraid to confront, but it's just constant confrontation; and I think it's better done in a group setting or situation. I think it takes a male to carry the credit and the power to have an effect.   (Therapist #123)

I much prefer a model in which men [work with] men who are batterers and abusers.   (Therapist #98)

The gender oppositions of trauma talk positioned women—therapists and clients—as vulnerable and powerless vis-à-vis male abusers. But raw emotions leaked into the interviews, contradicting this image. When it came to abusive men, some therapists felt a tide of righteous rage so powerful that a therapeutic encounter was impossible.

I don't work with rapists and my husband works more with perpetrators of sexual assault or family assault. I find I usually feel too angry with their behavior to really be able to be empathic enough. . . . I'm too sure of my own negative feelings about whatever they've done.   (Therapist #3)

I would not work with men who sexually abuse their children. . . . That's my own anger and I realize that I have this problem. It's like I want to cut off his balls. [Interviewer and therapist both laugh.]   (Therapist #225)

When we look critically at the gender antinomies of trauma talk, a number of questions emerge: Is compassion uniquely and universally womanly? Is confrontation uniquely and universally male? Is the former always and only good for victims? Is the latter always and only good for perpetrators? Are victims always women? Are victims always powerless? If we reject the idea that power is a static quality that individuals either do or do not possess, what alternative metaphors can we conjure? (Cf. Marecek and Kravetz 1998.) What new lines of vision open up? Suppose we borrow from Foucauldian theory and re-vision power as always negotiated, always provisional, and always in motion, circulating through personal relations, institutions, and knowledge structures (cf. Marecek, Fine, and Kidder 1997); how then would the terms *women/powerless/victim* and *man/powerful/victimizer* be realigned? Therapist #159 hesitantly confesses that she has moved toward new ways of working with power:

[Long silence] . . . I started off looking at it as a difference between men and women. You know where men had the power and women didn't. And I don't see it quite that way anymore. It's who's got the power? Where? And how are they using it? You could use it in benign ways. You could also use it in malignant and malevolent ways. I see that women do that. And I look at power of being a victim and how that victimization carries with it a lot of power—the power to control and manipulate.

Conclusion

My goal has been to trace how therapists' language practices construct clinical realities. I do not claim to have produced an exhaustive typology of therapists' language practices. Nor do I claim that all feminist therapists share the linguistic practices of my respondents. Rather, my aim has been to show how specific language practices create certain clinical realities, certain identities, and certain therapeutic practices.

In significant ways, the methods of an inquiry determine its results. Two features of the method deserve comment. One is the sample. The respondents are clinicians whose primary identities are as therapists and whose work is direct service. The voices of practitioners like these are not often heard in the professional clinical literature, nor does the research literature typically document their practices. Most of those who write about feminist therapy are positioned with one foot (sometimes two) in the scholarly world; studies surveying feminist therapists typically gather their respondents from the rosters of professional organizations. Only one of our respondents reported that she belonged to the Feminist Therapy Institute; no one, to the Association for Women in Psychology. Our respondents relied on occasional professional workshops, popular psychology books, and word of mouth for new ideas, not on scholarly or professional literature. Thus, this study complements others in the literature because it looks at a slice of the feminist therapy community that is usually hidden from view.

Another feature of the method is that students served as interviewers. For the most part, the student interviewers stuck closely to the interview protocol; they did not always seek the clarifications that we would have wanted. Nor did we have the opportunity to revise the protocol in response to unexpected trends. For instance, we did not anticipate how much the interviews would center on trauma and its treatment; had we known, we might have amended the interview protocol to ask about these issues directly. Moreover, the therapists were in dialogue with students and no doubt tailored their remarks to their audience. I stand outside their dialogues when I interpret them, working only from tapes and transcripts. This position involves an inescapable but uncomfortable power hierarchy.

A research process in which therapists could comment on and adjust my readings of their words would have been more satisfying.

Whatever the shortcomings of method, the study raises an important question: Why did trauma talk hold such appeal for the feminist therapists who took part in the research? What does it accomplish for feminists, and especially for feminist therapists?

One set of answers may come from situating the groundswell of trauma talk in its historical context. Trauma talk serves to overturn long-standing cultural practices of denying or minimizing the sexual and physical violations of women, practices of not believing (Haaken 1996). For many, trauma talk honors women's reality. As two respondents said:

> I can already hear myself going off onto this sort of lengthy discussion because to me, feminism [in therapy] is certainly primarily about women's issues and women's reality.   (Therapist #120)

> [Do you use feminist therapy in your support groups?] Most of the time, I don't have to say it because the women are saying it themselves and discovering that they are not crazy and they're not alone and maybe it's not necessary to take on so much responsibility for an abusive relationship or for a sexual assault or for what happened in childhood.   (Therapist #106)

The commitment to women's reality closely resembles a venerable epistemological stance in feminist theory: feminist standpoint theory (Harding 1986; Hartsock 1983; 1997). For standpoint theorists, women's knowledge of reality is different from men's. Following Marx, standpoint theorists argue that there are ethical and political reasons for privileging the knowledge of women and other oppressed social groups.

The current state of feminism forms another key part of the context in which our therapists practiced. Mari Jo Buhle (1998) captures what second-wave feminism has become in the 1990s: a "mix-and-match of diverse systems . . . devoid of strong moorings. Indeed feminism itself became in the process less and less a centering concept, turning instead into a secondary premise shifting with the ever changing political moods of the participants" (p. 276). Against this backdrop, the victimization of women offers solid ground, a space of certainty and solidarity, a flagpole around which all feminists (and perhaps all women) can rally. As Janice Haaken (1996) notes, the rubric of trauma holds out the promise of forging unity among feminists.

Feminists in the United States must also contend with an unrelenting media backlash, abetted by a profound cultural swing toward social and economic conservatism. Feminists in clinical practice confront backlash head-on in their everyday work. Many of our respondents, for instance, worried that their overt self-identification as feminists would alienate clients and colleagues, jeopardize referrals, discredit their words, and possibly even put their physical safety at risk. In response, they had come to relegate most feminist values to the far edges of therapy; the only feminist value that was safe to articulate was their intolerance of victimization and physical violence.

> Always I have to accept what [a couple's] mutually agreed upon goals are. Whether or not they would be my goals as a feminist, if those are their goals, then I know I can't impose on those views. What isn't OK with me is abuse and addiction.   (Therapist #98)

> My job as a therapist is to reach their goals as long as they don't involve abuse being let go or ignored.   (Therapist #116)

Exaggerated dichotomies of male and female and the celebration of women's virtue also can be situated in the context of the backlash against feminism. Janis Bohan (1993) has described how gender dichotomies that extol such traditional virtues as women's innocence, caring, and relational orientation can be seen as a response to the anti-feminist backlash of the 1990s.

As Judith Herman (1992) noted, public discussion of wife-beating, rape, and the sexual abuse of children cannot be sustained without a political movement. Acknowledgment of "the common atrocities of sexual and domestic life" (Herman 1992, p. 4) challenges myths of family harmony and patriarchal beneficence, as well as the norm that women should suffer in silence. Furthermore, challenging male violence condenses anxieties about the shifting relations of power between men and women. With its powerful and compelling vocabulary, trauma talk proclaims patriarchal abuse of power; its stark, simplifying rhetoric furnishes a political rallying point.

As a clinical discourse, trauma talk has its limitations. It does not suffice for capturing complexities of motives, meanings, and emotions or the shifting, layered, and ambiguous dimensions of personal relations. Furthermore, when trauma talk enters the clinician's office, it is imprinted with the professional culture of psychotherapy. From a systemic position, we see that oppositional knowledge, whether feminism, postmodernism, or trauma talk, inevitably takes its meanings from that which it opposes. Just as second-wave feminism takes its shape within late-twentieth-century capitalism, trauma talk in the office is framed within the medical model.

Oppositional politics always move under the sign of irony: they stage their fight on a terrain already mapped out by their antagonists.

The project of a feminist constructionist psychology is the critical examination of the practices of the discipline. Psychology's habits of authoritative expertise and its claim of privileged access a single Truth, even when practiced in the name of feminism, should be received with skepticism. This chapter is such a critical examination. I have tried to set up an abrasive interaction between taken-for-granted discourses and some counterdiscourses. I have called attention to therapists' language practices in hopes of showing not only that language constructs reality but also that different language practices shift that reality. As feminists, we need to embrace reflexivity, to incorporate a cultural analysis of our practices into those practices. Whether we are therapists, clients, or researchers, we labor to "get the story right," but we need to remember that there is no story that is right forever and for all.

NOTES

1. Diane Kravetz taught the class, trained and supervised the interviewers, and managed the recruitment of respondents and the collection of the interviews. For more information regarding the methods, see Marecek and Kravetz 1997.

2. The term *medical model* has many meanings in the mental health literature. Therapists in these interviews used the term as a kind of shorthand, without elaborating on what they meant.

3. Whether EMDR actually accomplishes lasting and significant change is highly disputed in the research literature. Moreover, controlled clinical research has found that the rapid eye movements are irrelevant to the treatment outcome. EMDR is thus more parsimoniously explained either as a placebo effect or in terms of well-established principles of exposure therapies (cf. Feske and Goldstein 1997). The brain mechanisms postulated by EMDR's originator (and echoed by our therapists) are almost certainly a red herring.

REFERENCES

Anderson, L., and Gold, K. 1994. "I know what it means but it's not how I feel": The construction of survivor identity in feminist counseling practice. *Women and Therapy* 15, 5–17.

Ballou, M., and Hill, M. 1998. Making therapy feminist. *Women and Therapy* 21, 1–16.

Baur, S. 1995. *Confiding: A psychotherapist and her patients search for stories to live by.* New York: Harper Perennial Library.

Bohan, J. 1993. Regarding gender: Essentialism, constructionism, and feminist psychology. *Psychology of Women Quarterly* 17, 5–22.

Brown, L. 1994. *Subversive dialogues: Theory in feminist therapy.* New York: Basic Books.

Buhle, M. J. 1998. *Feminism and its discontents: A century of struggle with psychoanalysis.* Cambridge, MA: Harvard University Press.

Eliasson, M. 1998. Book review of *Engendering Blame,* by Marian Meyers, *Women and Violence,* edited by Ros Thorpe and Jude Irwin, *Women, Violence, and Male Power,* edited by Marianne Hester, Liz Kelly, and Jill Radford. *Feminism and Psychology* 8, 226–229.

Enns, C. Z. 1997. *Feminist theories and feminist psychotherapies: Origins, themes, and variations.* New York: Haworth.

Feske, U., and Goldstein, A. J. 1997. Eye movement desensitization and reprocessing treatment for panic disorder: A controlled outcome and partial dismantling study. *Journal of Consulting and Clinical Psychology* 65, 1026–1035.

Guilford, P. 1996. The normalizing effects of managed care on patients and therapists: What would Foucault make of managed care? Paper presented at the meeting of the American Psychological Association, August, Toronto, Canada.

Haaken, J. 1996. The recovery of memory, fantasy, and desire: Feminist approaches to sexual abuse and psychic trauma. *Signs* 21, 1069–1094.

———. 1998. *Pillar of salt: Gender, memory, and the perils of looking back.* New Brunswick, NJ: Rutgers University Press.

Harding, S. 1986. *The science question in feminism.* Ithaca, NY: Cornell University Press.

Hare-Mustin, R., and Marecek, J. 1990. *Making a difference: Psychology and the construction of gender.* New Haven, CT: Yale University Press.

———. 1994. Feminism and postmodernism: Dilemmas and points of resistance. *Dulwich Centre Newsletter* 4, 13–19.

Hartsock, N. C. M. 1983. The feminist standpoint: Developing the ground for a specifically feminist historical materialism. In S. Harding and M. Hintikka (eds.), *Discovering reality: Feminist perspectives on epistemology, metaphysics, methodology, and philosophy* (pp. 283–310). Dordrecht, The Netherlands: Reidel/Kluwer.

———. 1997. Comment on Hekman's "Truth and method": Feminist standpoint theory revisited: Truth or justice? *Signs* 22, 367–374.

Herman, J. L. 1992 *Trauma and recovery.* New York: Basic Books.

hooks, b. 1989. *Talking back: Thinking feminist, thinking black.* Boston: South End Press.

Lerman, H., and Porter, N. 1990. *Feminist ethics in psychotherapy.* New York: Springer.

Marecek, J.; Fine, M.; and Kidder, L. 1997. Working between worlds: Qualitative methods and social psychology. *Journal of Social Issues* 53, 631–644.

Marecek, J., and Hare-Mustin, R. 1991. A short history of the future: Feminism and clinical psychology. *Psychology of Women Quarterly* 15, 521–536.

Marecek, J., and Kravetz, D. 1997. Power and agency in feminist therapy. In C. Heenan and I. B. Seu (eds.), *Contemporary feminist psychotherapies: Reflections on theory and practice* (pp. 13–29). London: Sage.

———. 1998. Putting power into practice: Feminist therapy as feminist praxis. *Women and Therapy* 21, 17–36.

Potter, J. 1996. Discourse analysis and constructionist approaches: Theoretical background. In J. T. E. Richardson (ed.), *Handbook of qualitative research methods* (pp. 125–140). Leicester, England: BPS Books.

Reinharz, S. 1992. *Feminist methods in social research.* New York: Oxford University Press.

Shapiro, F. 1995. *Eye movement, desensitization and reprocessing: Basic principles, protocols, and procedures.* New York: Guilford.

Siegler, M., and Osmond, H. 1974. *Models of madness, models of medicine.* New York: Macmillan.

Wyche, K. F., and Rice, J. K. 1997. Feminist therapy: From dialogue to tenets. In J. Worell and N. G. Johnson (eds.), *Shaping the future of feminist psychology: Education, research, practice* (pp. 57–72). Washington, DC: American Psychological Association.

Chapter Eight

Victims, Backlash, and Radical Feminist Theory

(or, The Morning after They Stole Feminism's Fire)

Chris Atmore

> Good social theorists are painfully aware of the complexity of the phenomena they seek to explain, and honest researchers tend to be suspicious of single-factor explanations, no matter how beguiling.
>
> (Sommers 1994, 234)

In the last few years, several popular cultural commentators who identify themselves as feminists or at least claim sympathy with feminist views have become prominent in the media: for example, Naomi Wolf, Katie Roiphe, Christina Hoff Sommers, and Camille Paglia. In one way the media feminist phenomenon is not new—Kate Millett, Gloria Steinem, and Germaine Greer were, somewhat controversially, feminist "stars" in the 1960s (although the media have proliferated considerably since then). However, some of the more recent media feminists have not simply espoused their particular views about women and gender but have publicly criticized individual feminists and aspects of feminist theory, in the process claiming a kind of dissident status for themselves—"I am a feminist, but...." This has been especially pronounced in relation to sexual violence. Paglia, Roiphe, Sommers, and Wolf, whom I refer to collectively from here on as "the media feminists," tend to single out this topic as the epitome of everything that they claim is "wrong" with much contemporary feminism, or "victim feminism" as they tend to rename it.[1]

Feminist reaction to this has been varied. Many women, especially those working against rape and child sexual abuse, have responded with anger and dismissal, characterizing the claims as media aspects of a larger "backlash" to feminist gains, more damaging this time because they come from women claiming feminist affiliation. However, any simple notion of backlash is quite problematic. Lumping together all four of the media feminists as backlash writers neglects the ways in which they differ from one another; for instance, it seems unfair to class Wolf with Paglia over the subject of date rape and intellectually wrong to equate the arguments of Sommers with those of Paglia. The work of each woman—including, importantly, not just published books but her media oeuvre—is also more helpfully read as embodying multiple and even contradictory themes; and here it may be more than coincidental that all these figures have become successful and influential in the popular arena.

There is a further reason for being cautious about the label of "backlash," which is linked to the idea that we are in a new era of sexual violence politics. Feminist theory and practice against sexual violence, like the abuse itself, are more accurately thought of as multiple phenomena, taking a range of shapes in many different places, with varying histories and landmark conflicts, including across intellectual disciplines and national boundaries. However, overall, in western societies such as the United States, Britain, Australia, and New Zealand, we can look back on three decades of feminist work (at least in what we might describe as the "modern phase"). As a result, western feminists are to some degree in a different position from the one we occupied in the 1970s. Sexual violences do not seem to have decreased in extent, but we have achieved some success in turning the "private" areas of intimate violence into public concerns.

It certainly cannot be argued any longer that the mass media ignore issues of violence against women and children. Not only are there more nonfictional representations than ever before—documentaries, talk shows and women's magazine articles—but subjects such as incest have become a ubiquitous plot device in made-for-TV movies, police dramas, and soap operas. It is difficult—and, I would argue, inappropriate—to try to classify all of this plainly as either a good or a bad thing for feminist initiatives against violence. Before we can try to make sense of the current proliferation of media images, we need to think about the changes that have taken place since the 1960s and the varying contexts in which they have occurred.

For instance, suppose we agreed that at least some of the media attention to sexual violence is positive—for example, a newspaper item that does not sexualize a young rape survivor but condemns the crime and concentrates on the fact that her convicted father was a "pillar of the community." The credit for this construction of the meaning of incest might lie partly with the court case and perhaps with the expert witness about the dynamics of father rape, since feminist theory and practice have at least begun to make some tracks through fields such as psychology and law. But we might also attribute this breakthrough to the increased presence of feminist journalists. To put it more broadly, the realms of "feminism" and "media" are not nearly so distinct from one another these days; it is no longer just about "the media" interviewing feminist collectives often quite hostile to the mainstream press but, more commonly now, a situation where many people are likely to be strategically media savvy—including, of course, the new kind of media feminists.

Finally, "backlash" already makes a judgment that we cannot possibly have anything to learn or be responsible for as far as the victim feminism charges are concerned, a theme that this chapter wants to explore rather than prejudge. To make the topic manageable, I focus on what the four media feminists have to say about victim feminism in relation to rape specifically. However, even that is a large topic, and as I have already suggested, in the complex modern field of sexual violence politics, it is not possible to produce one, monolithic account of the issue, appropriate for all contexts.

Another hypothetical but not unfamiliar example helps make this clear. A self-identified abuse survivor, her husband, and her therapist all appear on a TV talk show. A media feminist cites this as another form of proof of victim feminism. Even if we were to agree at least partly that the "survivor" came across chiefly as a victim (and it is hard to predict without knowing the details), where does the responsibility for that lie? The problem may lie in aspects of professional practice, in the discourses and therapies offered by mainstream, radical, and New Age psychologies and psychotherapies. As with the media, which are involved again here, these practices intersect with but are not identical to feminism by any means, as some other contributors to this book address.

To untangle these influences means also to think again about historical change; so it could be argued, along lines similar to Louise Armstrong's (1994), that this kind of talk-show appearance is typical of a much larger, end-of-millennium (particularly U.S.?) "victim culture," which is not ultimately shaped by the feminist interests that originally brought incest to public notice. Similarly, in other examples, victim feminism might be a media artifact due to the necessity for feminist campaigners to play the news game or a similar effect of feminist lawyers having to produce the perfect witness in court battles.

The idea that the North American context might be influential in the talk-show example also provides a note of caution about cross-cultural overgeneralizing in any exploration of what "victim feminism" might actually mean. Charges of victim feminism cross the borders of several western countries, often, in a complicated fashion yet to be charted, by way of some of the same American texts (see, e.g., Garner 1995; Guy 1996; Atmore, forthcoming). However, it is not clear to me, as a New Zealander working in Australia and contributing to an American book, that, as just one illustration, the politics and practices of campus feminism can be easily typified across national boundaries or even within them, although there are important and interesting connections. If we take the plurality of feminisms and sexual violences seriously, perhaps we should acknowledge, in a rethinking of "sisterhood as global," that variously focused inquiries are necessary, and consequently, where politics and theory are found inadequate, diverse strategies might be required.

I am particularly interested in what the media feminists actually take "victim feminism" to mean and what aspects of "victim theory" can be laid at the feet of radical feminist theorists, who were largely the original activists and thinkers on rape.[2] In other words, even if we concede that there are at least some grains of truth in the charges that the media feminists make, to what extent does the fault lie in the body of work from the late 1970s and 1980s, when writing and action against rape began to proliferate? My own, consequently limited investigation mainly concentrates on the victim theory charges as they are made in relation to the "original" radical feminist ideas about rape, in Camille Paglia's *Sexual Personae* (1990), *Sex, Art, and American Culture* (1992), and *Vamps and Tramps* (1994); Katie Roiphe's *The Morning After* (1994); Christina Hoff Sommers's *Who Stole Feminism?* (1994); and Naomi Wolf's *Fire with Fire* (1993). I start by considering the views that the media feminists appear to hold in common, before dealing in more depth with some of the particularities of their arguments, focusing especially on Paglia. Radical feminism is not an undifferentiated body of thought either, and I restrict myself to some ideas from one American theorist whose work I find especially interesting and who is often singled out as an archetypal radical feminist on rape, Catharine MacKinnon. I conclude by reflecting again on the relevance of the broader cultural context.

Reading the Media Feminists

Lest my resolve to approach the media feminist texts in a spirit of intellectual inquiry sound dispassionate, it is important here to make some comment about the process of reading this kind of work. As a feminist academic working on sexual violence issues in the 1990s and an activist against
rape, pornography, and child abuse in the 1980s, only recently could I bring
myself to read these books at all. I simply could not get past my fury and
distress any earlier, a reaction no doubt easily explained by the authors but
nonetheless characteristic of an era that still awaits more sympathetic cultural analysis. The texts themselves, to varying degrees, evoke at least for
this reader other, more public experiences of trying to "discuss" political issues when one's opponent (as that is how it is set up) does not fight fair.
There is a feeling of insufficient space, and the translation devices necessary
for meaningful dialogue have not been, and perhaps cannot be, invented.
At times, when reading the worst excesses of this anti-canon, I find myself
in the place to which I inevitably move when faced with a particular male
colleague who lets loose so many objectionable points on the way to his
main argument that sometimes the only recourse is to end the communication, for want of knowing how and where to begin.

If I had to rank the media feminists according to their proposals of a reactionary agenda, beginning with the most conservative, I would list Sommers (the most clearly tied to a broad, right-wing, anti-PC response, for
which "backlash" does seem apt), followed by Paglia, Roiphe, and Wolf. It
seems hard to let so many things pass unchallenged in pursuit of my own,
more limited goal. Yet, at the same time, I am surprised to find that there
are aspects in all the works that I can enjoy or at least some speck of truth
I can relate to, however small and uncomfortable. Even Sommers strikes the
odd chord for me, although Wolf discusses similar examples with more nu-
ance. As Adrienne Rich (1989) expresses it in "I read you always, even when
I hated you," the reader is offered a form of intellectual and political work-
out, signified also, in more benign form, by bell hooks's (1994, 92–93) evo-
cation of the productive energy that arose from her rigorous exchanges
with different feminisms as a teacher and learner. And I wonder if my
unanticipated response is an element of a new zeitgeist in which at least
some feminism now plays more of a part. Like the state of feminism and
media and sexual violence activism, it becomes less and less possible to talk
about distinct spheres and more and more necessary to engage across traditional boundaries, even if that is risky.[3]

Nevertheless, there is something excruciatingly galling about offering academic courtesy to some of these arguments. To take a perhaps extreme example: Camille Paglia's article in *Vamps and Tramps* "The Return of Carry Nation: Catharine MacKinnon and Andrea Dworkin" (Paglia 1994, 107–112) promises at first sight to be a direct address of radical feminist claims. But "Carry Nation," originally written for *Playboy*, is an extraordinary piece, even by Paglia's now well known standards. In it lies in miniature one of the key problems in Paglia's work as a whole: the reader traces the many crossed threads in the text to find that, ultimately, they have so many cut ends that they pull away, leaving little of any substance on which to base coherent criticism. The composition of "Carry Nation" in particular is an almost entirely and notably vicious personal invective, liberally laced with misogyny and anti-Semitism projected at MacKinnon and Dworkin. Perhaps my immersion in Janet Malcolm's (1990; 1995) literary-psychoanalytic journalistic investigations over the same time period as I interpreted Paglia influenced me in this, but it would surely be hard for even a cursory glance at "Carry Nation" to avoid a diagnostic reading of this vitriolic attack on "anti-porn feminists" and all they apparently stand (in) for in Paglia's psychic lexicon.

As with a small, bony fish that needs treatment before it can be digested, one begins the task only to wonder if the final sustenance justifies the effort. What is even more difficult to swallow is the fact of this type of work being taken up with alacrity by not only the media and publishing industry but some elements in academia. The flow-on effects include, as just one illustration, a published academic friend of mine having her article on date rape rejected by a prestigious psychology journal partly on the grounds that she had not considered Roiphe's book.

Consequently, my argument for treating seriously even the worst of the media feminist claims, and so indirectly adding to their circulation, rests mainly on their having made such a public splash, however unjust that is when one considers all the excellent feminist work that is only belatedly recognized, if at all. And while I do not want to suspend all judgment about merit and skill, there is a case to be made for treating popular and academic texts as equally important sources of ideas in their own rights. Many would say, in fact, that the former are more influential and that therefore those of us who work in universities should be doing more to engage in this forum, rather than treating the media with more traditional left-wing disdain (hooks 1994, 74–75, 89–90; Paglia 1992, ix).

As I read the media feminists closely, I found myself thinking about how to put them all onto some kind of chart. (Blame it on too many radical feminist brainstorming sessions, perhaps.) For example, Paglia the libertarian shares much with the revolutionary left that power feminist Wolf finds wanting; conservative Sommers and, in some ways, sexual radical Paglia agree on many things. Paglia's equal opportunity feminism, Sommers's nostalgia for true equity feminists, and Wolf's power feminism are cut from the same cloth. (In fact, liberal feminism is generally the only feminism allocated an honorable history, worthy of scholarly appreciation, in this writing.) Sommers, Paglia, and Roiphe seem to belong to a mutual admiration society, with Wolf more of an outsider—even at times reviled, especially by Paglia, for her earlier, more orthodox feminist work.

All the media feminists dislike, if not actively despise, postmodernist and poststructuralist theories[4] and the ways in which these have been taken up by some academic feminists (e.g., Paglia 1992, ix; 1994, xv; Roiphe 1994, 113–114; Wolf 1993, 136–137). In contrast, my approach here takes several useful conceptual tools from postmodernist feminism (Alcoff 1997). This nexus offers to me the possibility of feminist theories and practices that, as with the best of other kinds of feminist scholarship, are less totalizing in their categorization of gender and sexuality and opposed to simplistic binary choices, such as "agent or victim"—a strategy actually very much in line with the media writers' claimed commitments to a more open feminism.

In particular, the concept of "discourse" is useful to appreciate the contemporary field of sexual violence politics. A discourse can be understood as a historically, socially, and institutionally specific structure of statements, terms, categories, and beliefs (Scott 1988, 35). With the explosion of sexual violence issues into public life, relevant discourses have proliferated. For instance, radical feminism and psychology, in their different but overlapping ways, have helped produce what we might call a discourse of the raped woman, in which she is constructed as having been injured but not at fault. Certain forms of language—for instance, in court testimony, compensation claims, and autobiographical narratives—show signs of this discourse. (See also Gavey 1989.) Mainstream psychology and radical feminism then tend to part company, according to their own specific goals and strategies; employing their own discourses; so that, for example, the radical feminist discourse of the raped woman uses the term *survivor*, in contrast to the more common, psychological use of *victim*, even those two words alone implying significant differences. But as Michel Foucault (1980) first argued, no one can claim exclusive ownership of a discourse, and in fact, increasingly, they are taken up and reused as weapons against their original wielders. Of particular relevance here is the way in which the notion of victimhood has become associated not only with someone on the receiving end of violence but with figures such as the "falsely accused" father and the family represented as unfairly persecuted by child protection authorities (Atmore 1994a; 1996).

Discourses are therefore becoming more confused in the ways in which they overlap and contradict one another, and in a field of contestation such as sexual violence politics, we are all increasingly implicated in one another's logic—as with my use of Sommers's words in the epigraph to this chapter. This gives a more pertinent and complex meaning to the idea of backlash. Just as there is no longer any easily classifiable "them" versus "us" in relation to feminism and the media, there is no feminist discursive tactic that we can rest assured will remain exclusively "ours."

The postmodern strategy of deconstructive criticism can sensitize us to these traces of the same rhetoric in ostensibly opposing camps. Deconstructing a written narrative entails using contradictions and gaps in logic to "read against" the obvious story of the text for what other interpretations might be made of it—in other words, ferreting out the unofficial meanings (Grosz 1989; Norris 1988). The concept of deconstruction can therefore encourage the critic to examine accounts of sexual violence for the various political interests that may be, even unconsciously, advanced in them (Atmore 1995; 1997). Through this kind of analysis, we can examine both the media feminists' arguments and the endeavors of feminists working against sexual violence—and pay attention to the specific nuances of time and place that produced this state of affairs.

The Media Feminists on Radical Feminism and Rape

The themes of Paglia, Roiphe, and Sommers have much in common with arguments that have been used in sexual violence controversies in a range of cultural contexts since at least the early 1980s (Atmore 1995; 1996; Campbell 1988; Mead 1997). When it comes to their views on rape, several textual strategies tend to characterize the media feminists as a group, although Wolf is a partial exception. The attack on "gender feminists" (Sommers 1994), or "the current feminist sensibility" (Roiphe 1994, 7) tends first to center on accusing this group of producing and using false research statistics about the extent of sexual violence. These inflated figures are held responsible for the overzealous implementation of regulatory practices such as codes against sexual harassment, therapeutic treatment, and welfare agency intervention.

The media feminists argue that the root of the "wrong data" problem is the way in which the concept of rape is constructed. Gender feminists define the term so broadly that it becomes meaningless, so that even "normal" men and everyday heterosexuality are impugned. It therefore follows that this misleading and, in the view of media feminists, even willfully deceptive picture must be allied to "man-hating" or "man-bashing" feminism (read "radical feminism," lesbianism optional) and harnessed to a bigger feminist agenda. For instance:

> High rape numbers serve the gender feminists by promoting the belief that American culture is sexist and misogynist.   (Sommers 1994, 222)

The idea that a radically revised view of rape fuels radical feminist conspiracy appears in the way in which Paglia, Sommers, Roiphe, and to a lesser degree Wolf offer personal anecdotes about "Take Back the Night" demonstrations or anti-rape speak-outs (e.g., Roiphe 1994, 34–38). In these depictions, the media feminists express disquiet that all the stories begin to seem to sound the same, as if the women have been brainwashed into participating in "the spectacle of mass confession" (Roiphe 1994, 43).

This project is decried as a failed attempt to prove that the world is divided into a strict, dominator/dominated gender dualism, in which, for example, all men are said to be rapists and women are thereby deemed innocent victims, worthy of "special protections" (Sommers 1994, 52). For instance, Roiphe criticizes the image of women supposedly promoted by these feminists:

> women as victims, offended by a professor's dirty joke, verbally pressured into sex by peers . . . a delicate woman . . . her passivity, her wide-eyed innocence . . . perpetually offended by sexual innuendo . . . her excessive need for protection.   (Roiphe 1994, 6)

Similarly, Wolf describes "victim feminism" as "a set of beliefs that cast women as beleaguered, fragile, intuitive angels" (Wolf 1993, 147).

Obviously, many of the media feminist indictments relate to the fields of campus feminism, professional victim services, and research methodologies and must be addressed from those positions. But how precisely are radical feminist theorists implicated in the victim feminism charges as they relate to rape? Take Catharine MacKinnon, for example, as a representative of radical feminism. The media feminists do not focus on MacKinnon in much detail, apart from her anti-pornography work (e.g., Paglia 1994; Roiphe 1994). And even here, it is difficult to avoid the conclusion that her critics have drawn on their attendances at public lectures rather than an in-depth scrutiny of her published arguments. For example, Paglia (1994) describes MacKinnon's work as "totalitarian" but does not elucidate, though we perhaps get some clue in another statement that "all intrusion by authority figures into sex is totalitarian" (1994, 23). Paglia also characterizes MacKinnon's writing as "dry, bleached, parched" (1994, 109). This latter depiction seems at odds with the MacKinnon who claims that she is "not saying that viewpoints have genitals" (MacKinnon 1987a, 77)—an aphorism diametrically opposed to Paglia's view but still a pithy sound bite that the latter might wish to have authored in other circumstances.[5]

It is clear that the media feminists tend to misinterpret or ignore radical feminist theory. For example, Roiphe presents her *The Morning After* as "not a political polemic" (Roiphe 1994, 6–7) but goes on to say that she has

> written what I see, limited, personal, but entirely real. I have written my impressions. This book comes out of frustration, out of anger.   (7)

It would be hard for any feminist with more than a passing familiarity with second-wave feminism to hear the words *political* and *personal* without going on to associate them, as in "the personal is political." This link between individual women's lives and political theory was forged mainly through women-only consciousness-raising groups of the late 1960s and 1970s. In these groups, which MacKinnon (1989, 7–8) identifies as central to radical feminist method, women began by expressing individual feelings and then used collective scrutiny of those personal experiences to build feminist theory.

In a similar obfuscation of radical feminist ideas, Paglia (1990; 1992) argues that feminists are wrong to say that rape is about violence and power and not (also) sex. Here Paglia elides any possible differences among sources such as MacKinnon, Susan Brownmiller's (1975) *Against Our Will*, and graffiti in university women students' toilets,[6] and refers instead to "the feminist rape discourse" (Paglia 1994, 32). However, illustrating that all "gender feminists" are not alike, MacKinnon actually criticizes Brownmiller's analysis, arguing that it is epistemologically liberal rather than radical and that the problem of rape in masculinist societies is precisely that sex and violence/power cannot be radically distinguished. Rather, it is the myth that they can be that helps keep rape regulated rather than outlawed (MacKinnon 1989).

So Paglia and MacKinnon agree on the intertwining of sex and violence.[7] Some Paglian excerpts, with a little judicious editing, could, in fact, easily be mistaken for MacKinnon; for example:

> The problem with America's current preoccupation with child abuse is that cultural taboos automatically eroticize what is forbidden. Marking off zones of purity increases their desirability and ensures their profanation. . . . The enormous publicity about child abuse has certainly increased safety awareness, but I doubt it has lowered the crime rate.   (Paglia 1994, 34)

In comparison, MacKinnon argues that statutory rape laws are paternalistic in their protectiveness and also eroticize sexual contact with children as "taboo" (MacKinnon 1983, 648; 1989; 175–176). Such ostensible prohibition "may serve to eroticize what would otherwise feel about as much like dominance as taking candy from a baby" (MacKinnon 1987b, 71).

What, then, makes Paglia's view different from MacKinnon's radical feminism? The media feminists claim that victim feminism subscribes to gender dualism—men as somehow always rapists and women, just as inevitably, as preyed upon. In its crudest form, gender dualism is biologically essentialist, implying that men and women are just "naturally" the way they are and so things cannot change. Men, unqualified, everywhere, can't help being more aggressive—it's their hormones, their evolutionary drive to procreate, ad hominem (literally). But if MacKinnon's stance is to be characterized by Paglia as victim theory, it certainly cannot be on the grounds of biological essentialism, without implicating Paglia herself. Paglia claims "the truth in sexual stereotypes" and "the biologic basis of sex differences" (Paglia 1990, xiii, 24), whereas MacKinnon states categorically about gender inequality, "The good news is, it isn't biological" (1987b, 80).

MacKinnon therefore also disagrees with Brownmiller again, as do many feminists working against sexual violence, over the latter's tendency to offer a biologically essentialist explanation about the origins of rape. While, to be fair, Brownmiller does not devote much attention to the question, she suggests that when men discovered they *could* rape women due to the differences between male and female anatomy, they then proceeded to do so.[8] But Paglia's stance is similar to Brownmiller's here: the description of women as "physically lack[ing] the equipment for sexual violence" comes from *Sexual Personae* (Paglia 1990, 24), not from Brownmiller's *Against Our Will*. Paglia therefore argues that rape and sadism occur throughout history and cultures, and this is because violent impulses come from nature, not society, which must do its best to regulate them:

> When social controls weaken, man's innate cruelty bursts forth. The rapist is
> created not by bad social influences but by a failure of social conditioning.
> Feminists, seeking to drive power relations out of sex, have set themselves
> against nature.   (Paglia 1990, 2)

If Paglia's overt biological essentialism distinguishes her from radical
feminism, aspects of her stance on rape also separate her from her media
feminist peers. The argument against victim feminism from Roiphe, Sommers, and Wolf centers on its claim that oppositions between evil rapists
and innocent women assume a basic, innate gender dualism. In contrast,
for Paglia, some basic notion of opposite sexes grounded in nature puts the
zing into everything from personal interactions to the creation of sky-
scrapers and great art (e.g., Paglia 1990, 17). As sex and violence are also in-
terwoven in Paglia's—here decidedly unliberal—worldview, she must still
distinguish her position from the "high rape numbers" victim camp, which
suggests that the endemic character of rape is part of a broader domina-
tor/dominated dynamic in which the man/woman dualism plays a crucial
part. Paglia's view is potentially open to charges of an even greater pes-
simism, given that rape comes from nature and so, presumably, is inevitable.

Paglia therefore argues, in effect, that rape is not so bad, both in terms of
redefining individual experiences that radical feminists would want to call
rape and in terms of rape's broader impact on societies. Rape, for Paglia, is
part of the larger rough-and-tumble of the relationship between the genders, or "the sex game" (Paglia 1992, 54), without which there would be no
potent forms of sexual attraction or (male) creativity. Rape becomes the
price "we"—society—pay for great art, as only men can be sex murderers
because only men can be great creators, and vice versa (Paglia 1990,
246–247). In addition, if Paglia had her way, only rape by a stranger or in-
volving the "forcible intrusion of sex into a nonsexual context" (Paglia 1994,
24) would deserve the name.[9] In feminist social science terms, this is the
atypical rape. The definition of rape is therefore greatly narrowed (just like,
one assumes, the incidence of truly great art). Rape becomes restricted to
the acts of comparatively few, but sane, "criminals" (Paglia 1994; see also
Sommers 1994), men who have not been successfully trained to be "ethical"
(Paglia 1992, 72).

Further undermining any claim about victimization as a significant gendered phenomenon, Paglia agrees with her media feminist peers that notions of "good" and "evil" have no predictable group affiliation. In particular, even if women cannot rape, Paglia does not see sexual domination as a

one-way dynamic of man over woman. For instance, during sex itself, "one domination dissolves into another. The dominated becomes the dominator" (Paglia 1990, 26).

As for Sommers (1994, 194–200) and other revisionists of the figures on domestic violence, if each "side" does it to the other, Paglia takes this to undercut any legitimate claims about "victims," and therefore "special protections for women" are "infantilizing and anti-democratic" (Paglia 1994, x). As "the sexes are eternally at war" (Paglia 1990, 26), this also means that even those women who are raped are targeted because women are powerful: rape is "male power fighting female power" (Paglia 1990, 23):

> Rape is an act of desperation, a confession of envy and exclusion. . . . Every boy must stagger out of the shadow of a mother goddess, whom he never fully escapes.   (Paglia 1994, 32)

Indeed, Paglia suggests that women are more powerful than men; for example:

> Women must accept their own ambivalence in order to wield their birthright of dominion over men.   (Paglia 1994, 38)

> Nature gives males infusions of hormones for dominance in order to hurl them against the paralyzing mystery of woman, from whom they would otherwise shrink. Her power as mistress of birth is already too extreme.
> (Paglia 1990, 24)

For this argument to make any sense,[10] it must rest again on a small incidence of "real" rape—the price women pay for being powerful, apparently:

> "She made me do it": this strange assertion by rapists expresses man's sense of subservience to woman's sexual allure. The rapist feels enslaved, insignificant: women seem enclosed, impervious. . . . Men are tormented by women's flirtatiousness.   (Paglia 1994, 35)

> Sex crime is revenge against women as an abstract class for wounds already suffered by men as a class—the wound of birth and its consequent galling dependencies.   (Paglia 1994, 37)

"Sense of subservience"? "Enslaved, insignificant"? "Tormented"? "Wounds"? "Dependencies"? The male rapist becomes the victim. Paglia's apparent reframing is typical of the broader contemporary reuse of the original feminist discourse of victimization.[11]

At the same time, even here Paglia's claims resonate with some radical feminist insights. When I read that women are raped because of their powerful, provoking link to nature and mystery, which the rapist feels compelled to try to unveil, as exemplified by the actions of Jack the Ripper (Paglia 1990, 22–23), I think of Deborah Cameron and Elizabeth Frazer's underappreciated analysis of sexual murder and its connections to western thought, *The Lust to Kill* (1987), and the stance of feminist critic of masculinist science Evelyn Fox Keller (1982; 1983; 1986). These feminist scholars, along with MacKinnon, argue that the problem of male domination and its links to sexual objectification and violence goes much deeper than power disparities between flesh-and-blood men and women. Science, philosophy, literature, and, indeed, perhaps any powerful contribution to western cultural frameworks are built on a romanticized notion of the questing, "objective" male hero, who wrests knowledge and truth from a feminized object, often sexually dominating "her" in the process.[12] Sexual violence here becomes more than only individual, one-against-one acts and instead is deeply implicated in the broader culture, which produces and celebrates "the joy of violation and destruction" and an "aesthetics and erotics of profanation" (Paglia 1990, 24).

Paglia makes these links in order to celebrate them but then risks falling down her own slippery definitional slope, trying to keep "real rape" in place as uncommon and as unrelated to the normative. As a last resort, she would say that it is only natural, after all, and so, drawing from the same well as artistic creativity and heterosexual attraction, is not nearly as great a problem as radical feminists argue. But what happens if we take the props of "nature" and "biology" away?

The key difference between Paglia and MacKinnon-esque feminism here is that Paglia takes dominant practices and worldviews as the way things simply must be. In contrast, here is MacKinnon answering the charge that a radical feminist view of sexual violence stereotypes women as victims:

> If this [victim] stereotype is a stereotype, it has already been *accomplished*,
> and I come after.   (MacKinnon 1987a, 220, my emphasis)

In MacKinnon's view, male power "extends beneath the representation of reality to its construction" and so confirms "its way of being and its vision of truth, as it creates the social reality that supports both" (MacKinnon 1989, 122). To put it more succinctly, male power is "a myth that makes itself true" (MacKinnon 1989, 104). MacKinnon's theory is therefore concerned with the question of how to know the world differently—including how to understand rape—when that world is "gendered to the ground"

(MacKinnon 1983, 655). This means the available tools of critique, such as scientific "objectivity" toward studying nature, artistic appreciation, and intellectual inquiry in general, are also not untainted in any simple way.

Radical Feminism on Rape: Catharine MacKinnon

MacKinnon states quite emphatically that not only is society gendered to the ground, as the related critiques of science and broader Enlightenment thought argue, but gender is also social, all the way down. The gender binary is actually constructed and enforced, rather than inevitable, and this includes biology-as-we-tend-to-know-it. Gender, through processes of sexuality, is something that is "done"; hence it is at least possible for it to be undone, or perhaps done differently, in ways that do not automatically involve dominance. This suggests that male and female bodies are not the resisting bedrock to a revolutionary deconstruction of gender that they are made out to be by conservatives and liberals alike.

MacKinnon argues that rape is central to this understanding of gender. She sees the man/woman dualism as inextricably associated with the respective positions of dominator and dominated, and she ascribes a motor force to processes of sexuality in the constitution of gender. Putting these two arguments together, "forced sex as sexuality is not exceptional in relations between the sexes but constitutes the social meaning of gender" (MacKinnon 1989, 178). MacKinnon goes on to quote Carolyn Shafer and Marilyn Frye:[13]

> "Rape is a man's act, whether it is a male or a female man and whether it is a man relatively permanently or relatively temporarily; and being raped is a woman's experience, whether it is a female or a male woman and whether it is a woman relatively permanently or relatively temporarily." To be rapable, a position that is social not biological, defines what a woman is.
>
> (MacKinnon 1989, 178)

I concentrate for the moment on what the argument about gender implies for the overall argument about rape, rather than the other way around. Taking into account the vast incidence of sexual violence that does follow the blueprint of the rapist in a male body and the raped person as biologically female, it seems logical to describe rape as a feminizing act for the victim and a masculinizing one for the rapist. But this is still the case when the sex of the bodies is a different combination, as it sometimes is (and bearing in mind that there are many more men who are raped than women who are rapists). So, for example, we are not surprised when a man who has been raped attributes some of the trauma to being "made to feel like a woman," while it is highly unlikely that a female rape survivor would describe her experience in "opposite sex" terms. Rape is something that involves and even creates gender, independent of, or at least partly autonomous from, the bodies of rapist and raped—and thus, "a man relatively permanently or relatively temporarily," "a female or a male woman."[14]

At the level of individuals, therefore, gender is fluid to some extent; just as it is a construction in broader societal patterns. Gender involves a domination dynamic that travels—across bodies and from individual practices to traditions of objectivity and further to broader Enlightenment thought. This contrasts to the rather more pedestrian view of gender adhered to by Paglia, Sommers, and Roiphe, and which is the basis for these critics to bring up examples of "women as violent too" and of men raping men, as if this must necessarily undermine the radical feminist critique of rape as a gendered—and gendering—process.

It is therefore no coincidence that the media feminists ignore, or at best misinterpret, the other concept crucial to radical feminist arguments about male violence against women: compulsory heterosexuality. Adrienne Rich's (1980) theory of heterosexuality as an institution that is political but critically neglected (including by feminist theorists) implicates the widespread use and threat of force by men against women as a key strategy in maintaining women's participation in heterosexual relationships. In turn, MacKinnon suggests (drawing on Rich, who herself cites MacKinnon's 1979 *Sexual Harassment of Working Women*) that the assumed naturalness and superiority of heterosexuality is closely bound up with the domination of masculine over feminine, in which "the sexes" are not just complementary but in a hierarchical relationship (MacKinnon 1982; 1983; 1987b). Gender as hierarchy is therefore eroticized; or as MacKinnon puts it, inequality is sexy.

In this closed system, it does not make sense to call something rape when it also appears to be sex-as-usual and when it involves normative ideas about gendered behavior. Hence MacKinnon's (1989) well-known critique of whether consent can be regarded as a meaningful concept when sex is taken to mean something that men do to women. One need not read this, as it appears the media feminists do, as saying that women are incapable of consent but rather as pointing out that in a context of normative heterosexuality, with its close ties to masculinist domination, even feminist-motivated tinkering with how "consent" is thought about will take us only so far.

In contrast, the media feminists subscribe to an at best liberal tolerance of alternatives to an implicitly privileged heterosexuality; a classic live-and-let-live attitude to "minorities." The subtext of all of these works is an assumed and unquestioned heterosexual attraction as the basis for the vast majority of women needing to get along with men, and hence the liberal feminist dilemma.[15] Even Naomi Wolf (1993, 74–78), who at least criticizes "dyke baiting," does so because she views it as a distraction from feminist issues, rather than, as Rich argues, central to an understanding of them.

Problematizing MacKinnon's Approach

Certainly, radical feminist arguments have problematic aspects. For instance, MacKinnon's analysis clearly prioritizes gender over other forms of oppression, rather than producing a theoretical framework of cross-cutting dimensions of power, perhaps variably relevant depending on the particular context (cf. hooks 1990, 57–64; Crenshaw 1993). Even within this gender reductionist stance, the oppression of women is constantly traced back to coercive sexuality as the primary cause. At first glance, it looks as if it might be possible to sidestep many of these kinds of criticisms by saying that such objections are not clearly made by the media feminists, and that I am interested more here in what MacKinnon says about rape than in her overall theory of women's subordination. From this perspective, it could be said, as Mark Davis (1997) does about similar "victim feminism" charges leveled at an anti-rape pamphlet, that in the context of an argument against rape as endemic, it is hardly surprising not to find the life-enhancing aspects of sexuality and sexual practices being extolled. However, as is evident by now, larger processes of gender and sexuality are deeply implicated in MacKinnon's analysis of sexual coercion, and the more so the more common we concede rape to be, especially in the light of MacKinnon's question:

> Is sexuality throughout life, then, ever not on some level a reenactment of, a
> response to, that backdrop? (MacKinnon 1987b, 86)

The media feminist condemnation of "victim feminism" relates more directly to MacKinnon's argument that gender and heterosexuality "as we know them" involve the eroticization of hierarchy and therefore have everything to do with the existence and prevalence of rape. Several questions then arise. Must the eroticization of hierarchy always be a bad thing? Paglia's answer is that it is what makes the world go around—an obvious no. Other media feminists, such as Naomi Wolf, struggle with whether aspects of heterosexual desire that might be deemed hierarchical are compatible with feminism (and it is not only heterosexual desire that is implicated, if the dominance dynamic is a movable one across biological bodies).[16] But Wolf's answer is a classic liberal retreat: she suggests that the problem of when desire might involve the eroticization of dominance and subordination simply stops being political (and therefore, by implication, a problem) if it can be traced back to the psyche (Wolf 1993). Yet as bell hooks (1994) argues, we can reject notions of individual guilt and attempts at repression or thinking that the status quo is easy to change without denying that the ways in which our psyches are formed are also political issues.

At the same time, is gender always so inevitably reducible to hierarchy and forced sex? Can women ever be agents rather than on the receiving end of masculine power, even if partially and contradictorily so? And if this is possible, is there space for positive experiences, including of sex with men? If not, are at least heterosexually inclined women meant to wait for the magical overhaul of the entire social system, and how will this ever happen?

It is these kinds of issues that have resulted in MacKinnon's arguments being described as "victim" theory, not only by media feminists but by feminists more influenced by postmodernist theories (e.g., Harding 1986; Cocks 1989). Postmodernist feminists commonly charge MacKinnon (if, indeed, not radical feminism *in toto*) with essentialism, even its biological variant (e.g., Flax 1987; Fraser and Nicholson 1988), which is plainly a misinterpretation. In similar fashion, Wolf shies away from the implications of MacKinnon's work by partly misreading her argument. Wolf is at least initially generous when she calls the actions of the other media feminists "slick and dangerous" in the face of a rape "epidemic" (Wolf 1993, 147–148). She includes MacKinnon's and Rich's work among the "influential theories" that "opened up the way we could think about gender" (Wolf 1993, 132), and she goes on to say that due to a "tendency to rigidity" in the women's movement, these arguments have been translated too literally, resulting in them being transmitted

> poorly into popular conversation . . . perceived as political road maps, rather than as intellectual provocations.   (Wolf 1993)

This has included theorists being "quoted out of context" (Wolf 1993, 132)—in other words, the fault does not lie with the theories themselves.

But Wolf goes on to characterize victim feminism as including casting "women themselves as good and attack[ing] men themselves as wrong" (Wolf 1993, 149; her emphasis), without making clear whether this criticism, most commonly leveled at political theory and practice labeled as "cultural feminism,"[17] should apply to MacKinnon and Rich or not. Wolf perhaps more legitimately criticizes MacKinnon and Dworkin for "their vision of overweening male oppression and female lack of choice" (1993, 156) but then argues that their focus "on female victimization at the expense of female agency, derives from conditions that once applied more than they do now" (154). This latter claim is tenable only from a liberal position, which both MacKinnon and Rich are disputing and which becomes more obvious subsequently, in Wolf's assertion that the problem of victim feminism is that it sees phenomena such as aggression as gendered, rather than as just two different human approaches (1993, 157–159).

The question of why the work of radical feminists such as Rich, Dworkin, and especially MacKinnon is so often apparently misread by other feminists is a subject that deserves further investigation. Certainly, at least some of the misdirected aspects of the criticisms of MacKinnon's work by postmodernist and media feminists alike may be understood as a protest about the seeming inevitability of the oppressive gender and sexual status quo in her model. As MacKinnon puts it:

> Confronting the pervasiveness and tenacity of male dominance frequently seems to inspire this peculiar combination of reassurance with despair: if it is that hard to change, it must be natural, but since we know it is not natural, it must not be that hard to change.   (MacKinnon 1984, 186)

In MacKinnon's radical feminism, the fact that women's oppression is hard to change does not stop women from trying, even if women's agency therefore tends to be underplayed in her account. MacKinnon's own work testifies to her activism within the masculinist legal realm, and she continually footnotes other feminist action against sexual violence. Relating back to her epistemological critique of male power as myth that makes itself true, MacKinnon suggests that women's resistance that does not buy straight back into more of the same could be understood in radical feminist terms as an expression of how "women's consciousness erupts through fissures in the socially knowable.[18] It is a phenomenon underemphasized and ultimately insufficiently explained from within the terms of MacKinnon's overall project, but still present. When critics such as Paglia (1992) and Wolf (1993) urge women to take their own revenge and fight back against the would-be rapist, it is therefore as if a whole tradition of radical feminism, including self-defense and "turning fear into anger," had passed them by—which it must, in order for the media feminist characterization of "victim feminism" to appear without contradiction.[19]

Radical Feminism, Modified

Nevertheless, the victim feminism critiques remain only partly addressed, as MacKinnon (along with Rich) still tends towards the one, overarching narrative, in which there is little room for contradictions and ambiguities. A partial rejoinder might be offered in other aspects of MacKinnon's work, where she uses a Marxist analogy, pointing out that a good job or day at the factory does not make the relations of capitalism nonexploitative as a whole (MacKinnon 1987a, 218; see also Wolf 1993, 153). In other words, as Wolf (1993, 133) suggests, we need to distinguish between arguing that "sex occurs in a context of social inequality," as MacKinnon does, and wrongly attributing to her the idea that all heterosexual sex is rape.[20] It might be helpful here to explore the ramifications of MacKinnon's original "to be rapable defines what a woman is," not for its suggestion that being a woman means (and only means?) being vulnerable to rape but for the more specific connotation that being vulnerable to rape puts one in the position of "woman." This may give a little more conceptual space in which to think about gender-as-hierarchy as the dominant but not sole mode—as MacKinnon's own epistemological critique of male power actually implies.

Here, radical feminism could usefully meet up with feminist postmodernism. From radical feminism we should retain the notion that rape is extremely common, even endemic; it is very much about normative masculinity and heterosexuality; and it is crucially bound up with the dominant binary view of gender as we know it. But postmodernist feminist theory is more attuned than radical feminism to pre-existing gaps, contradictions, and changes in the dominant system and is more sympathetic to a genuine feminist politics of difference, which does not subsume any one form of oppression to any other.[21] Feminist postmodernism also offers some extensions and challenges to radical feminist ways of understanding gender: if gender for MacKinnon is something done, for a feminist postmodernist such as Judith Butler (1990), gender is performative. The concepts of gender as socially constructed and gender as performed obviously share much, but the postmodernist stance suggests that the gender dichotomy as we tend to know it can be, and indeed already is being, disrupted, to a greater extent than radical feminism would allow. Might this open up at least some space to address the limitations of radical feminist analysis, while building on its strengths?[22]

If there is one truly useful insight in the media feminist contributions, it may lie in the fact that they already presume this alliance between radical and postmodernist feminist arguments.[23] To return to the broader contemporary cultural context of discourses and politics about sexual violence, producing a revamped feminist theory adequate to the task of opposing rape will be possible only if we can get past the binary legacies of the 1980s feminist "sex wars." An exchange between radical feminism and feminist postmodernism might help us keep resisting—as both bell hooks (1994) and Naomi Wolf (1993), the latter in her only partly successful attempt, express it—the temptations of "either/or" criticism. In the dominant dichotomous framework supposedly offering a choice, Wolf (1993, 211) argues, either rape is treated "like a bad evening" (an obvious reference to Paglia's views) or, which happens far less often, a bad evening is treated like rape.

At present, though, while radical and postmodernist feminist theory and politics do not subscribe to mainstream constructions as fully as the media feminists do, they, too, tend to get caught within these kinds of binary terms. So, for example, radical feminists often express antipathy toward postmodernist views (e.g., Bell and Klein 1996). This hostility is not without foundation where rape is concerned: as I have briefly suggested, feminist postmodernist typifications of radical feminist ideas, while justified to some extent, also can have more than a little in common with media feminist attitudes. More generally, it seems that the engagement of feminism with postmodernist theories has developed along with a decentering of sexual violence from feminist theory.[24] The reasons for this are complex (see, e.g., Atmore 1993), but it seems likely that there has been some sort of mutually constitutive effect arising out of, on the one hand, the ways in which radical feminism tends to get interpreted, characterized, and consequently dismissed even by those postmodernists who are feminists, and on the other, the centrality of sexual violence to the cogency of radical feminist analysis.

Conclusion

To return to the themes of my introduction, feminist arguments about rape are enmeshed in a much larger web of late-twentieth-century preoccupation with issues of sexual violence—a web about which one grand story cannot be told. The high profile of these topics may not always have much to do with specific feminist goals of ending rape. Just as talk shows might feature incest "victims" to get ratings, so, too, usually critically rigorous, "high" feminist theory may call a feminist anti-rape activist a "victim theorist" for reasons that are only partly about direct struggles for the meaning of rape, and in the same way as the assertions about rape in Christina Hoff Sommers's book serve a broader, anti-PC agenda. Again, then, there is no longer any easy counterposition of "them" to "us," and all kinds of political interests get served through making claims and counterclaims about sexual violence.

Examining "victim feminism" charges in their distinct contexts means considering what specific forces may have combined to produce the kinds of claims that are being made and the responses to them, including feminist ones. For example, any particular conflict over media feminist accusations of victim feminism must, like sexually violent practices themselves, be shaped by historical legacies and cultural milieux—the salience of PC (political correctness) as a scare term, for instance. Similarly, the respective influences of feminist postmodernism and radical feminism and the associated implications for who does work against sexual violences, how, and where, vary considerably across and within western countries. Each situation depends on factors such as recent shifts in academic power nexuses, including the selective and uneven uptake of postmodernist theories and the relationship of this to feminisms inside and outside particular universities.

These kinds of considerations also undercut yet again media feminist claims about some kind of homogenous "gender feminism" that has put everyone under the spell of the victim slant on rape. For instance, the media feminist overlap with feminist postmodernist typifications of radical feminism suggests that Paglia and company are not quite the marginal dissidents they claim to be, or certainly not in some contexts.[25] The notion of dissent, like the idea of "victim" itself, is context dependent, and never more so than when rhetoric about rape has become such a medium of bids for power.

And so, perhaps in some situations at least, we have got to the point that Germaine Greer recently implied when, responding to a suggestion that her work was positioning women as victims, she commented, "Talking about victims these days is so un-PC."[26] PC itself can be traced back to two now-mingled, but previously distinct, places of origin: radical groups' in-house, mainly tongue-in-cheek relation to their own theories and more recent conservative attempts to claw back progressive gains in the public sphere (O'Sullivan 1993). Who gets to claim to dissent from the "party line" depends on what it is, and hence, to some extent, on where the dissenter is locally situated—a university women's studies department, a rape crisis center, a current affairs panel. And it also depends on other factors: Would Greer's statement make sense at this time if she were not who she is, where she is?

We could not begin to answer these questions from within the restrictive talk-show format of "victim feminism: for or against." But at the same time, as far as radical feminism and feminist postmodernism are concerned, the potentially more productive public conversations have barely begun.

NOTES

1. Referring to these four as "the media feminists" is not meant to imply there are no other feminists prominent in the contemporary media or that all those who are share the stance of those four. I am interested mainly in the claims made by media feminists against feminist theory and practice about sexual violence. It also seems clear that someone like Camille Paglia has a lot more popular exposure than a far more "progressive" media contributor like bell hooks, at least from my Australian vantage point.

2. It is too simple to say that anyone who does work against sexual violence that I might tag "radical feminist" must be one. But any political manifesto that ranks taking sexual violence seriously, as a key item, has strong affinities with radical feminist thought and activities. For example, while many Black feminists may not choose to identify with the tag "radical feminist" because of its public association with White-dominated feminism, which emphasizes gender at the expense of race, Black feminist traditions of organizing against sexual violence have some important overlaps with what are more "officially" known as radical feminist tenets. (See, e.g., hooks 1990, 57–64; Crenshaw 1993.)

3. See, for example, Louise Armstrong's critique of "the incest industry" from her perspective as one of the first survivors to publicize incest as a feminist issue (Armstrong 1994; Kitzinger 1995).

4. Like Alcoff (1997), for ease of expression I refer to these theories as "postmodernist" in the rest of the chapter.

5. The phrase was sufficiently provocative for one student in my lecture on MacKinnon's feminism to return the following day with it stenciled on her T-shirt. See also Roiphe's (1994, 138–160) view on MacKinnon's prose, which differs from Paglia in at least the "dry" categorization.

6. See Paglia 1994, 31–32. The treatment of graffiti on toilet walls as an index of

radical feminist hegemony over thinking about rape is a common feature of media feminist writing. See also Roiphe 1994, 18–19.

7. However, they differ in their relationship to liberalism. Paglia's stance on liberalism is more ambivalent than MacKinnon's, as the former claims to critique contemporary liberalism (e.g., Paglia 1994, 246) but still uses many liberal arguments. For instance, Paglia argues, in typical liberal fashion (Atmore 1995), that victim feminists have fallen down a slippery slope of definitions: "When feminist discourse is unable to discriminate the drunken fraternity brother from the homicidal maniac, women are in trouble" (Paglia 1994, 33). Yet as I have suggested, a similar lack of conceptual discrimination appears in Paglia's own typification of feminist arguments about rape.

8. See Brownmiller 1975, 4. Cf. MacKinnon 1982, 528 n4; 1983, 646; Eisenstein 1984, 27–30; Russell 1984, 111–13; Woodhull 1988.

9. However even "the forcible intrusion of sex into a nonsexual context" is "excusable if a sexual overture is welcomed" (Paglia 1994, 24), begging the question of what "forcible" can actually mean in this logic.

10. It has obvious parallels with the now-criticized idea of personal homophobia as simply a fear of the other, when the homophobe can also be a gay-basher or even a murderer.

11. hooks (1994, 99, 105) makes a similar point about aspects of Wolf's and Roiphe's arguments. Another reversal of discourse is apparent in the assertion that it is the feminist view on rape that puts women in danger (Paglia 1994, 255; see also Roiphe 1994, 10, 28), because women are consequently not "prepared to go it alone" (Paglia 1994, 24).

12. See MacKinnon 1982, 537–541; 1983, 636 n4. Again, this makes Paglia somewhat different from a liberal like Sommers (1994, 66, 71–72), who scoffs at feminists such as MacKinnon and Fox Keller as if it were self-evident that relating mainstream science to critiques of sexual objectification must be far-fetched.

13. C. Shafer and M. Frye, Rape and respect, in M. Vetterling-Braggin, F. Elliston, and J. English (eds.), *Feminism and philosophy* (Totowa, NJ: Littlefield, Adams 1977), 334.

14. The same logic applies in MacKinnon's and Andrea Dworkin's anti-pornography ordinance, which allows for the possibility that men or transsexuals will occupy the position more commonly reserved for legally recognized women. I suggest, as with the argument about rape, that it would be a similar rather than an identical position, although that is an issue needing work beyond the scope of this chapter.

15. While Paglia's version is slightly different, she expresses doubts that gay people make up even as much as 10 percent of the population (Paglia 1994, 73–74). Paglia also insists on women recognizing that sex is "in the air" every time a woman goes on a date with a man (Paglia 1994, 243), but this sexual possibility is not emphasized for other combinations of genders.

16. For example, it is not clear how MacKinnon implicates lesbians in the existing system, given her insistence on gender as to some extent independent of physical bodies. See MacKinnon 1989, 178–179.

17. However, even critiques of cultural feminism more sophisticated than those from the media feminists (Echols 1984a; 1984b) may tend to set up a straw woman and need more examination.

18. See MacKinnon 1979, xii. This tension is similar to the one that Wolf (1993, 118) tries to confront but ends up simply denying, as she responds to the radical feminist challenge of Audre Lorde's (1983) "the master's tools will never dismantle the master's house" by simply claiming that fire can be fought with fire. hooks (1994, 96–97) also points out the inadequacy of this reading of Lorde by Wolf.

19. See also Roiphe 1994, 44; and in contrast, Bart and O'Brien 1985; Atmore 1995. Paglia (1994, 420) does briefly refer positively to Valerie Solanas and her Society for Cutting Up Men, but without linking it to the radical feminism she denigrates.

20. Similarly, Wolf argues that Rich's analysis has wrongly "trickled down" to an assumption that all heterosexuality is coercive and that straight women are falsely conscious (Wolf 1993, 133–134).

21. For example, bell hooks's more recent work (hooks 1994) can be interpreted as feminist postmodern theory, or at the very least has affinities with it.

22. The possibilities of such a theoretical exchange raise a host of issues that cannot be pursued here; but see, as one beginning, my use of Butler's (1990) concept of "the heterosexual matrix" in order to analyze media representations of rape (Atmore 1994b).

23. For instance, Paglia (1992, 174, 187–188) treats Foucault with the same scorn as she does MacKinnon. Sommers (1994, 113–114, 229–232) collapses "gender feminism," Faludi, Foucault, and Derrida into one seamless theory.

24. As just one example, in a work titled *Gender trouble*, Judith Butler's major focus is on aspects of gender performativity, such as drag. Her one reference to rape is in a footnote, in which she describes the practices of rape, other sexual violence, and "queer-bashing" as examples of "the violent enforcement of a category violently constructed" (Butler 1990, 166 n26). Even more striking is that part of Butler's theoretical framework can be understood (as she acknowledges) as a feminist postmodernist updating of Adrienne Rich's theory of "compulsory heterosexuality," to which sexual violence was seen by Rich to be crucial.

25. Contradictions and previously unlikely alliances are not unusual in this climate. I had the interesting experience recently of listening to two Filipina activists use radical feminist Kathleen Barry's (1979) *Female sexual slavery* to indict prostitution. This took place without comment in the kind of "high theory" women's studies center that more typically, in other seminars, berates radical feminism for victim theory or at best ignores it, charging that radical feminists are the worst offenders in claiming (wrongly) to speak for all women.

26. Germaine Greer, The new assault on women (keynote speech, Melbourne Writers' Festival, 15 October 1997).

REFERENCES

Alcoff, L. 1997. The politics of postmodern feminism, revisited. *Cultural Critique* (Spring), 5–27.

Armstrong, L. 1994. *Rocking the cradle of sexual politics: What happened when women said incest.* New York: Addison-Wesley.

Atmore, C. 1993. Feminism's restless undead: The essential(ist) activist. Paper presented at "Bring a Plate: The Feminist Cultural Studies Conference," University of Melbourne, December.

———. 1994a. Witch hunts, icebergs and the light of reason: Constructions of child sexual abuse in recent cultural controversies. In H. Borland (ed.), *Communication and identity: Local, regional, global: Selected papers from the 1993 National Conference of the Australian Communication Association* (85–96). Canberra: Australian and New Zealand Communication Association.

———. 1994b. Brand news: Rape and the mass media. *Media Information Australia* 72, 20–31.

———. 1995. The Mervyn Thompson controversy: A feminist deconstructive reading. *New Zealand Sociology* 10(1), 171–215.

———. 1996. Cross-cultural media-tions: Media coverage of two child sexual abuse controversies in New Zealand/Aotearoa. *Child Abuse Review* 5, 334–345.

———. 1997. Loving another science: Some musings on the complexities and productivities of cross-disciplinary feminist work against sexual violences. Paper presented at "Transformations: Thinking through Feminism Conference," Centre for Women's Studies, Lancaster University, UK, 17–19 July.

———. Forthcoming. Sexual abuse and troubled feminism: A reply to Camille Guy. *Feminist Review* 61.

Barry, K. 1979. *Female sexual slavery.* Englewood Cliffs, NJ: Prentice-Hall.

Bart, P., and O'Brien, P. 1985. *Stopping rape: Successful survival strategies.* New York: Pergamon Press.

Bell, D., and Klein, R. (eds). 1996. *Radically speaking: Feminism reclaimed.* North Melbourne: Spinifex Press.

Brownmiller, S. 1975. *Against our will: Men, women and rape.* New York: Simon and Schuster.

Butler, J. 1990. *Gender trouble: Feminism and subversion of identity.* New York: Routledge.

Cameron, D., and Frazer, E. 1987. *The lust to kill: A feminist investigation of sexual murder.* New York: New York University Press.

Campbell, B. 1988. *Unofficial secrets: Child sexual abuse—The Cleveland case.* London: Virago.

Cocks, J. 1989. *The oppositional imagination: Feminism, critique and political theory.* London: Routledge.

Crenshaw, K. 1993. Whose story is it, anyway? Feminist and antiracist appropriations of Anita Hill. In T. Morrison (ed.), *Race-ing justice, en-gendering power* (pp. 402–440). London: Chatto and Windus.

Davis, M. 1997. *Gangland: Cultural elites and the new generationalism.* St. Leonards, New South Wales: Allen and Unwin.

Echols, A. 1984a. The new feminism of yin and yang. In A. Snitow, C. Stansell, and S. Thompson (eds.), *Desire: The politics of sexuality* (62–81). London: Virago.

———. 1984b. The taming of the id: Feminist sexual politics, 1968–83. In C. Vance (ed.), *Pleasure and danger: Exploring female sexuality* (50–72). Boston: Routledge and Kegan Paul.

Eisenstein, H. 1984. *Contemporary feminist thought.* London: Unwin.

Flax, J. 1987. Postmodernism and gender relations in feminist theory. *Signs* 11, 621–643.

Foucault, M. 1980. *The history of sexuality.* Vol. 1: *An introduction.* Translated by Robert Hurley. New York: Vintage.

Fox Keller, E. 1982. Feminism and science. *Signs* 7, 589–602.

———. 1983. Gender and science. In S. Harding and M. Hintikka (eds.), *Discovering reality* (187–205). Boston: D. Reidel.

———. 1986. Making gender visible in the pursuit of nature's secrets. In T. de Lauretis (ed.), *Feminist studies/critical studies* (67–77). Bloomington: Indiana University Press.

Fraser, N., and Nicholson, L. 1988. Social criticism without philosophy: An encounter between feminism and postmodernism. *Theory, Culture and Society* 5, 373–394.

Garner, H. 1995. *The first stone: Some questions about sex and power.* Sydney: Picador.

Gavey, N. 1989. Feminist post-structuralism and discourse analysis: Contributions to feminist psychology. *Psychology of Women Quarterly* 13, 459–475.

Grosz, E. 1989. *Sexual subversions: Three French feminists.* Boston: Allen and Unwin.

Guy, C. 1996. Feminism and sexual abuse: Troubled thoughts on some New Zealand issues. *Feminist Review* 52, 154–168.

Harding, S. 1986. *The science question in feminism.* Milton Keynes, England: Open University Press.

hooks, b. 1990. *Yearning: Race, gender, and cultural politics.* Boston: South End Press.

———. 1994. *Outlaw culture: Resisting representations.* New York and London: Routledge.

Kitzinger, J. 1995. Jenny Kitzinger on *Rocking the cradle of sexual politics: What hap-*

pened when women said incest, by Louise Armstrong. *Feminism and Psychology* 5, 389–391.

Lorde, A. 1983. The master's tools will never dismantle the master's house. In C. Moraga and G. Anzaluda (eds.), *This bridge called my back: Writings by radical women of color* (98–101). 2d ed. New York: Kitchen Table.

MacKinnon, C. 1979. *Sexual harassment of working women: A case of sex discrimination.* New Haven: Yale University Press.

———. 1982. Feminism, Marxism, method and the state: An agenda for theory. *Signs* 7, 515–544.

———. 1983. Feminism, Marxism, method and the state: Toward feminist jurisprudence. *Signs* 8, 635–658.

———. 1984. Reply to Miller, Acker and Barry, Johnson, West, and Gardiner. *Signs* 10, 184–188.

———. 1987a. *Feminism unmodified: Discourses on life and law.* Cambridge: Harvard University Press.

———. 1987b. A feminist/political approach: "Pleasure under patriarchy." In J. Geer and W. O'Donohue (eds.), *Theories of human sexuality* (65–90). New York: Plenum.

———. 1989. *Toward a feminist theory of the state.* Cambridge: Harvard University Press.

Malcolm, J. 1990. *The journalist and the murderer.* New York: Vintage.

———. 1995. *The silent woman: Sylvia Plath and Ted Hughes.* New York: Alfred A. Knopf.

Mead, J. (ed.). 1997. *Bodyjamming: Sexual harassment, feminism and public life.* Milsons Point, New South Wales: Vintage.

Norris, C. 1988. Deconstruction, post-modernism and the visual arts. In C. Norris and A. Benjamin (eds.), *What is deconstruction?* London: Academy Press.

O'Sullivan, S. 1993. Where does political correctness come from? Does it drop from the sky? In D. Bennett (ed.), *Cultural studies: Pluralism and theory* (89–196). Melbourne: University of Melbourne, Department of English.

Paglia, C. 1990. *Sexual personae: Art and decadence from Nefertiti to Emily Dickinson.* London and New Haven: Yale University Press.

———. 1992. *Sex, art, and American culture: Essays.* New York: Vintage Books.

———. 1994. *Vamps and tramps: New essays.* London and New York: Viking.

Rich, A. 1980. Compulsory heterosexuality and lesbian existence. *Signs* 5, 631–660.

Rich, A. 1989. Negotiations. In A. Rich, *Time's power* (9). New York: W. W. Norton.

Roiphe, K. 1994. *The morning after: Sex, fear, and feminism.* London: Hamish Hamilton.

Russell, D. 1984. *Sexual exploitation: Rape, child sexual abuse, and workplace harassment.* Beverly Hills: Sage.

Scott, J. 1988. Deconstructing equality-versus-difference: Or, the uses of post-structuralist theory for feminism. *Feminist Studies* 14, 33–50.

Sommers, C. H. 1994. *Who stole feminism? How women have betrayed women.* New York: Simon and Schuster.

Wolf, N. 1993. *Fire with fire: The new female power and how it will change the twenty-first century.* London: Chatto and Windus.

Woodhull, W. 1988. Sexuality, power, and the question of rape. In I. Diamond and L. Quinby (eds.), *Feminism and Foucault: Reflections on resistance* (167–76). Boston: Northeastern University Press.

Index